THE AFTERLIFE OF UTOPIA

THE AFTERLIFE OF UTOPIA

Urban Renewal in Germany's Model Socialist City

Samantha Maurer Fox

CORNELL UNIVERSITY PRESS

Ithaca and London

First published 2026 by Cornell University Press

Library of Congress Cataloging-in-Publication Data

Names: Fox, Samantha, 1985– author
Title: The afterlife of utopia : urban renewal in Germany's model socialist city / Samantha Maurer Fox.
Description: Ithaca : Cornell University Press, 2025. | Includes bibliographical references and index.
Identifiers: LCCN 2025019598 (print) | LCCN 2025019599 (ebook) | ISBN 9781501785108 hardcover | ISBN 9781501785115 paperback | ISBN 9781501785122 epub | ISBN 9781501785139 pdf
Subjects: LCSH: Urban renewal—Germany—Eisenhüttenstadt—History | City planning—Germany—Eisenhüttenstadt—History | Eisenhüttenstadt (Germany)—History
Classification: LCC DD901.E29 F68 2025 (print) | LCC DD901.E29 (ebook) | DDC 307.3/526094315—dc23/eng/20250825
LC record available at https://lccn.loc.gov/2025019598
LC ebook record available at https://lccn.loc.gov/2025019599

Contents

Abbreviations

AWG (/'aː.fa.geː/)	Workers' Housing Cooperative (Arbeiterwohnungsbaugenossenschaft)
EWG (/eːˈfa.geː/)	Eisenhüttenstadt Housing Cooperative (Eisenhüttenstädter Wohnungsbaugenossenschaft)
GeWi (/'geː.viː/)	Eisenhüttenstadt Real Estate Company (Eisenhüttenstädter Gebaudewirtschaft), in which the city government is the only shareholder
GDR	German Democratic Republic, or East Germany
KPD	German Communist Party (Kommunistische Partei Deutschlands)
OFFIS	Place for a Forum and Information in the City Center (Ort für Foren und Informationen im Stadtzentrum), which houses the Agency for Engagement
SED	Socialist Unity Party (Sozialistische Einheitspartei Deutschlands), the ruling party of East Germany

FIGURE 1. Map of Eisenhüttenstadt within Germany. Illustration by the author; source data provided by the German Federal Agency for Cartography and Geodesy.

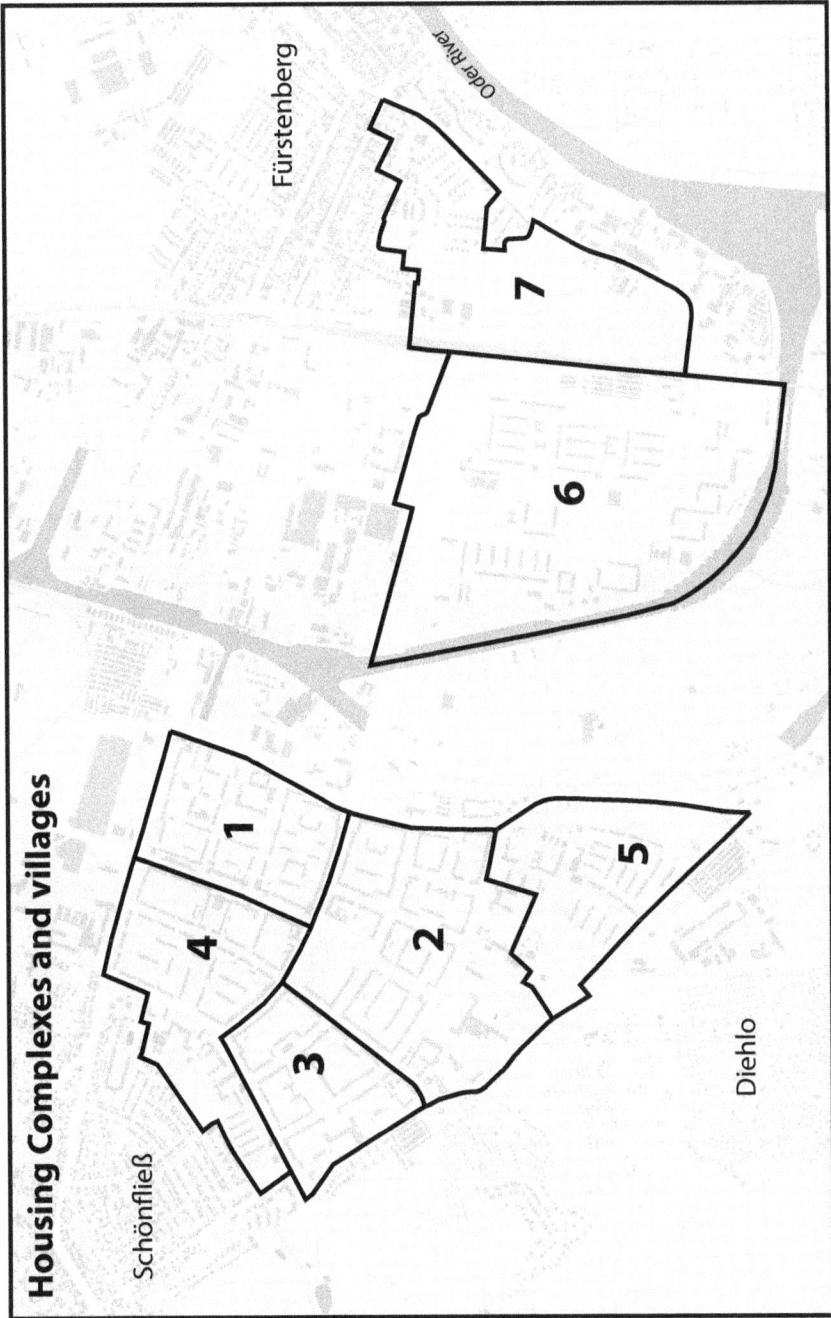

Housing Complexes and villages

Schönfließ

Fürstenberg

Oder River

1

4

3

2

5

6

7

Diehlo

FIGURE 2. Housing Complexes and villages within Eisenhüttenstadt. Illustration by the author; source data courtesy of Stadtverwaltung Eisenhüttenstadt, 2024.

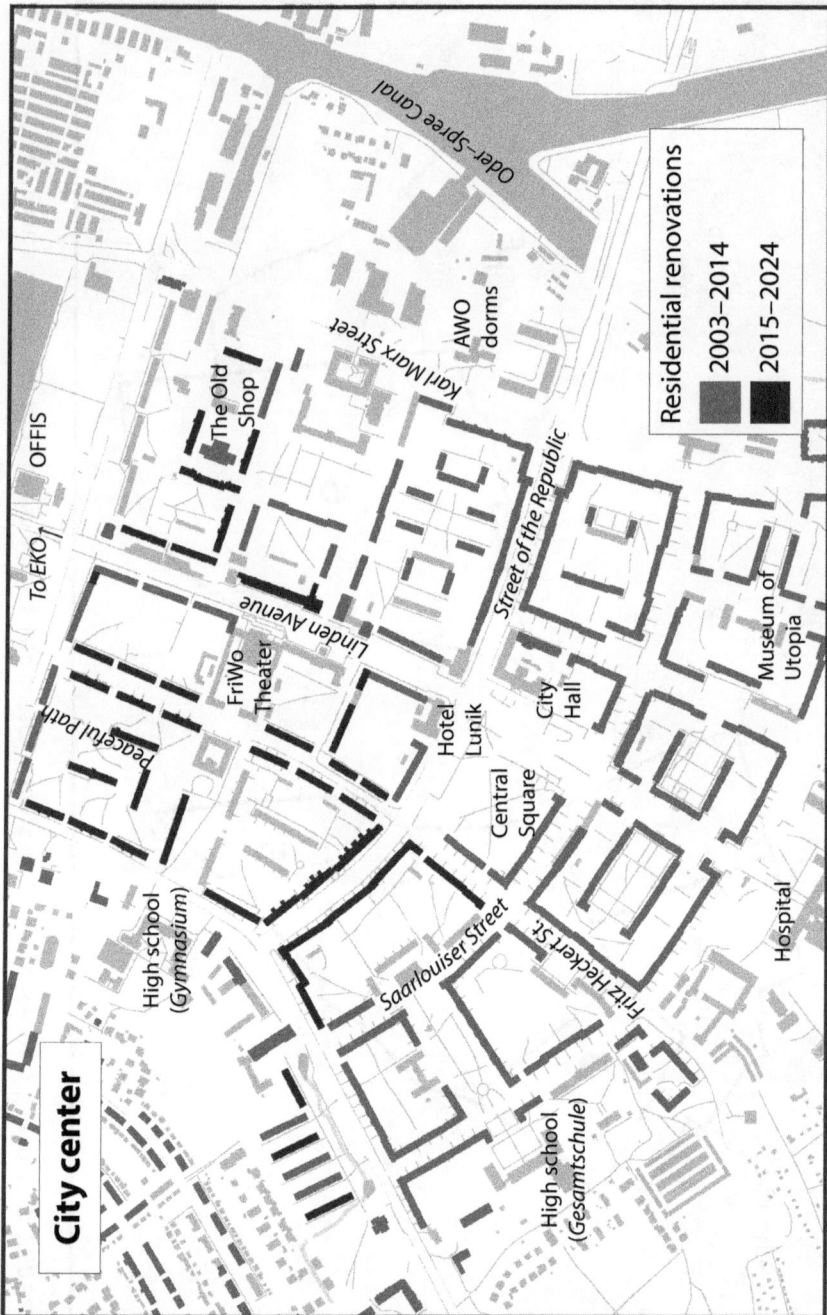

FIGURE 3. City center detail. Illustration by the author; source data courtesy of Stadtverwaltung Eisenhüttenstadt, 2024.

Map labels:

City center

Oder–Spree Canal

OFFIS

To EKO

The Old Shop

Karl Marx Street

AWO dorms

Street of the Republic

Linden Avenue

FriWo Theater

Peaceful Path

High school (Gymnasium)

Hotel Lunik

City Hall

Central Square

Museum of Utopia

Saarlouiser Street

Fritz Heckert St.

High school (Gesamtschule)

Hospital

Residential renovations
2003–2014
2015–2024

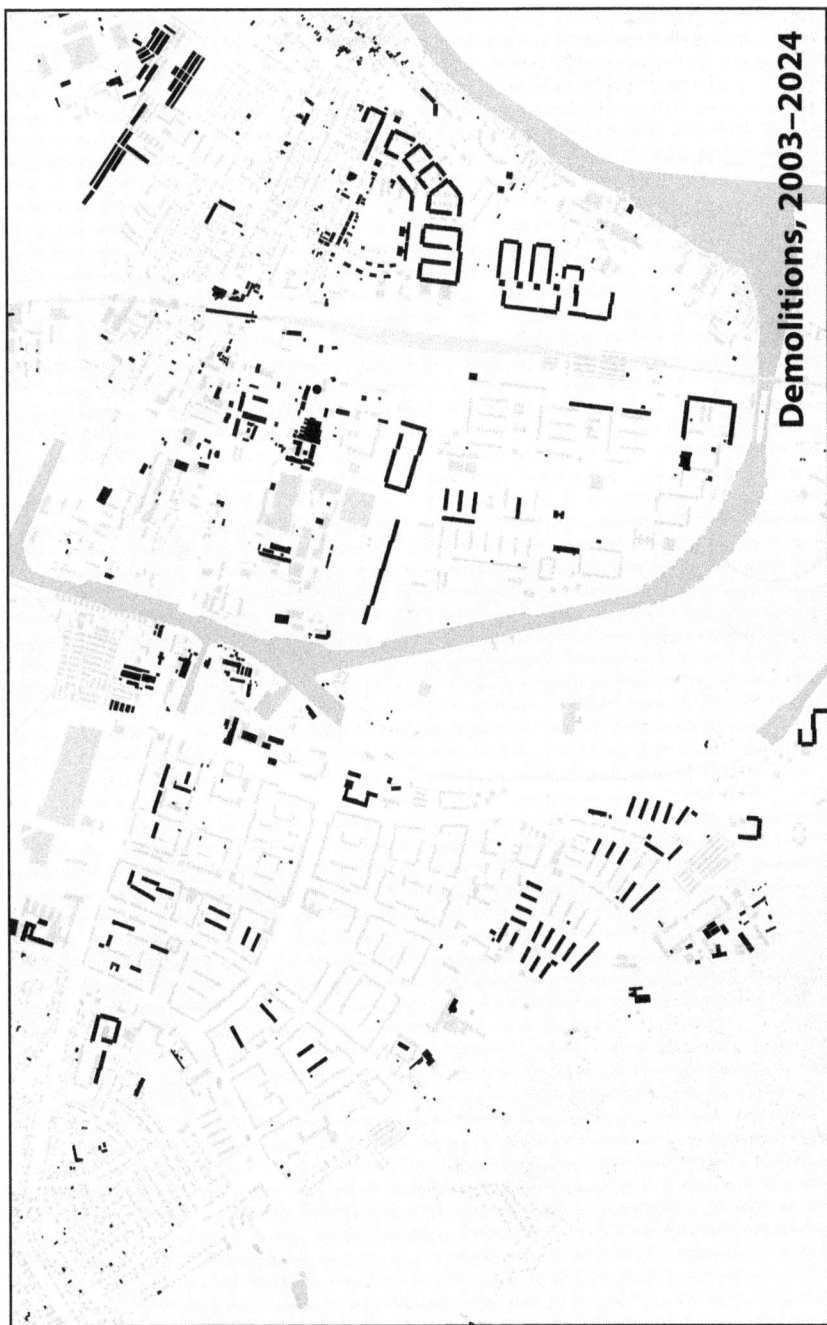

FIGURE 4. Demolitions carried out between 2003 and 2024. Illustration by the author; source data courtesy of Stadtverwaltung Eisenhüttenstadt, 2024.

Demolitions, 2003–2024

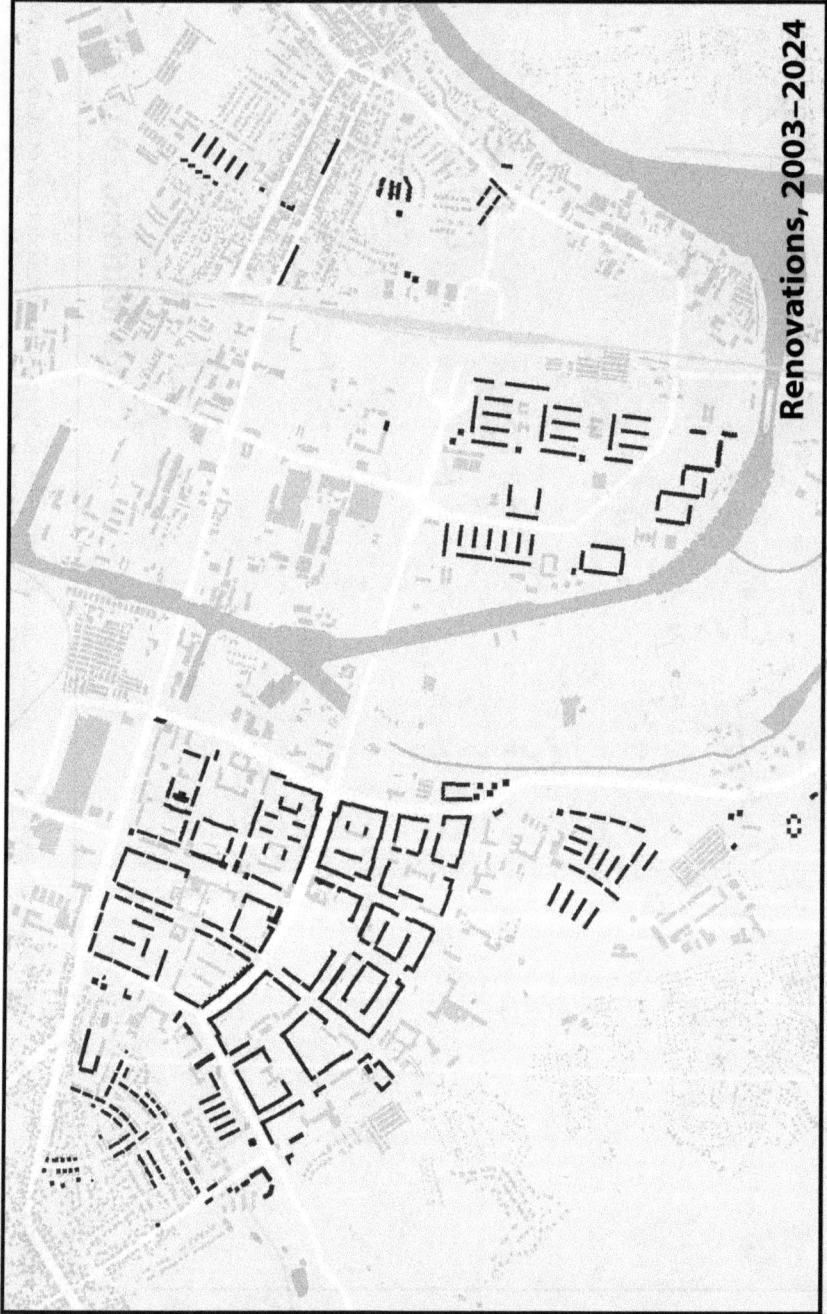

FIGURE 5. Renovations carried out between 2003 and 2024. Illustration by the author; source data courtesy of Stadtverwaltung Eisenhüttenstadt, 2024.

THE AFTERLIFE OF UTOPIA

INTRODUCTION
The Afterlife of Utopia

Eisenhüttenstadt was founded in 1950, originally called Stalinstadt and officially known as "Germany's First Socialist City." While it is often considered utopian (Wakeman 2016; Ludwig 2000; Richter et al. 1997), a utopian city is something of a contradiction in terms. Derived from the Greek *ou* (no) and *topos* (place), the term was first used by Sir Thomas More to describe a fictional island where private property had been abolished and diverse groups lived in harmony—an obvious impossibility (More [1516] 1965). Yet utopia remains a powerful concept, slipping between the real and the imagined. The urban historian Lewis Mumford began his career with *The Story of Utopias*, in which he describes a "utopian" as someone who aims to "reconstruct" both the built environment and cultural norms (1922, 21). In Mumford's telling, there is only reconstruction, never construction. Circumstances always impose constraints, but Mumford cautions against letting them deter utopian pursuits. He writes, "We need not abandon the real world in order to enter these realizable worlds; for it is out of the first that the second are always coming" (Mumford 1922, 25).

Located about seventy-five miles east of Berlin, along the German-Polish border, Eisenhüttenstadt was conceived as a totalitarian planned city, a steel manufacturing hub that would be integral to East Germany's first Five-Year Plan. Its products would enable the rise of Eastern Bloc industry, and its design, focused on the needs of young families, would showcase humane urbanism: Cultural amenities, walkable neighborhoods, and ample green space would be available to all. Throughout the East German era, the city thrived. Then, in 1990, came German reunification. In the following decades, the city's population fell by over

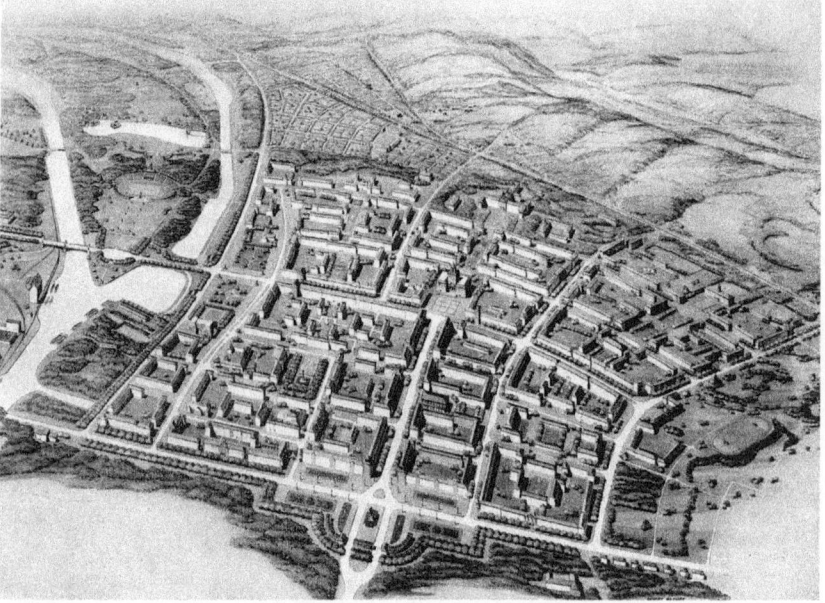

FIGURE 6. Rendering of Eisenhüttenstadt (then Stalinstadt) as planned in 1954, from Kurt W. Leucht, *The First New Town in the German Democratic Republic* (Berlin 1957), courtesy of Stadtarchiv Eisenhüttenstadt.

FIGURE 7. May Day parade, May 1, 1960, Housing Complex 2. Courtesy of Terje Hartberg.

half, from close to sixty thousand in 1989 to around twenty-three thousand in 2023 (Lötsch 2023a). But municipal leaders were prescient: In the early 1990s, they incorporated city-owned real estate in order to prevent its sale to Western speculators. As a result, urban renewal projects have been carried out at a scale unmatched in comparable late-industrial cities. And after decades of large-scale, structural transformation—demolitions, renovations, utility reconstruction, and investments in social programs—urban renewal projects are now yielding success. Eisenhüttenstadt thus exemplifies an "ecological" economics (Daly [1977] 1991, xi) from the ground up: a turn toward sustainable, communitarian urbanism made possible by the city's socialist history.

In examining developments since the turn of the millennium, this book shows how Eisenhüttenstadt's planners have forged a new iteration of urban utopia, a reimagining of mid-century collectivism that stands to bolster the city against contemporary challenges. When urban renewal efforts began in 2002, Eisenhüttenstadt had a residential vacancy rate of around 20 percent, with some neighborhoods close to 60 percent vacant (Howest 2006, 102). By 2006, demolitions had not kept up with population loss, and the vacancy rate rose to nearly 30 percent. The abandoned urban landscape prompted *The New York Times* to ask about Eisenhüttenstadt, in 2013, "What becomes of a model city when the model goes bust?" (Eddy 2013). Since then, however, vacancy has steadily decreased; it was around 8 percent in 2023 (Lötsch 2023b).[1] Unemployment, too, fell from a high of over 25 percent in the 1990s to just under 7 percent in 2020, which was finally in line with the national average and below average for the former East Germany. In 2018, the city government eliminated the structural deficits that had long plagued its operating budget (Destatis 2022a; Stadt Eisenhüttenstadt and BBSM 2022, 16–18). In 2021, *Der Taggesspiegel* profiled Eisenhüttenstadt with the headline, "After a Long Decline, the City Shines Again" (Lippitz 2021). Later that year, the multinational corporation ArcelorMittal announced that it would invest over €1 billion to make Eisenhüttenstadt one of the world's first carbon-neutral steel manufacturing sites by 2050 (Evans et al. 2021)—a move that both reflects and enables the city's newly imagined longevity.

Eisenhüttenstadt is also home to the largest historically protected site in Europe, preserved as an exemplar of East German architecture and urban planning (Stadt Eisenhüttenstadt 2021). Low-rise apartment buildings with neoclassical detailing and spacious proportions, built before the advent of prefabricated architecture, are connected by pedestrian pathways and surrounded by monumental civic buildings: schools, a theater, a hospital, and the city hall. Large-scale mosaics and sculpture gardens dot the urban landscape. Inside the historically protected zone, apartment building facades, often painted in pastel shades of pink, blue, and yellow, must be meticulously maintained, while outside this area, concrete high-rise towers have been steadily demolished by the state. As this process unfolds, displaced residents are relocated to the city center in what is widely perceived as the necessary undoing of late socialist-era expansion. At the same time, Eisenhüttenstadt's socialist origins are preserved in the Museum of Utopia and the Everyday, an institution founded in the early 1990s as the Documentation Center for Everyday Culture in East Germany. Its museum and curatorial offices are housed in the defunct Kindergarten 2, while a former high school holds the collection of around 150,000 everyday objects from East Germany—everything from canned food to rotary phones to busts of Lenin. As a result, Eisenhüttenstadt exemplifies tensions between East Germany's ambitious origins and its later shortcomings, and between the preservation of architecture and culture, outside and inside, the material remains of socialist urbanism and the social world that was housed within it.

In light of these tensions, planners and municipal officials often draw on—and sometimes reinvent—the ethos of socialist urbanism on which their city was founded. Residents, too, are sensitive to the polyvalent nature of urban space—the layering of histories, temporalities, and social worlds that Henri Lefebvre ([1974] 1992, 86) likened to a "mille-feuille pastry," and which scholars have long recognized as a defining feature of urban space in the former East Germany (Huyssen 2003; Young 2000; Till 2005). Such social frameworks (Goffmann 1974; Halbwachs [1925] 1992) are key to the "production" of urban space (Lefebvre [1974] 1992), and as urban renewal projects have been carried out, the sense of collective endeavor integral to the socialist project has begun to emerge in new forms. For example, social infrastructures originally built for young families have been transformed to accommodate the needs of the elderly and disabled. Walking and bike paths, built when individual car ownership was rare, are recast as instruments of carbon reduction and, simultaneously, as conduits for the serendipitous interactions that strengthen civic commitments. The city's two estate companies, both socialist-era entities, work cooperatively to ensure that their ownership stakes in renovated properties are equitably distributed. These efforts speak to a model of governance focused on long-term well-being—on "development" rather than growth (Daly [1973] 1980).

Urban studies has traditionally defined the urban as the site of expansion: of population, freedom, wealth, material, and industry (Mumford 1961 ; N. Smith 1996; Joyce 2003). Yet Eisenhüttenstadt illustrates how imaginations of human flourishing can take shape in places where the dream of endless population growth has been replaced by an imagination of sustainability: of zero-emissions steel production and after-work walks through the city's green spaces. Eisenhüttenstadt's leadership states that their vision of successful urban renewal is "not simply dependent on 'growth'" (scare quotes in the original). Success "exists only

FIGURES 8A AND 8B. Scenes from the archive of the Museum of Utopia and the Everyday, 2010–23. Photographs by the author.

FIGURES 9A AND 9B. Scenes from the archive of the Museum of Utopia and the Everyday, including portraits of East German leader Erich Honecker, 2010–23. Photographs by the author.

in the interplay" between metrics that are too often celebrated out of context, without regard to right-sizing and other local contingencies (Stadt Eisenhütten-stadt 2018). As this book shows, such comments are not an attempt to obfuscate what may otherwise be perceived as failure.

Anthropologists, too, have called for new modes of social analysis in our current era of polycrisis (Graeber and Wengrow 2021; Knox 2020; Günel 2019; Livingston 2019)—and they are perhaps uniquely suited to the task of forging them. Trained to examine the Other, anthropologists traditionally found their objects of study in the foreign cultures of the Global South (the "savage slot" [Trouillot (2003) 2016]) or in the abjected communities of the Global North (the "suffering slot" [Robbins 2013]). But as Mauss ([1925] 2002, 100) long ago established, "total social facts" shape both sociopolitical systems and the cultural lenses through which we understand their success or failure. Anthropology can thus examine political economy through the holistic lens of culture, and an anthropology of "the good" (Robbins 2013) can provide unique insight into sociocultural systems that push back against taken-for-granted hierarchies and social injustices.

From a cultural perspective, ecological economics seems to reconcile a desire for the recuperation of socialist collectivism with the need to accept the intractability of global capitalism. Drawing on the first and second laws of thermodynamics—the conservation of energy and matter—ecological economists argue that the economy is a subsystem of the biophysical world and, as such, is constrained by entropy: A biophysical system is inevitably depleted as energy is transformed into matter and back again. As we unheedingly deplete the earth's resources, the limits of economic activity shift from human ingenuity to the availability of resources themselves—from the efficiency of fishing implements to the number of fish in the sea (Daly [1973] 1980, 7; 2014). As such, we must develop new models of governance focused on improving quality of life—"development"—rather than increasing surplus capital at the expense of the planet (Daly [1973] 1980). After all, recent decades have shown that rising GDP often fails to bring about an overall increase in human welfare—and certainly fails to do so on a global scale. These ecological models of governance would, in theory, move away from the capitalist-socialist divide. Rather than focus on the presence and scope of private enterprise, they would seek to maximize social good, however defined, without exceeding the planet's ecological limits.

Eisenhüttenstadt's ecological governance is focused on consolidating urban space and shrinking the city's resource consumption, but it also draws on a history of utopianism that reorients the city toward the future. As such, Eisenhüttenstadt exemplifies the tendency of "post-cities" to incubate historically novel urban imaginaries (Ringel 2018; Schwenkel 2020; Dzenovska 2020; Ahmann 2022) as citizens reject the yoke of "post-ness," which orients places inexorably toward the past (Chari and Verdery 2009; Ringel 2022).[2] Moreover, as scholars of ruination and colonialism have observed, the traces of defunct regimes are not only material (crumbling monuments, devalued currency) but also social and psychological: habits, expectations, and emotional responses (Stoler 2013, 2016; Dawdy 2010, 2016; Edensor 2005; Buchli and Lucas 2001). Ruins are not moribund transmitters of pastness but rather are active forces. Indeed, Ann Laura Stoler (2016, 348) asks us to consider ruins as "not what we are left but what we are left *with*." Eisenhüttenstadt thus provides one answer when it comes to the ruination of Eastern Bloc socialism: We are left with a new paradigm of urban governance—a mimetic reproduction of socialist urbanism, refracted through the lens of contemporary sociopolitical concerns.

Over the course of this introduction, I examine how Eisenhüttenstadt's relationship to the socialist past has changed in the decades since reunification, as well as how the city's preservation of its "socialist scaffold" (Zarecor 2018, 99) has enabled a novel form of ecological governance. I then draw on anthropological scholarship to consider cultural engagements with the city's utopian origins, which point to a resurgent interest in legacies that can mitigate the more destructive aspects of our current social order.

Shifting Frameworks

In the early 2000s, as outlying areas of the city began to be demolished and the population shifted toward the historically protected center, city officials and residents alike discussed a return to East German planners' original vision. Yet understandings of that vision, as well as of the socialist past more broadly, have changed radically since reunification. In the 1990s, Eisenhüttenstadt's leaders worked to scrub socialist memory from the urban landscape, with socialism understood as a failed sociopolitical system. But in the twenty-first century, amid geopolitical and sociocultural instability, city officials publicly celebrate the East German state's utopian origins and hopeful orientation toward the future.

In 2021, the local government officially announced that Eisenhüttenstadt's Documentation Center for Everyday Culture in East Germany, whose state funding had been dwindling and precarious for years, would reopen as the Museum of Utopia and the Everyday: Everyday Culture and Art from East Germany in Beeskow and Eisenhüttenstadt (LOS 2021). The collection would be merged with a museum of East German art in the nearby town of Beeskow, the Oder-Spree County seat. The relaunch had been in preparation since 2019 and resulted in new curators, a stylish website redesign, and a flurry of activity, including a podcast with Friedrich Liechtenstein, an electronica musician and Eisenhüttenstadt

FIGURES 10A AND 10B. Scenes from the city center, 2014–16. Courtyards are accessed through ornate entryways, and bicycle transportation is common. Photographs by the author.

FIGURES 11A AND 11B. Scenes from the city center, 2014–16. Courtyards are accessed through ornate entryways, and bicycle transportation is common. Photographs by the author.

native best known as the star of the grocery chain Edeka's 2014 "Super Awesome" (*Super Geil*) ad campaign.

In June 2021, a few months after the museum's reopening, curator Florentine Nadolni gave a podcast interview in which she described her curatorial vision. East German cultural history, she said, "does not lie entirely in the past," and in fact remains an active part of the present, deeply embedded in many German life histories, beliefs, and cultural norms. Moreover, she went on, "when we speak about the past or about the present, it is also important to remember the view forward, toward the future, that is always contained within—this is what we hope to highlight in our use of the term 'Utopia'" (Nadolni 2021). The museum's collection focuses on East German material culture, but its curators attend equally to East Germany's immaterial legacies: the lifeworlds with which the collection once coexisted, and which it now evokes, in which utopian futurity featured prominently.

Socialist orientations toward the future have long been the object of scholarship (Buck-Morss 2000; Yurchak [2005] 2013; Boyer 2006; Bach 2002), but they are rarely singled out in public discourse as a defining feature of socialism's legacy. Thus, I consider my ethnographic attention to the socialist past to be a practice of "social stratigraphy" (Dawdy 2016, 8) analogous to the stratigraphic work of an archaeologist: Stratigraphy is the practice of examining the earth's strata in order to understand the past, analyzing the remains layer by layer. The past is "an unstable entity subject to taphonomy" or fossilization (Dawdy 2016, 28), and, like material or geological remains, it settles unevenly, reproducing some social topographies while erasing others. The present comes to us with these erasures and transformations already in place, and it is up to the ethnographer to identify patterns that indicate the presence of something buried or otherwise transformed, just as an archaeologist may identify a potential dig site based on its elevation relative to the surrounding area. Yet the ethnographer is also constrained by the uneven ways in which the past is materially, archivally, and socially preserved (Trouillot 1997; Stoler 2009), as well as how those preserved traces intersect with the heterogeneous points of view that inhabit an urban landscape (Schwenkel 2020; Tsing 2017).

Eisenhüttenstädters have become acclimated not only to the inherent heterogeneity of the urban landscape but also to the ways in which that heterogeneity makes urban meaning-making slippery—a slipperiness exacerbated by memories of both regime change and life under totalitarianism. Named Stalinstadt in 1953, the city was renamed Eisenhüttenstadt (Ironworks City) in 1961 during a period of de-Stalinization across the Eastern Bloc. Over the course of my fieldwork, people whose birthplace was recorded as Stalinstadt often made a show of pulling out their driver's license, usually with a remark about how comically

FIGURES 12A AND 12B. Detlef Juckel's family photographs depict the "building generation." Courtesy of Detlef Juckel.

arbitrary it felt when the city where they were born—founded only a decade prior—suddenly had a new name. One woman told me, laughing, "I was born in Stalinstadt, my brother in Fürstenberg"—a medieval village later subsumed into the city—"and we both grew up in Eisenhüttenstadt, all without moving house." After reunification, a popular joke noted that all of East Germany could be said to have "moved without moving house" (*umzug ohne umziehen*). It has long been clear in this region that seemingly immutable epistemic systems—geopolitics, geography, national identity—are subject to change from above and without notice (Yurchak [2005] 2013; Humphrey 2002a; Verdery 1996; Borneman 1992). Nearly overnight, Eisenhüttenstadt transformed from a well-resourced city at the center of the Eastern Bloc to a shrinking city on the nation's periphery.

Yet Eisenhüttenstadt's relationship to unstable systems of value goes beyond renaming and regime change. As a post-city and sociomaterial organism, the city is subject to the "uneven temporal sedimentation" of social and material ruins (Stoler 2016, 348). As a shrinking city, it faces the simultaneous transformation of meaning and material that tends to result from breakdown in the built environment (Fennell 2015; Buchli 1999). As a totalitarian planned city, it can be considered a "promissory utterance," ingrained with the expectation that it would, consistently, change radically over time as the building process unfolded (Abram 2014; Abram and Weszkalnys 2013). This was doubly true of Eisenhüttenstadt's "building generation" (*Aufbaugeneration*),[3] said to have "built" a new society while also contributing to the material construction of their city. The double meaning underscores an entanglement between social and material urban space that continues to be instrumentalized as urban renewal programs are carried out.

A New Model of Governance

Eisenhüttenstadt is unique among former socialist cities in that, as in socialist times, it still embodies an unusual degree of top-down administration in urban planning. The East German government expropriated large landholders, and land was returned to its former owners following reunification. But Eisenhüttenstadt's land had belonged to the Märkische Electric Company, which was long defunct. As a result, its ownership remained with the descendants of socialist municipal entities: the Eisenhüttenstädter Gebaudewirtschaft, or Eisenhüttenstädter Real Estate Company, known by the acronym GeWi (/ˈɡeːˌviː/), and the Eisenhüttenstädter Wohnungsbaugenossenschaft, or Eisenhüttenstädter Housing Cooperative, known by the acronym EWG (/eːˈʔfaˌɡeː/). As of this writing, the GeWi and EWG own close to 80 percent of the city's real estate, inclusive of commercial and industrial holdings, and around 75 percent of residents rent an apartment from one of the two companies (Stadt Eisenhüttenstadt and BBSM 2015, 18, 20).[4] This enables the city government to demolish and renovate residential neighborhoods on a scale that would be impossible to implement with multiple landlords in play—or at least impossible to implement with an equivalent degree of satisfaction across various stakeholder groups.

Although Eisenhüttenstadt was called the "First Model Socialist City," it would in fact prove to be the only one of its kind. Subsequent model cities, comprising prefabricated concrete architecture, were built adjacent to preexisting towns and cities, and their effects were diverse; while some, such as Halle-Neustadt, functioned as satellite neighborhoods adjacent to an established urban landscape, others transformed previously rural towns—namely, Hoyerswerda and Schwedt—into large industrial centers. Scholars tend to consider Eisenhüttenstadt, Hoyerswerda, Schwedt, Halle-Neustadt, and Wolfen-Nord, adjacent to Bitterfeld, to be East German socialist "New Towns," build according to the principles outlined by the East German Building Ministry (Bernhardt 2005). Eisenhüttenstadt is considered unique primarily for its architectural significance—the city center was built before cost-cutting measures forced a switch to prefabricated architecture—but it is also unique in the degree to which the circumstances of its founding have translated into what is effectively a two-party real estate market comprising the GeWi and EWG.

In such a consolidated market, the two real estate companies are able to collaborate closely on large-scale development projects. They sell each other property as needed to ensure that both companies remain solvent as plans are carried out, and they coordinate with the city government to ensure that funding is split equitably between them. For instance, most of the EWG's holdings have traditionally been outside the historically protected zone, in neighborhoods now slated for demolition; in the 2010s, the EWG effectively traded these buildings with GeWi buildings in the city center that were slated for renovation (BWSB 2018). As EWG chair Verena Rühr-Bach explained, this decision allowed the EWG to reap the long-term benefits of federal renovation funding—lower vacancy rates, higher property values—and the GeWi, too, would benefit if the city as a whole thrived. After all, the EWG's collapse would increase unemployment and urban decrepitude, ultimately a net negative for the GeWi. Thus, while ecological economists tend to argue that "a rising tide lifts all boats" is often a fig leaf for trickle-down policies (TEDx Talks 2014), the GeWi and EWG's cooperation shows that the logic of rising tides can in fact hold when corporate and state actors embrace a commitment to mutual aid and the equitable distribution of financial and material resources.

Moreover, the companies work together to assist the residents of buildings slated for demolition. Around two years prior to each demolition, residents are invited to view comparable apartments across each company's holdings. Because nearly all apartments in the city are owned by the two landlords, residents do not have to scour real estate listings and apply for housing with numerous landlords or companies, a process that would be difficult to navigate for the city's large proportion of elderly residents. When it comes time for residents to move, the two real estate companies use demolition funding to hire moving services— urban renewal funding programs aim to relocate residents with as little friction as possible. Many informants who were relocated prior to demolitions told me that their experience had been wholly positive, and that they were grateful for the help they received in relocating from their increasingly vacant, disinvested neighborhoods.[5]

Large-scale projects in Eisenhüttenstadt are funded primarily by the federal government or by multistate initiatives, with funds procured at the city level. Since 2002, the GeWi, EWG, and city government have collaborated on an Urban Renewal Plan (Stadtumbaukonzept, or STUK) that details plans for large-scale structural changes, including the demolition of outlying areas and the revitalization of the city center. The most recent Urban Renewal Plan was published in 2015 and covers plans through 2025, many of which are described in this book. Since 2006, the STUK has also been complemented by an Integrated Urban Development Strategy (Integrierte Stadtentwicklungskonzept, or INSEK), which forms the basis of everyday urban administration as well as funding applications to the Brandenburg State. The INSEK is "the overriding instrument for urban planning at the city level" and takes "interdisciplinary consideration of different fields of urban development" (Stadt Eisenhüttenstadt and BBSM 2022, 8). The current iteration of the INSEK, published in 2022, was first developed between 2006 and 2008 and was revised between 2012 and 2014. The 2022 iteration outlines planned developments through 2035 and reflects on how ongoing projects can help the city meet its social and environmental goals.

Although Eisenhüttenstadt's leaders are certainly influenced by market forces when choosing where to invest their renovation or demolition funding, the city is uniquely set up to deprioritize growth in its real estate sector. The GeWi is a private company in which the city government is the only shareholder, and cost sharing between city and state governments is, in most cases, determined proportionally by the city's income. If the GeWi were to produce profits in excess of what the city could reinvest—an unlikely possibility—the city government would take on a greater share of urban renewal costs vis-à-vis the state, but the overall concept for urban renewal would remain largely unchanged. The EWG, by contrast, is a real estate cooperative, and, as such, any profits it generates have always been reinvested into the upkeep of its holdings. Eisenhüttenstadt therefore provides unique insight into what urban planning may look like when structural forces enable a municipality to prioritize a holistic vision of urban well-being—one that includes financial solvency—over the endless accumulation of surplus capital.

Eisenhüttenstadt's real estate market bears a striking resemblance to what Herman Daly ([1973] 1980, 1993) calls a "steady-state economy," a modern reinterpretation of John Stewart Mill's stationary state. Classical economists of the eighteenth century predicted that what they termed the progressive state, in which profits, wages, and accumulated wealth were continually rising, would eventually give way to a stationary state, in which saturated markets failed to produce increasing amounts of surplus capital year over year. Yet while Adam Smith and other classical economists dreaded the stationary state, Mill recast it from a mark of failure to one of achievement. Given a stationary population— Mill does not elaborate on how to achieve the necessary "prudential restraint on population" (Mill [1848] 1986, 319)—any surplus capital could be reinvested to pursue "mental culture" or "moral and social progress." As a result, "there would be . . . much room for improving the Art of Living, and much more likelihood of its being improved, when minds ceased to be engrossed by the art of getting on" (321). Mill questions the need of growth for growth's sake. "Towards what ultimate point is society tending by its industrial progress?" he asks, "When the progress ceases, in what condition are we to expect that it will leave mankind?" (318).

Daly, too, finds that classical economists have lost sight of the economy's ultimate ends. Its intermediate means (resources) are put toward intermediate ends (need fulfillment), but we pay heed neither to ultimate means (the sum total of the earth's resources) nor to ultimate ends (the Art of Living). And while redefining prosperity has long been a priority for economists (Sen 2001), more recent scholarship on the subject points to the urgency of our current moment (Jackson 2016, 2021). As climate change progresses and our ultimate means shrink, it becomes increasingly important to attend to the sustainability of our ultimate ends, and to ask whether those ends justify the diminution of ultimate means that results from their pursuit. Through this lens, ecological economics shares with East German socialism a definition of sustainability that emphasizes providing for future generations. Both emphasize using intermediate means—labor, materials—to fulfill ultimate ends: creating the conditions of possibility under which future generations might thrive. This form of sacrificing the present for an imagined future—one whose realization is impossible to verify—is not unlike the "cruel optimism" that powers capitalism (Berlant 2011): We imagine that our desired outcome will materialize if only we continue to live as we do in the present, however uncomfortable that may be. In doing so, both socialism and environmentalism imbue daily practices with a sense of purpose, an obligation toward imagined others that brings an attention to ultimate ends into the realm of the everyday.

A City Without a Past

Despite their innovative intellectual frameworks and lauding by industry experts, Eisenhüttenstadt's developments are not always perceived in a positive light. On the ground level, it can be difficult to generate excitement over plans that focus on managing shrinkage. In 2015, when Eisenhüttenstadt's mayor announced at a public gathering that plans had been approved to build a nursing home in Central Square, the empty lot across the street from City Hall, an audible gasp went through the crowd. Despite anxieties about the empty lot, originally intended for a Culture Palace and informally used as a parking lot for City Hall employees— and despite the fact that residents often complained about the decrepit state of the existing nursing home, which was too small to meet demand and was located on the city's outskirts—residents did not want indicators of decline or obsolescence in such a central location. In part due to the public's response, the new nursing home, like the Culture Palace before it, never materialized.

As the collective gasp evinced, Eisenhüttenstadt's residents are wary of being marked indelibly not only with the socialist past but with pastness more generally. One informant told me that while Eisenhüttenstadt began as "a place with no past, a place with only a future"—a place to which no one was native, and which had no wartime history—it had now become a place defined by its past. Anthropologist Dominic Boyer (2006, 361) describes this temporal transformation as futurity "turned inside-out," in which the future(s) of postsocialist places are perceived in light of the socialist past. The gasp reflects a desire among Eisenhüttenstadt's residents to fix their inside-out futurity and "occupy the same historical time as their cosmopolitan contemporaries" (Schwenkel 2020, 19)—a position common to residents of places marked by pastness, and one that can feel difficult to achieve amid material reminders of a defunct regime (Scott 2014; Buck-Morss 2000).

The narrative of Eisenhüttenstadt as a city without a past—repeated often by informants and in local media (Erler 2015)—is fantasy. During World War II, the area's transportation connections to both Berlin and the Eastern Front fostered a cottage industry in Nazi military manufacturing. A chemical weapons factory run by the company Degussa, which held the patent on Zyklon B, was built near Fürstenberg in 1940 and produced explosives, plastics, and formaldehyde. In 1944, a short-lived metallurgy factory run by Rheinmetall-Borsig began production of onboard aircraft guns. Allied prisoners of war were held in prison

FIGURES 13A.   City Hall, 2023. Photograph by the author.

camp Stalag III B and were forced to man a granite transshipment point on the Oder–Spree Canal, which connects the Oder River with the Spree in Berlin. Concentration camp prisoners brought in from Ravensbrück and Sachsenhausen, as well as Jews from the Lodz Ghetto, were pressed into labor at all three sites, as well as in the nearby Märkische Electric Company power plant. By the end of 1945, Allied bombings and Russian troops had destroyed much of this industrial infrastructure (Drieschner and Schulz 2008), though East German urban planners cited the local "orientation toward industrial work" (Bauakademie der DDR 1951) as an advantage when choosing where to situate the model city.

When Eisenhüttenstadt's construction began in 1951, the East German national newspaper described the area where it would be built as "where the hares and foxes bid each other goodnight"—a turn of phrase meant to evoke a site utterly untouched by human development, save perhaps the quaint medieval villages a few miles away (Pfannstiel 1951). Yet for people old enough to remember the Nazi barracks that stood until the mid-1960s; or who know the history of the ruined Märkische Electric Company power plant, whose inactive smokestacks still rise behind the city; or who have walked along the banks of the Oder and seen the foundations of the old bridge that was blown up by the Wehrmacht in an effort to stop the advancing Red Army—for those people, present-day changes, like the construction of the city itself, are considered just one more iteration in

FIGURES 13B. Central Square, early 1960s. Photograph by M. Fricke, courtesy of Stadtarchiv Eisenhüttenstadt.

a churn of sociopolitical projects, each of which imposes its own reading of the urban landscape, and each of which is eventually erased.

As a result, many of my informants exhibit an attunement to what Nancy Munn (2013) calls the "becoming-past of place," an imagination of the present within history's *longue durée* in which one glimpses one's own eventual erasure. I was surprised when, on two separate occasions, informants told me that the hills around the city had been formed by Ice Age glacial deposits. The comments seemed intent on portraying human existence as dwarfed by geologic time, and I wondered whether my informants meant to insinuate that, as Eisenhütten-städters, they were inheritors to far more than socialist urbanism: the natural world, which long preceded human habitation. Later, one of those informants told me that after experiencing so much regime change in her lifetime—she had lived through both the Nazi and East German eras—she felt much more of an allegiance toward those ancient hills than to any abstract notions of nationhood. Like a slowly melting glacier that exposes new layers of debris over time, the past accretes and becomes exposed to us unevenly. And as different pasts become apparent to us, we must understand not only what we do with our inheritances, but also what we do in recognizing our inheritances as such.

This book examines such reckonings with pastness and futurity in order to understand the layering of sociopolitical worlds, both real and imagined, that guide urban development and urban practices over time. It is about the interplay between plans and actualization, which always produces gaps where unexpected contingencies can grow (Holston 1989; Rabinow [1989] 1995). It is about how the same space can be used to house radically different social worlds—in opposition to the mechanistic Corbusian imagination with which Eisenhüttenstadt was planned. And, at its core, it is about time: time as taphonomic transformer, time as the driver of obsolescence, time as the creator of emergency, time as cruelly linear and cruelly cyclical (to paraphrase George Carlin, the planet will survive—its people will not). We can neither exist outside time nor exhaust its potential, so we would do well to better understand its effects on both cities and the social.

Rethinking Late Socialism

As the postwar era wears on, it has become increasingly clear that post-cities need new futures (Ringel 2022; Zeiderman and Dawson 2022). Within this discursive imagination, the effects of a post-hyphenate—postsocialist, postcolonialist—are presented as moribund, lying thoroughly in the past. Effects are strongest following a regime's collapse and then recede over time—a progression quite unlike the one that has actually played out since the mid-twentieth century, in which post-effects have proved alternately latent and long-lasting (Shapiro and Kirksey 2017; Ahmann 2018). Hence, scholars prefer to describe the deindustrialization of the Global North as "late industrial," a term that accounts for industrialism's shifting geography and ongoing impacts (Fortun 2012).

Post-ness also binds places to particular historical eras without regard for how that era's legacies are manifested.[6] In the early 2000s, Felix Ringel conducted an ethnography of Hoyerswerda, East Germany's Second Model Socialist City and, at the time, its fastest shrinking. (Hoyerswerda is 110 kilometers southwest of Eisenhüttenstadt, about a ninety-minute drive.) As in Eisenhüttenstadt, the socialist past laid the groundwork for much of Hoyerswerda's postreunification shrinkage. But pasts and futures exist in and for the present, and Ringel found that Hoyerswerda's imagined futures were influenced less by the socialist era than by the decades spent grappling with its loss. As residents struggled with deindustrialization and the neoliberalization of the East German economy, they rejected postsocialist narratives of inevitable decline, instead embracing "the fact that futures can be lost and exchanged for other futures [as] an essential part of Hoyerswerda's story" (Ringel 2018, 12)—and as an essential starting point for urban revitalization.

In this context, "late socialism" is perhaps a more appropriate descriptor for the postsocialist present. The term is often used to describe the 1960s through the 1980s in the Eastern Bloc, but "late socialism" as an analogue of "late capitalism" and "late industrialism" suggests that socialism continues to exist in radically altered form—one in which socialist governance is largely absent. Late socialism creates a conceptual space needed to acknowledge that some forms of radical experimentation within the confines of capitalism—Eisenhüttenstadt's stasis-generating real estate market, for instance—can be read as manifestations of socialism's continued effectual force. Indeed, Eisenhüttenstadt illustrates how socialism's lessons and legacy create social change that might never have come to pass absent this particular history.

We would also do well to remember the lessons of "transitology," commonly defined as the study of regime change. During the immediate postsocialist period, political leaders and public intellectuals imagined that formerly socialist countries would move inexorably toward free-market capitalism (Fukuyama [1992] 2006; Friedman 2005)—transitology's object was the transition from socialism to capitalism. But as Katherine Verdery (1996, 15) has pointed out, transitology is simply the study of transformation, and postsocialist anthropologists rejected such teleological suppositions (Berdahl 1999; Verdery 1996). After all, efforts to naturalize capitalist expansion as inevitable and desirable are a product of capitalism itself.

Nostalgia for the Future

East German culture remains distinctive within Germany. When East and West Germany unified in 1990, reunification was portrayed as the union of two equals, a "vision of solidarity" with neither side dominating (Gook 2015, 282). Within months, the East emerged as the losing side. Its state-owned businesses were dismantled, resulting in massive unemployment and outmigration. And as East and West Germans encountered the foreignness of each other's clothes, habits, and consumer goods, a former East German identity began to emerge, colloquially called *Ossi* or occasionally *Zoni*, referring to the former East (Ost) and its origins as the Zone of Soviet Occupation (Sowjetische Besatzungszone). West Germans stereotyped Easterners as uncultured, poor, and out of touch with contemporary practices. East Germans stereotyped Westerners, or *Wessis*, as uptight and materialistic; they were sometimes called *Besserwessis*, or know-it-all Westerners, for their condescending attitudes toward Easterners (Berdahl 1999, 168). Despite the irreverent-sounding nicknames, the division of Germans into Ossis and Wessis was in fact often experienced as traumatic. Dominic Boyer (2006, 371) writes that "the greater trauma was not the collapse of the GDR and its lifeworld but, rather, the discovery that post-unification public narratives reduced the GDR to the prison camp of a criminal regime and reduced [former East Germans] to this camp's abject inmates."

As Ossi culture began to develop, East Germans rejected the assumption that Western goods were superior—the "real" version of goods toward which socialist goods aspired (Bach 2017, 22; Borneman 1991, 146–47). Nostalgic representations of East Germany began to proliferate, ushering in a culture of *Ostalgie*— a neologism of "East" (*Ost*) and "nostalgia" (*nostalgie*)—that celebrated East German aesthetics and material culture. Since the early 2000s, internationally acclaimed films and television shows, including *Good Bye, Lenin!* (2003), *The Lives of Others* (2006), *Weissensee* (2010), and *Deutschland 83* (2015) have portrayed East Germany for a national audience. (Many of the set pieces for these productions came from Eisenhüttenstadt's Museum of Utopia and the Everyday.) As a result, the texture of everyday life in East Germany—from polyester clothes and melamine dishes to Young Pioneer uniforms and Stasi surveillance tactics— has become familiar within the wider German culture.

Ostalgie is, in some ways, a remedy for the erasure of East German culture that took place in the early 1990s, a period when anthropologists of the Eastern Bloc perceived a mandate "to describe the nature of a vanishing society" (Borneman 1991, 250). The consumption of Ostalgie has been popularly understood as a way for former East Germans to express nostalgia for the culture of their upbringing without expressing support for the East German state as such. Furthermore, Ostalgie offered Germans of all backgrounds the chance to reexperience East German culture after it could no longer be experienced firsthand. Andreas Ludwig, a West German historian who founded what was then called the Documentation Center for Everyday Culture in East Germany, told me that he was inspired to found the museum when, in the early 1990s, he began to see trash heaps filled with the colorful plasticware that was once ubiquitous in East German homes— shortly after reunification, many East Germans replaced their possessions with the Western goods they had long been denied. He told me that in the 1990s, visitors to the Documentation Center were mostly former East Germans looking to revisit their recently vanished material culture or share that culture with Western friends and relatives. Often they marveled at how strange it was that what had recently seemed contemporary was suddenly relegated to the past.

Yet anthropologists have perceived another layer to Ostalgie: a longing for a time before widespread disillusion with capitalism, when utopian impulses still seemed possible (Bach 2002, 2017; Boyer 2006). During the socialist era, East Germans expressed faith that their eventual reunification with West Germany—and their adoption of Western culture—would enable them to pursue the self-actualizing life courses that had been stifled by the socialist regime. But capitalism turned out to be stifling in unexpected ways, as predatory lending practices, coupled with the rushed and mishandled sale of state-owned enterprises, led to a severe economic downturn in the former East. Thus Ostalgie, as a form of what Bach (2017, 18) calls "modernist nostalgia," is "less a longing for an unredeemable past as such than a longing for the fantasies and desires that were once possible in that past . . . a longing for a *mode* of longing that is no longer possible." Before access to capitalism was a reality, East Germans could imagine that it promised an eventual panoply of possible futures. Reunification was a source of hope—even if its imagined futures were never actually attainable. Daphne Berdahl (1999, 138) describes an informant looking at a photograph of herself from the East German era: "I used to wear that dress every day just because it was from the West," she told Berdahl. "Now, of course, I know they just sent us the things they didn't want any more."

Capitalist consumption loomed large in the East German imagination, and its lack shaped East German subjectivity. John Borneman writes that socialism, with its constant material shortages, infused everyday life with a nonspecific form of desire—a diffuse desire, roughly, for Western abundance—that reunification offered to sate. Capitalism, in contrast, trained its subjects to desire an endless supply of specific, immediately attainable things (Borneman 1991). Thus, the retrospective realization, among those who had hoped for access to capitalism, that the socialist era was in fact suffused with a deep sense of hopefulness reflects a duality within Ostalgie: the "diffuse desire" for capitalist consumption—perhaps enabled by reunification—layered onto the optimism inherent to the socialist project.

Since reunification, traces of the socialist era have come to function as dialectical images (Dawdy 2010; Buck-Morss 1991) and, as such, are able to evoke the future orientation that was integral to life under socialism. Eastern Bloc socialism sought mastery over time, its victories "described in terms of historical progress rather than territorial gain" (Buck-Morss 2000, 23). Architecture was an effort to bring that revolutionary orientation into "the phenomenal world of the everyday" (Buck-Morss 2000, 42), but so, too, were everyday objects. As Krisztina Fehérváry (2009, 428) notes, because the distribution of goods was tightly managed in the Eastern Bloc, "the socialist state [was] a material entity—robustly present in everything from Cuban oranges and East German paper napkins to the pseudo-Modernist built environments that became its signature." These products were tactile reminders of the state's promise for a better life and of the incremental changes that would take place as socialism progressed (Pence and Betts 2008)—an entanglement of materiality and futurity mirrored in the duality of the building generation.

The Museum of Utopia and the Everyday does not specify which socialist-era future it seeks to revive—the hope for capitalist possibility, the hope for the achievement of Communism, or an entanglement of the two wrapped in a "mode of longing" (Bach 2017) for something other than the future at present. Perhaps this ambiguity is itself, in part, one legacy of socialist doublethink (Yurchak [2005] 2013; Humphrey 2004). Regardless, the material endurance of Eisenhüttenstadt, like other cities that have outlived the regimes that built them (Schwenkel 2020), speaks to the fact that new urban futures emerge by necessity under changing sociopolitical circumstances. After all, post-cities have by definition traded away at least one erstwhile future, and their continued presence is a testament to their ability to withstand seismic sociopolitical shifts.

Rising from the Ruins

In 2020, Niklas Nitschke, an artist based near Eisenhüttenstadt, founded a symposium series titled *Between Model and Museum*, inspired by the city's utopian past. "The promise of a different, 'ideal' society [is] preserved in the urban fabric," Nitschke (2021) writes, and the symposia, conducted in 2020 and 2021, brought together artists and academics to interrogate utopianism through the lens of Eisenhüttenstadt and its history. Nitschke acknowledges that Eisenhüttenstadt, as a utopian city, is something of a contradiction in terms—a materially stolid instantiation of a temporally fluid thing. After all, utopia, like futurity, ceases to be the thing *qua* thing as soon as it is made material. In its concreteness, Eisenhüttenstadt is a reminder of utopian thinking and, simultaneously, a check on future utopian ambitions—an obstacle to utopian achievement exemplary of the internal contradictions that continue to define the former Eastern Bloc.

Yet perhaps the attention currently being paid to utopian impulses—as well as to the impossibility of their achievement and the trauma of their loss—offers us reassurance that we, too, will weather the next catastrophic historical rupture, even if we must do so in a way that falls short of our ideals. As part of the 2021 symposium, Nitschke collaborated with artist Armin Harteinstein to curate an exhibition in an abandoned preschool building. There, a text painting by Harteinstein, around six feet tall and starkly visible, stood at the end of a long corridor, reading, "AND ORIENTED TOWARDS THE FUTURE" (Und der Zukunft zugewandt). The words are taken from the opening line of the East German national anthem, "Rising from the Ruins" (Auferstanden aus Ruinen), which begins, "Rising from the ruins and facing the future." The song describes the nation's triumphant birth amid the wreckage of the Second World War. The future that East Germany faced was presumed boundless.

Yet all modern nation-states foster an imagination of eternal endurance (Anderson [1983] 2016). The Third Reich, too, operated under the assumption that its temporal horizon would be infinite; indeed, the long-term future was central to Nazi ideology. Albert Speer's "Theory of Ruin Value" held that Germania—as Berlin would be renamed after its transformation into a monumental Nazi capital—should be built such that its eventual ruins, thousands of years hence, would evoke a grandeur comparable to that ascribed to classical Greece and Rome, eternal evidence of Nazi superiority (Huyssen 2006). Granite destined for Germania now paves sidewalks in Eisenhüttenstadt (Drieschner and Schulz 2004), a testament to the irony of eternal endurance.

For a viewer familiar with East German history, Hartenstein's artwork playfully engages with the "future past" (Koselleck 2004). Moreover, it evokes a temporal landscape we have seen repeated often since the mid-twentieth century: Imaginations of linear progress and eternal endurance—of a regime, socioeconomic system, or epistemic outlook—meet an end that is widely experienced as abrupt and unexpected. Such disruption can be experienced as traumatic even by those who had advocated for change. Writer Jana Hensel attended Monday Demonstrations as a thirteen-year-old in Leipzig but was nonetheless shocked by the reality of German reunification.[7] She writes that although she had once hoped that East Germany would disappear—and quickly—"now it was as if East Germany had never even existed, and as if it wasn't supposed to hurt to have everything familiar suddenly torn away" (Hensel 2002, 14).

The text painting, with its modernist aesthetics and site-specific emplacement, acts as both a reference to East Germany's temporal-historical orientation and a repetition of it. The artwork invites its viewer to reinhabit the East German sensibilities that were once cultivated in the abandoned school building, reenacting socialist practices as they read the text. Next to the typographic painting, the curators exhibited a painting by Nitschke depicting two figures walking along the Street of the Republic; in the weeks leading up to the symposium, Nitschke displayed the painting in a makeshift gallery set up in the school's foyer, where he invited residents to engage in conversation about the city's development. Yet when paired with Hartenstein's text painting, the two artworks produced a new ambiguity. Does the viewer ascribe the phrase "facing the future" to the East German figures and imagine *their* future orientation? Or do they take on the words as their own, centering themselves and the contemporary future through the inherent subjectivity of language (Benveniste [1958] 1971)? The ambiguity becomes productive as the viewer considers their own relationship to futurity alongside the imagined futurity of the depicted East Germans—and perhaps that of the fascists whom the East Germans replaced.

In imagining the layered urban futures simultaneously in play, one may find that the contemporary Euro-American temporal landscape bears a striking resemblance to that of Eastern Bloc socialism—if Eastern Bloc socialist

FIGURE 14. Text painting by Armin Hartenstein in an exhibition curated by the artists, Eisenhüttenstadt, 2021. Photograph by Niklas Nitschke.

FIGURE 15. Text painting by Armin Hartenstein (*right*) and painting by Niklas Nitschke (*left*) in an exhibition curated by the artists, Eisenhüttenstadt, 2021. Photograph by Niklas Nitschke.

temporality could be accessed from a future anterior position. Knowledge of socialism's eventual collapse is a bell that cannot be unrung, and even valorizations of socialist futurity carry that knowledge within them. Socialist futurity, no matter how hopeful, always feels melancholic in the present. As one informant from Eisenhüttenstadt told me, "We thought to ourselves [under socialism], 'We're going straight into paradise.' And after reunification it was paradise lost." Thus, to reinhabit socialist futurity in the present is to look to the future with hope while also accepting the possibility of a sudden, irrevocable disruption to contemporary ways of life.

We must grapple with the fact that global capitalism, though seemingly intractable, is incompatible with the continuation of human existence into an indefinite future. On a global level, we continue to engage in practices that the earth cannot sustain: air and space travel, resource extraction, and the production of plastics, among many others. Yet unlike East Germans in the mid-twentieth century, we know that a day will come when we have no choice but to radically reinvent our social, political, and economic systems. The temporal pattern that one observes layered in Eisenhüttenstadt and the symposium exhibition, in which seemingly eternal ways of life are suddenly and permanently upended, is frighteningly similar to the most likely scenario for our own near future.

Perhaps, then, to recover lost utopian impulses is to recover faith in human ingenuity. Twice before—following World War II and following reunification—people in Eisenhüttenstadt forged a new future when none seemed possible. Who is to say that cannot happen again—even if we do not yet know what that future will look like? In light of climate change's existential threats, one could argue that human beings should desire *a* future, not a particular one. And in Eisenhüttenstadt, as "a place with only a future," as one informant put it, empty placeholders of futurity abound. For a time in the early 2000s, the city's slogan was "Future Eisenhüttenstadt." Stamped on the spines of binders whose contents document the city's nadir, "Future Eisenhüttenstadt" now feels like both a plea and a promise. In 2015, an amateur photography club set up a display in the city's main shopping center depicting the theme "Future Eisenhüttenstadt" through photo collage. The exhibition was dominated by hyperindustrialized, sometimes Seussian imagery, and by signifiers of modernity that were unlikely to be built: a major airport and train station, new high-rise buildings, the skyline glittering at night. While such futures are at odds with the ones put forth by city officials, they nonetheless evince Eisenhüttenstädters' desire to imagine alternative futures—to counter assumptions that shrinking cities have "no future" (Ringel 2018, 25) by exercising and externalizing their imaginations of futurity.

The multiple, sometimes opposing futures evoked in Eisenhüttenstadt— the industrial powerhouse, the right-sized pastoral city—may be read as "indeterminate," which scholars distinguish from comparable terms such as "indecipherable" or "undecided" (Alexander and Sanchez 2018). Something that is indeterminate, in their formulation, fails to conform to existing systems of value, particularly the system that dominates under capitalism, which relies on a binary distinction between productivity and waste. The indeterminate signals the existence of other, yet unknown systems of value. Indeterminacy is essential to our current moment because any future that includes human beings must introduce a radically new way of assessing and understanding value—or else risk catastrophic outcomes in the pursuit of productivity. Perhaps these new systems will be achieved by shifting our focus to development, as Daly suggests. Or perhaps methods yet to be developed will enable them. Capitalism, unlike socialism, does not imagine its own successor, and no likely contender has emerged thus far.

Economist Kate Raworth suggests that we let go of the capitalist-socialist binary altogether and embrace what she calls "doughnut economics." Unlike the linear projections that have characterized socioeconomic visualizations until now—the rise and fall of metrics such as age or income—Raworth proposes that municipalities should monitor a dashboard of doughnuts, wherein the inner rings represent various aspects of municipal well-being (employment or poverty rates, for instance) and the outer rings represent the associated ecological costs (Raworth 2017). The goal would be to extend the inner rings as far inward as possible, representing increases in well-being, without the outer rings, which grow outward as negative ecological impacts increase to the point that they exceed planetary limits. In such a model, political leaders would be forced to ask, "At what cost?" when, for instance, their low unemployment numbers are dependent on an ecologically destructive industry. Their goal would be to stay within the doughnut.

"Doughnut initiatives" have recently launched in major cities such as Copenhagen, Toronto, Glasgow, and Barcelona (DEAL 2022)—places where both budgets and political will allow local governments to hire forward-thinking experts. Eisenhüttenstadt, by contrast, has a limited municipal operating budget, is economically reliant on industrial manufacturing, and has seen rising support for right-wing political parties since the late 2010s. Yet, as I show over the course of this book, as municipal leaders attend to their city's history—sometimes by choice, often by circumstance—they reinvent East German urbanism through the lens of contemporary politics. After all, scholars remind us, remembering is always an act of the present (Huyssen 2003; Ricoeur 2009; Augé 2004). And as Eisenhüttenstadt's leaders navigate life and governance in a city whose burdensome historical superlatives—Germany's First Socialist City, Germany's Largest Historically Protected Site—often seem at odds with contemporary notions of

THE AFTERLIFE OF UTOPIA   29

urban thriving, they have been forced to contemplate how urban thriving may be redefined as they carry out revitalization efforts.

The Art of Living

Eisenhüttenstadt's renovation efforts since the 2010s mean that the urban land-scape no longer bears the marks of its tumultuous history, save the abandoned Hotel Lunik that looms over the informal parking lot across from City Hall. Still, it is not Berlin, where buildings that were utterly derelict in the 1990s now sell for millions. Although artists and filmmakers occasionally visit, it is no bustling cre-ative center. It is not a bastion of ardent socialism, nor is it a paragon of financial success. It is a small, well-kept city of low-rise buildings dominated by the elderly. People from the region are more likely to describe it as a quiet working-class town than as a radical commune. In many ways, it also fails to conform to our imagination of what a successfully revitalized city should be, with young people, entrepreneurs, hip cafés, nightlife—in a word, growth.

In his early twenties, John Stuart Mill suffered from a long bout with depres-sion, the resolution of which he credited to literature—namely, the poetry of Wil-liam Wordsworth. Economist Tim Jackson, who recounts Mill's story, suggests that poetry helped Mill precisely because in it, he "found a balm that lay beyond the intellect" (Jackson 2021, 64). Poetry brought Mill in touch with a transcendent sense of shared humanity. It expressed inarticulable emotional experiences, com-mon to the human condition, in words greater than the sum of their parts. And later in life, as he struggled to write his autobiography, poetry revealed to him the paradox at the heart of utilitarianism: That which is unquantifiable—the sense of fulfillment wrought by spirituality, human relationships, or connection to the natu-ral world—is left out of the technocratic statecraft intended to increase human well-being. In an unpublished draft of his autobiography, Mill wrote, "In our schemes for improving human affairs, we overlook human beings" (quoted in Jackson 2021, 55).

Like poetry, ethnography attempts to capture what William James ([1890] 1983, 247) called the "unclassified residuum," the fullness and complexity of lived experience that cannot be assimilated into the reified notions spawned from dis-ciplines such as economics or urban planning. This ethnography portrays a city that does not easily conform to existing categories and models: a capitalist city without private homeownership, a steel town promising carbon neutrality. In 2022, the EWG won its fifth "Living Well: Fit for the Future" commendation, an award granted by the Berlin-Brandenburg Housing Association (Verband Berlin-Brandenburgischer Wohnungsunternehmen), despite the fact that nearly a third of Eisenhüttenstadt's population is over the age of sixty-five (EWG 2022b).

Socialism, like capitalism, defined urban success in terms of growth. When the East German state collapsed, Eisenhüttenstadt's leaders were planning Housing Complex 8; they projected a population of 110,000 by 1999 (Heilmeyer 2021, 19). But this erstwhile promise of urban expansion has been replaced by the promise of a balanced life lived in proximity to nature. A 2021 advertisement from the EWG called "Welcome Home" depicts groups of residents frolicking through the city's green spaces and, as of this writing, has twenty-two thousand views on YouTube—a number that comes close to the city's total population. Over the course of the well-produced commercial, the protagonists, played by actors of various ages, visit Eisenhüttenstadt's Diehlo Mountain Park, first as children and then as increasingly older adults. Interspersed are depictions of after-work bike rides and picnics along the banks of the Oder, as well as a cameo from the chair of the EWG, who plays a mother disciplining her teenage son. He moves out, signaling the availability of apartments suitable for young people (EWG eG 2021). Other videos by the EWG, also with thousands of views on YouTube, profile young residents who have returned to Eisenhüttenstadt after stints in larger cities. The message, it seems, is that these young people, both real and fictional, have found in Eisenhüttenstadt an appreciation for the good-enough life, one in which being bound to the local landscape and community is considered more valuable than proximity to wealth and power. They have found, in other words, a new imagination of urban thriving at a time when new imaginations are urgently needed.

Structure and Methods

The structure of this book tacks between examinations of urban development and cultural history. Chapter 1 recounts Eisenhüttenstadt's founding and architectural development, as well as the development of the East German architectural emic. Chapter 2 explores contemporary efforts in demolition and renovation, focused on Urban Renewal East and the revitalization of the Housing Complex. Chapter 3 discusses historiography in the reunification period, as residents reconsidered the city's socialist past and its legibility within the urban landscape. Chapter 4 returns to contemporary developments, examining how socialist-era legacies have undergirded cooperation between the city's two real estate companies. Chapter 5 looks at the city's history of collectivism and its development amid social change, including the increase in migration to Europe that occurred in 2015.[8] Chapter 6 discusses contemporary efforts to reduce the city's carbon footprint and transform Eisenhüttenstadt into the world's first carbon-neutral steel manufacturing city.

FIGURE 16. The residents of Linden Avenue 18 (then Lenin Avenue) socialize on their roof deck in an undated photograph, circa 1980s. Courtesy of Helga Boehm.

FIGURE 17. Linden Avenue 18 (*bottom center*) in a postcard from 1963. Courtesy of Detlef Juckel.

Throughout the book I include images, including documentary photographs and visual materials collected from informants: family photographs, newspaper clippings, and postcards, which played a particularly central role in East German culture. Ben Kaden, an Eisenhüttenstadt native and library scientist, has observed that, in a country with limited phone and telegram service, postcards provided an essential form of everyday communication. Kaden's extensive collection of East German postcards includes banal messages such as "I'd like to pay you a visit on Sunday" and "I won't be returning home on Friday as planned," with postmarks indicating that the cards were sent short distances within Brandenburg. Yet postcards also played an important role in the fledgling nation's political imaginary. The East German regime controlled the production, distribution, and delivery of postcards and used them to circulate images that would build its national identity and visual culture (Kaden 2017, 2020a). In Eisenhüttenstadt, postcards were particularly important for cultivating the reputation of the model city—Kaden notes that postcards "transport narratives of the city into the world" (Kaden 2020b). Many of my informants collected postcards of their hometown, and those that were removed from circulation now reflect both informants' personal attachments and the idealistic narratives put forth by the defunct regime.

This book draws on ethnographic fieldwork conducted between 2010 and 2023, a time when Eisenhüttenstadt was undergoing dramatic change. During the 2010s, around seven thousand apartments were demolished across the city. Renovation efforts on the remaining buildings had only just begun when, in 2015, the sudden arrival of thousands of migrants upended urban renewal projects. I lived in Eisenhüttenstadt from 2014 to 2016. As a city resident, I participated in public life, attended community events and town hall meetings, and conducted numerous informal interviews with neighbors and acquaintances. I also interviewed municipal leaders, including architects and urban planners, and conducted participant observation with the elderly, high school students, and asylum seekers, in part as a volunteer with the local charity Workers' Wellness (Arbeiterwohlfahrt, or AWO). I conducted archival research at the Eisenhüttenstadt City Archives, as well as at the Brandenburg State Archives in Potsdam and the German Federal Archives in Berlin. Some names have been changed to protect the privacy of informants. Where requested, informants are referenced by their first name and last initial, a common practice in German media.

THE FIRST NEW TOWN

In 2012, the actor Tom Hanks was a guest on *The Late Show with David Letterman*. He had been making a film in Berlin, and he told Letterman about his visit to "Iron Hut City": Eisen Hütten Stadt. Eisenhüttenstädters have been trying to capitalize on the mistranslation ever since, and the city's tourism bureau still sells Iron Hut City souvenirs. "An amazing architectural place where they are trying to rebuild it so that young and old people—fascinating place," Hanks said. Eberhard Harz, the former GeWi chair, had been Hanks's tour guide, and his influence was apparent.

"A lot of concrete?" Letterman interrupted.

"A lot of concrete," said Hanks. "We saw Housing Complex Number 1, and Housing Complex Number 2, and walked over to Complex Number 3." He then leaned into stereotypes about socialist city building. "No cars, no people, just a dearth of everything."

Yet Eisenhüttenstadt defies most stereotypes about late socialist urbanism. Its low-rise apartment buildings are surrounded by landscaped courtyards and a diverse array of public art. It has a cobblestone main avenue and monumental neoclassical civic buildings; adjacent medieval villages also fall within the city limits. Like many towns and cities in Brandenburg, Eisenhüttenstadt has a well-defined urban border, outside which lie nature preserves and agricultural fields, crossed by well-maintained hiking and bike paths. Outside the compact, walkable city center is a mall (ironically called City Center, in English), a movie theater, and a few scattered businesses, car dealerships, and abandoned buildings. The actual city is situated around the axis formed by Linden Avenue and City Hall.

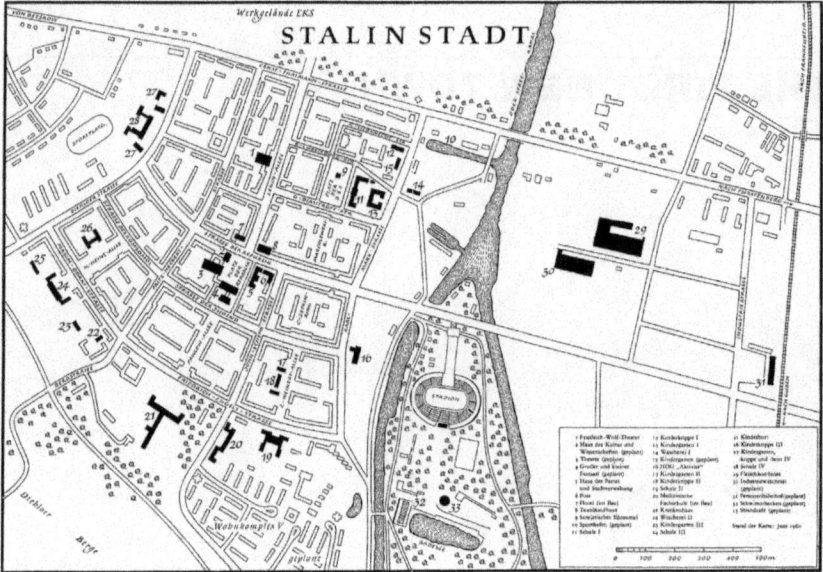

FIGURE 18. Map of Eisenhüttenstadt (then Stalinstadt), 1960. Courtesy of Stadtarchiv Eisenhüttenstadt.

Housing Complexes 1 through 4 are arranged in quadrants around City Hall, numbered in the order in which they were built. Housing Complexes 5, 6, and 7, comprising prefabricated concrete buildings called *Plattenbauten*, are on the city's periphery and are, for the most part, in the process of being dismantled. Housing Complexes were the building blocks of socialist urban planning, intended to be self-contained, walkable neighborhoods that fulfilled residents' daily needs—smaller versions of the Soviet *microrayon*. Those in the city center were planned for around five thousand residents each; apartment buildings are arranged around courtyards with playgrounds, picnic tables, and sculpture gardens, while walking paths connect the complex's internal components. During the socialist era, each Housing Complex had its own day cares, schools, shopping area, and other services, though most are now closed. Each was also built in a distinctive architectural style such that it would be unlikely for a resident to look around and, for instance, confuse Complex 2 for Complex 3. Moreover, Housing Complexes are foundational to residents' spatial awareness and navigation. Ask an Eisenhüttenstädter where they live, and you are likely to hear "I live in Complex 1," or simply "I live in the second," referring to Housing Complex 2. In the course of everyday conversation, residents may refer to the high school in Complex 4 or the convenience store in Complex 3, rather than use street names.

FIGURE 19. The mosaic *Production in Peace* by Walter Womacka (1965), more commonly called the Peace Dove, along Linden Avenue (then Lenin Avenue), on a postcard from 1974. Courtesy of Ben Kaden.

Linden Avenue, originally Lenin Avenue, is the city's main boulevard, acting as a dividing line between Housing Complexes and a visual axis connecting City Hall to the steel plant on the horizon. Its low-rise buildings house coffee shops, bakeries, stores, and businesses such as insurance agencies and the offices of the local newspaper.[1] At its end are two high-rises, Hotel Lunik and what was formerly the Magnet Department Store, now renovated as an office building, with the municipal library occupying its top two floors. The back of Magnet faces Linden Avenue and, since 1965, has featured an intricate five-story mosaic; the flags of Poland, East Germany, and the Soviet Union, featured in the design, are said to represent the Soviet engineering and Polish coal that powered the city's steelworks. City Hall sits across the street, exemplary of the Stalinist wedding cake style of architecture, named for its tiered, cake-like upper stories and decorative cornices. Its grand entrance faces Central Square, now an untended lot. Nearby is Leisure Time Island, a peninsula in the Oder–Spree Canal with parks, walking trails, playgrounds, and sports fields, as well as a skate park, an indoor swimming pool, a miniature golf course, a petting zoo, snack bars, and a beer garden. The nineteenth-century railway station, located close to two miles from the city center, often provides visitors with their first impression of the city. On one side of the building, graffiti reads "Refugees Welcome!," while on the other, "I'm not a racist, I hate everyone" has been there since I first visited in 2010—a reflection of Eisenhüttenstadt's varied facets and iterations.

Housing Complexes 1 through 3 and Linden Avenue constitute Europe's largest historically protected zone, which has been protected since 1984 as the most complete and comprehensive exemplar of East German architecture and urban planning. Built before the Eastern Bloc's cost-saving turn toward prefabricated concrete architecture, Eisenhüttenstadt's city center is a monument to early socialist architectural grandeur. Its closest analogue is Berlin's Karl Marx Avenue, where the East German state held televised parades and reserved housing as a reward for exemplary service. Buildings have neoclassical architectural detailing and socialist-realist friezes depicting themes appropriate to the "farmers' and workers' state." In Eisenhüttenstadt's protected zone, the city must maintain facades and remove graffiti—a side job handed out by the head of the Fürstenberg Museum—and any architectural changes must be approved by the county historic preservation board. Since 2002, the city has also identified two areas of "consolidation" where residents will be expected to move as Complexes 5 through 7 are demolished: the medieval village of Fürstenberg,[2] which lies along the Oder on the city's eastern edge, and the city center, comprising Complexes 1 through 4. In recent years, as outlying areas of the city are increasingly emptied of both people and buildings, urban renewal programs have begun to focus on renovating the city center. And as residents repopulate the area, city officials have begun to discuss a return not only to the city's original geographic footprint but also to its founders' original vision more broadly.

Eisenhüttenstadt's planners were deeply influenced by prewar modernism, and their approach to urban design is indebted to Walter Gropius's conception of the *Gesamtkunstwerk*, or total work of art. While earlier practitioners of Gesamtkunstwerk tended to produce theater and opera—the term was popularized by Richard Wagner in the nineteenth century—modernist Gesamtkunstwerke focused on the everyday. The Bauhaus State School, which Gropius founded in 1919, sought to break down the disciplinary boundaries and hierarchies that had theretofore characterized artistic production in Europe.[3] Students were required to take foundational courses in crafts—blacksmithing, woodworking, weaving—while also learning fine arts, such as painting and sculpture, and other disciplines such as material science, anatomy, and bookkeeping. Architecture and urban design were elevated as instruments of holism as the Bauhaus sought to shape—rather than merely decorate—the built environment. All three of the Bauhaus School directors were architects (Gropius was succeeded by Hannes Meyer and Mies van der Rohe before the school was shut down in 1933), and from their point of view, the building represented art's apotheosis. Upon the Bauhaus School's founding, Gropius ([1919] 2019) wrote, "Let us together will, conceive, and create the new building of the future, which will unite everything in a *single form*—architecture *and* sculpture *and* painting—and which will one day rise heavenwards from the hands of a million craftsmen."

Eisenhüttenstadt continues to bear the hallmarks of Gesamtkunstwerk, and its planners took great care to curate the visual perception of their city. Residents pointed out to me that the Street of the Republic, a central thoroughfare, has a barely perceptible curve so that pedestrians do not suffer a monotonous view. Building entrances tend to face interior courtyards, and residents enter their Housing Complexes through colonnades or archways, guiding residents' perceptual experience.[4] The city's hospital, located in Housing Complex 2, was built with the same Stalinist neoclassical grandeur of City Hall and is surrounded by ornate gardens. Like many municipal buildings, its interior has distinctive mid-century-modern architectural flourishes, including brass door handles, banisters, and chandeliers; walls are decorated with wood paneling and mosaics. The hospital's top floor also has a lookout point that provides a clear line of sight toward the steelworks on the horizon, as do most of the city's high-rise apartment buildings and the parks at Rose Hill and Diehlo Mountain, south of the city. During the socialist era, Rose Hill had a sculpture garden that was collectively maintained by residents, but the sculptures have since been relocated to protect them from vandalism.

Residents often suggested to me that Eisenhüttenstadt was replete with public art because, in its early years, the city had few trees—a pine forest had been razed to make way for construction and newly planted greenery was yet to mature. While scholars suggest that public art was long essential to socialist urban planning (Buck-Morss 2000, 42), photographs from the 1950s and 1960s often depict an ecologically barren urban landscape—spindly trees, sparse garden beds—that likely felt as if it needed enlivening. Large-scale, colorful mosaics can be found throughout the city, depicting astronauts, animals, atomic scientists, and smiling socialist families, among other motifs. There are 112 bronze and sandstone sculptures, many of life-size human figures, which have been moved throughout the city over the decades (Gericke 1998). In the early 2000s, a series of four brass animal statues, each about two feet tall, were moved from the park at Rose Hill to Linden Avenue; the monkey and lion have shiny gold patches where generations of residents have affectionately patted their heads. In 2000, the city held a contest for sculptures inspired by the steel industry, funded by ArcelorMittal, and shortly thereafter installed the winners: an abstract shape resembling a Rubik's Cube in Complex 2, and "Germania," an unbeloved skeleton charioteer who towers over the city's northern edge on a forty-foot pedestal.

FIGURES 20A AND 20B. Two postcards from the 1950s depict Housing Complex 2. Courtesy of Ben Kaden.

FIGURE 21. A postcard from the 1960s depicts the view from Rose Hill. Courtesy of Detlef Juckel.

FIGURE 22. A postcard from the 1960s depicts the Hotel Lunik (*left*) and the Magnet Department Store (*right*). Courtesy of Detlef Juckel.

Developing the East German Emic

The East German architectural emic emphasized a holistic, totalizing form of urban planning, a logic both reflected in and enabled by the Eastern Bloc's particularly expansive form of biopolitics. During the 1920s and 1930s, the Soviet Union developed an ideology around "city building [*gradostroitel'stvo*]" that anthropologist Stephen Collier (2011, 2) frames "as an alternative to a liberal framework for understanding and governing life in industrial cities." Collier notes that Foucault's conception of biopolitics was developed under the influence of French liberalism, which positioned government as "a relationship between the juridico-legal domain of the state and the quasi-natural order of 'population'" (17). Under liberalism, the state manages certain aspects of human biology and health in order to enable or disable the autonomous actions of its citizens. But, as will be discussed in greater detail, the Soviet state was concerned with the provisioning of the population insofar as it was concerned with the management of that population's outputs.

Because the Soviet Union perceived its citizens not as autonomous actors but as embodied labor, the provisioning and management of bodies was considered a key element in the broader project of city building. Urban planners were tasked with shaping citizens' milieu as an instrument of biopolitical control (Foucault 2007, 20). As such, nearly all arenas of life were subject to the Soviet state's totalizing gaze: food production, childcare, living arrangements. East Germany, as a Soviet satellite, followed suit. During my fieldwork, the permanent exhibition at the Documentation Center for Everyday Culture in East Germany featured large-scale photographs of the collective toilet training that took place in East German day cares and preschools—a provocation to Western visitors and a testament to the totalizing force of Soviet-style city building. From the perspective of architects, East German and Soviet architects' totalizing approach to urban planning was also made possible through the abolition of private property. As Eisenhüttenstadt's former Chief Architect Kurt Leucht said in a 1994 interview with the magazine *Red Flag*,[5] "Marx said that there would be a time when the surplus would be differently distributed. That time became a reality" (*Rote Fahne* 1994, 21).

Leucht was one of many architects who influenced Eisenhüttenstadt's development, but he was the project's general director during the development of the historically protected zone, and he is often credited as the city's developer. In his book introducing Eisenhüttenstadt to the public, *The First New Town in the German Democratic Republic*, Leucht (1957, 13) writes that the city, then called Stalinstadt, was one of "numerous examples throughout history" of well-designed, livable cities. Its Housing Complexes, examined in detail in chapter 2, offered green pathways and play areas for children; the "restorative landscapes" of Diehlo Mountain and Leisure Time Island were at most a twelve-minute walk from residents' homes (14). But "the most outstanding feature of socialist urban planning," according to Leucht, was that "the structure of composition of the city, its functions and buildings, would not be designed and built in the interest of capitalist profits, but rather for the whole of society [die Gesamtheit der Gesellschaft]" (9).

Leucht had not always been an ardent socialist. In 1933 he joined the Nazi Luftwaffe, where he helped design airfields, including Berlin's Tempelhof, and he was briefly held in an Allied prison camp. In 1937, he visited the World Exposition of Art and Technology in Modern Life, in Paris, and became acquainted with the modernist architects with whom he would later publicly associate himself, including Ernst May and Mies van der Rohe. In 1945, at the war's end, Leucht took a job as an architect for the city of Dresden. Historian Jörn Schütrumpf suggests that Leucht's plan for the city's rebuilding shielded him from scrutiny of his Nazi past; in 1948, Dresden's mayor arranged for Leucht to join the local branch of the German Communist Party (KPD), despite the fact that KPD members had been persecuted by the Nazis and KPD leadership had spent the war in exile (Schütrumpf 1997a).

When Leucht was interviewed by documentarians in 1991, he made no mention of his Nazi past. Instead, when asked to reflect on his life's work, he credited his professional development to his study of European modernism. Leucht described having been deeply influenced by the Athens Charter, developed at a meeting of the International Congress of Modernist Architects (Congres Internationaux D'Architecture Moderne, or CIAM) in 1933. The CIAM Athens conference had been oriented around the development of the Functionalist City, a techno-modernist utopia of standardizable urban planning. This architectural genealogy is now perhaps most closely associated with failed US public housing projects—the 1972 demolition of the Pruitt-Igoe Homes in St. Louis was famously called the day "Modern Architecture died" (Jencks 1977, 9).[6] But modernist functionalism did not necessarily translate to bleak, poorly maintained high-rises. Indeed, the Athens Charter ultimately informed the East German Building Ministry's emphasis on humane, human-scale urban design.

The charter notes that European cities of the nineteenth and early twentieth centuries had developed chaotically, according to the whims of private developers and the demands of industrial production. CIAM proposed modern cities, rationally developed, that would offer relief from the density, pollution, and inequity of rapidly urbanizing centers across Europe, such as Paris, Moscow, and Berlin. Modern cities would offer their citizens easy access to work, leisure, and transportation within a reasonable distance from home. And while members of CIAM operated in capitalist contexts, the charter emphasized that urban design should principally serve the public good, not only through investments in public spaces but also through cohesive urban planning that disfavored private development. The Athens Charter is an enumerated list, ending with point 94: "Private interests should be subordinated to the interests of the community" (CIAM 1946).

Leucht would later compare his work in East Germany with work conducted under capitalism—he designed a school in West Germany in 1958—and he emphasized how remarkable it had been, across both systems, to design a city in its social and material totality. "Look here," Leucht said to his interviewer. "People's basic needs are housing and conveniently located workplaces, and then there is the question of culture and recreation. . . . I placed great importance on the fact that at the same time [as housing was constructed], there was also a theater, and a well-appointed restaurant where you could celebrate weddings, and shops, and pubs. That was never done again, not even in the GDR." Indeed, later East German New Towns such as Hoyerswerda lacked Eisenhüttenstadt's greenery and grand neoclassical public buildings, as well as its cultural amenities. Yet Leucht described the culmination of his work as "this lively city, with its streets and green areas where you can sit on a bench" (Leucht 1991, 4). The city, it seemed, was made manifest in the interstitial spaces where one could appreciate its *Gestalt*, and in the atmospherics produced by the social life therein.

In April 1950, the East German Building Ministry sent a delegation of architects, Leucht included, on a roughly six-week trip to Moscow to learn from their Soviet counterparts.[7] The group studied the postwar rebuilding of Moscow, Leningrad, and Kyiv, as well as the founding of New Towns and the practice of Soviet city building. In July 1950, the East German Building Academy published the nation's Sixteen Principles of Urban Planning, which would guide urban development throughout the country. While historians present the Sixteen Principles as an outcome of the Moscow trip (Schütrumpf 1997a; Schretzenmayr 1998), Leucht remembered things differently. The Soviets, he recalled, shared many of the East Germans' concerns: "the problems of regional planning, the founding of towns, the reconstruction of the towns and settlements that had been destroyed . . . how we can overcome monotony in urban planning . . . transportation planning, land use planning, landscape design, urban space." But Leucht saw the Moscow trip as merely a starting point in a broader conversation. As the Moscow Group began to codify their conversations into a set of guiding principles, Leucht recalled, he discussed the matter with Building Minister Lothar Bolz, who encouraged the group to shape their principles in the Athens Charter's image. Bolz, like the Moscow group, had been influenced by "the famous book by Le Corbusier [in which] urban planning is a sense of harmony between the house, tree, and person, as a symbol, so to speak, as a square, as a street, as a complete city, as a whole." Leucht stressed that the Sixteen Principles were in conversation not only with Russian or Soviet architecture but with European modernism more broadly (Leucht 1991, 3).

Like the Athens Charter, the East German Sixteen Principles consist primarily of high-level instructions for urban design: Monumental buildings should be in a city's center, cities should have multipurpose town squares and multistory buildings, heavy traffic should be separated from residential areas, housing density should allow for the provision of light and air. But they are most instructive in their broad proclamations, which evince a commitment both to Soviet-style city building and to the modernist holism that informs the socialist emic. Principle 1: "In terms of its structure and architecture, the city is an expression of the political life and national consciousness of the people." Principle 2: "The principles of urban planning are based on natural conditions, the social and economic foundations of the state, the highest achievements in science, technology, and art, the requirements of the economy, and the use of progressive elements in the people's cultural heritage." Principle 3: "Cities in and of themselves do not arise. . . . The growth of the city, the number of inhabitants, and the area are determined by the city-forming factors, that is, by industry, administration, and culture. The determination and recognition of city-building factors is ultimately the decision of the state" (BpB 2005).

Thus, teleologically planned socialist cities serve the dictates of the state while also being provisioned by the state with the precise number of everything from schoolteachers to buses to consumer goods, according to the state's teleological imagination. If the city should be an expression of political life, then the texture of everyday life would be political—or at least would be understood by inhabitants as a manifestation of statecraft, as indeed it often was (Fehérváry 2009; Pence and Betts 2008). Yet the Sixteen Principles also reflect the emancipatory possibilities of early twentieth-century modernism. Le Corbusier's "famous book," *Towards a New Architecture*, suggested that architecture "affects our senses to an acute degree and provokes plastic emotions," as the architect "determines the various movements of our heart and of our understanding" (Le Corbusier [1931] 1986, 1). As East German citizens came to experience their access to housing and recreation as expressions of their deservingness in the eyes of the state, leaders hoped to instill a sense of pride in the socialist project. Architecture has the capacity to express social priorities in how it allocates resources and for whom it enables a humane course of everyday life (Anand 2017; Von Schnitzler 2016)—hence Le Corbusier wrote, "It is a question of building which is at the root of the social unrest of today: architecture or revolution" (Le Corbusier [1931] 1986, 8).

But perhaps the clearest distillation of the socialist emic is embodied by a mosaic, *Space Earth Men*, designed by Otto Schutzmeister in 1969. The artwork depicts two space travelers floating against an abstract background; their colorful

FIGURE 23. The mosaic *Space Earth Men* by Otto Schutzmeister (1969) in Housing Complex 5, 2015. Photograph by the author.

uniforms lack any information that might indicate their nation of origin. One day in 2010, I was walking through Eisenhüttenstadt with Ben Kaden, the library scientist and postcard enthusiast, who, at the time, also wrote a popular blog about the city. As Kaden showed me around on an informal tour, we stopped to look at *Space Earth Men*, and I remarked that I liked the astronauts. "Those are not astronauts," he told me. "We're in Eisenhüttenstadt—they're cosmonauts." The exchange was in jest, but it reflected a fundamental difference between socialist and capitalist planning. An astronaut explores astral bodies, isolated points of interest in a blank field. A cosmonaut explores the cosmos, taking in his or her surroundings in their totality.

The First Five-Year Plan

East Germany was founded in the aftermath of World War II. In 1945 the Allies split Germany into four zones of occupation—British, French, American, and Soviet—the borders of which were negotiated among Allied leaders at the Yalta and Potsdam Conferences. Shortly thereafter, tensions between the Soviet Union and the other Allied powers led the British, French, and American zones to operate in conjunction with each other and independently of the Soviet zone. In April

1949, the British, American, and French merged their zones and transitioned from a military occupation to an independent German government that would be overseen by the Allied High Commission. The Basic Law of this new government was established the following month (US Department of State 1949). In October 1949, the Soviet military occupation ceded control of is zone to a provisional German government, which established the East German constitution and elected Otto Grotewohl as the first minister president of the newly founded People's Parliament ("Das Deutsche Volk Formt Selbst Sein Schicksal" 1949). The Soviet Zone of Occupation thereby became the German Democratic Republic, an origin that led to the country being nicknamed "the Zone" and its people "Zonis."

In July 1950, the People's Parliament hosted the Third National Party Congress of the Socialist Unity Party (Sozialistische Einheitspartei Deutschlands, or SED), East Germany's national political party. Drawing on the Soviet Union's practice of planning the nation's economic goals in five-year increments, officials announced East Germany's first Five-Year Plan, which would be enacted between the years 1951 and 1955. Its focus was on increasing industrial output and agricultural production, and on training workers to fulfill ambitious goals. The fields of metallurgy, machine building, precision engineering, and textile manufacturing were slated to grow by over 200 percent, and the output of oleaginous and fibrous plants by 708 percent (Protokoll des III. Parteitages der SED 1950). Western officials estimated that East Germany produced about half the targeted outputs described in its first Five-Year Plan (Lowenthal 1957, 296).

As part of this push, officials announced that they would build a new city, a model of socialist living, devoted to the production of steel. At the time, East Germany was facing three intersecting crises that the new city promised to resolve: a housing shortage, the result of wartime destruction; a workforce shortage, due to a lack of training for the industrial jobs on which the new economy would rely; and a lack of access to steel to use in the furtherance of farming, construction, and industry. The German steel industry had long been based in the western Ruhr valley—only 7 percent of the country's steel came from the area that became the GDR—and West Germany had enacted a trade embargo with the East in February 1950 (Döring 2015, 122).[8] Moreover, the East German government suffered from shortages of raw materials of all kinds. While some officials suggested importing steel from the Soviet Union, officials at the Third Party Congress agreed to invest 347 million Ostmarks toward building a domestic steel industry. On July 24, 1950, the Party Congress finalized its decision to build the steel plant and city, which would help prepare the nation for its second Five-Year Plan (Ludwig 1999, 56–57).

FIGURE 24. The Friedrich Wolf Theater (*at left, with columned entryway*) on Linden Avenue (then Lenin Avenue), where the steel plant in the background acts as a visual anchor on the horizon, 1960. Courtesy of Terje Hartberg.

Archival documents from the socialist era do not question the necessity of domestic steel production or its primacy among the new nation's priorities. In the technologically driven culture of the Eastern Bloc, steel represented possibility, and it made possible other forms of industrial production. Historian Stephen Kotkin (1997, 30) writes that, given the centrality of steel to Eastern Bloc economies, "socialism meant making machines to make machines." Even after construction began on Housing Complex 1 and initial work orders called for only stone, clay, and cement (Bauprogramm Wohnstadt 1952), the SED took for granted that steel would be essential to a modern nation—an assumption embedded in the Western imagination of iron as the progenitor of technological modernity (Benjamin 2002, 4).

The steel plant was further celebrated as an engine of job creation. Although employment would be mandated for every GDR citizen, the first Five-Year Plan noted a shortage of workplaces. Following the Third Party Congress, East German President Wilhelm Pieck announced, "I am confident that with this steel plant . . . two enormous and burdensome worries will disappear. The first is the question of finding placements for our workforce, and the second is the vexing housing question" (quoted in Döring 2015, 125). The party organ *Neues Deutschland* wrote that for the people of eastern Brandenburg, the steel plant had "one meaning: Here there will be jobs" (quoted in Döring 2015, 125).

The decision of the Third Party Congress did not give the city a name. Like a child referred to only as "the baby," the city was referenced in party documents as Germany's First Socialist City, Germany's Socialist Model City, or EKO Residential City (Wohnstadt), because of its role in housing the workers of the steel plant, provisionally named EKO, an acronym for Eisenhüttenkombinat Ost, or Eastern Steelworks. The name Stalinstadt was chosen in 1953, two years after the city's construction began and immediately following the Soviet leader's death, and EKO was briefly renamed the Josef W. Stalin Steelworks. It wasn't until 1961 that the city became Eisenhüttenstadt in response to a directive from the Soviet Union's Twenty-Second Party Congress, which urged countries across the Eastern Bloc to erase Stalin's name from their cities and streets. When the city was renamed, the neighboring villages of Schönfließ and Fürstenberg were annexed as the boroughs of Eisenhüttenstadt West and Eisenhüttenstadt East, respectively (SVV Stalinstadt 1961).

The city's handful of apartment buildings would do little to solve the nationwide housing crisis, and it was not until 1985 that the steelworks began producing the finely milled steel used in automobiles and other consumer goods. Still, the city's founding was a symbolic victory for the SED and the new nation. Not only did it reflect the nation's postwar ethos—a physical embodiment of the East German national anthem, "Rising from the Ruins"—but government reports applauded the city as an embodiment of the new social order. Publications such as *Stalinstadt: New Lives, New People* (Colditz and Lücke 1958) celebrated the city's utopian character; the book's text is in multiple languages, as if the new city needed to be introduced on a global scale, and the authors write, in English, that "a crumb of German Earth harbored a whole new world" (Colditz and Lücke 1958, 4). Indeed, scholars have noted that by the 1960s, a strong mythology around the construction of the new socialist person had already taken hold in Eisenhüttenstadt (Ludwig 2000, 55).

This dualism, simultaneously constructing personhood and place, is also reflected in the life histories of the individuals who moved to the new city. Nearly all were young adults, given the nature of the work required, and most had experienced the war as children—Eisenhüttenstadt's construction began in 1951, six years after the war's end. Many informants told me how transformative it had been to find a safe, stable home after traumatic wartime and postwar experiences. Others told me about being attracted to the city after personal traumas, often experiences of domestic abuse; the future-oriented city with no wartime history would be the perfect place to start over. And informants often saw their own lives and careers grow as the city itself grew. They moved into ever larger, newer Housing Complexes as the steel plant added stages to its refinement process. And they perceived, in their everyday lives, the emancipatory possibilities that signaled the arrival of socialist progress. Eisenhüttenstadt had twenty-four-hour day cares to accommodate the fact that the steel factories were continually operational; residents were allocated gardens and collectively cultivated perennial crops such as strawberries and asparagus.

At the same time, as one historian notes, the state "began to celebrate itself as a personalized project," publicly commemorating the nation's tenth birthday, then twentieth, with a narrative that anthropomorphized East Germany's childhood, adolescence, and maturity (Wierling 2009, 208). Unlike citizens in more repressive regimes, including the Soviet Union, Eisenhüttenstädters experienced what historians have called a "welfare dictatorship" (Jarausch 1999) or "participatory dictatorship" (Fulbrook 2005, 12). The East German state restricted its citizens' individual freedoms—to travel, to participate in the market economy—yet citizens did not always experience their state as repressive; millions of them, around 8 to 16 percent of the population, played an active role in governmental organs, from trade unions to cultural organizations. While some interpret participation in state-organized activities as an expression of either self-interest or coercion, Mary Fulbrook notes that many East Germans believed in the possibility of social change through sociopolitical participation, and that despite state surveillance, it was possible "both to have participated in the structures of power, and yet simultaneously to have been openly critical of the regime—even well before 1989" (Fulbrook 2005, 236). But she also identifies a growing alienation of East Germans from "their" state over the course of the 1970s, as younger East Germans came to see their country not as a socially conscious alternative to capitalism but rather as an inferior, more repressive version of Western democracy (Fulbrook 2005, 2016). The generation that came of age in the 1970s did not express the same sense of allegiance to utopian socialism as the "building generation" had (Pfaff 2006). And with that shift came a dissipation of the imagination of the East German state as a receptive engine for social improvement. One study of East German environmental activism notes that in 1972, slightly over 30 percent of environmental petitions were suggestions and proposals for positive change, rather than complaints about environmental degradation. But by 1976, the proportion of positive petitions had fallen to 14 percent, and by 1981 it had fallen to zero (Quinn 2002, 101, 342, quoted in McLellan 2006).

A City, Not a Settlement

When the East German government announced its plan to build the Model Socialist City, architectural plans had not yet been drawn up. Five potential sites for EKO Residential City were initially proposed: sparsely populated areas near the towns or villages of Küstrin-Kietz, Eberswalde, Ueckermünde,

Frankfurt Oder, and Fürstenberg, the last of which was chosen. The Ministry for Construction ultimately settled on this land along the banks of the Oder River because of its transportation infrastructure, the purported suitability of its population for industrial work, and its room to accommodate any potential expansion of the city (Ministerium für Aufbau 1950, 1). Fürstenberg, a town of around ten thousand, was a small medieval village first inhabited by Slavic settlers in the fourth century; the thirteenth century saw the town's official founding, in 1250, as well as that of the cloister in nearby Neuzelle. Toward the middle of the nineteenth century, increasing industrialization brought a rail connection in Fürstenberg on the line between Berlin and Breslau, now Wroclaw, Poland. Fürstenberg became known for its glassblowing and basket-weaving industries, and for its location along the Oder–Spree Canal, built in 1891 (Gansleweit 1986).[9] Neighboring Schönfließ was the site of lignite mining, which led the Märkische Electric Company to purchase much of the surrounding land to mine for coal that would fuel its power plants (Drieschner and Schulz 2008, 33). Even after Eisenhüttenstadt's founding, the region remained lightly populated, and throughout the GDR era it had one of the lowest population densities in the nation (Ludwig 1999, 58–59).

Beginning in 1939, Fürstenberg was also the site of a Nazi chemical weapons factory run by the company Degussa (Deutsche Gold- und Silber-Scheideanstalt). The qualities that made the site appealing to GDR planners had also made it appealing to Degussa's director; in a letter to the architect who would help him construct the factory, he extolled the site's accessibility to the railroad and canal that could transport the factory's products, and the room it afforded to expand industrial development (Schütrumpf 1997b). Later in 1939, in Fürstenberg, the Nazis built Stalag III B, a POW camp, which housed at times up to twenty thousand prisoners in thirty-four barracks (Durth et al. 1998, 1:358). The following year, the Rheinmetall-Borsig company established a weapons factory nearby; both factories were operated by Allied prisoners, and, together with the Märkische Electric Company's power plant, built before the war, they "defined Fürstenberg, by the war's end, as a highly industrialized region," according to historian Jörn Schütrumpf (Schütrumpf 1997b). On land owned by the Märkische Electric Company, there was also a transshipment point for granite, manned by Stalag III B prisoners; the stone was to be moved via the Oder–Spree Canal to the new world capital Germania. Although these factories ceased operation at the end of the war, the East German Building Ministry made oblique references to them in describing the local "orientation toward work" that would make them suitable for industrial labor (Ministerium für Aufbau 1950, 1).

When construction on Eisenhüttenstadt began, Fürstenberg was recovering from postwar Soviet occupation. It is a compact town of cobblestone streets, lined with one-story medieval houses huddled near the banks of the Oder and grander, two- or three-story nineteenth-century townhouses near the train station and village square. In 1950, it was in disarray. Most of the town lacked running water and had significant structural damage and massive overcrowding. German refugees from Silesia—now western Poland and the northern Czech Republic—had fled the advancing Red Army and were taken in by villagers in Fürstenberg and other nearby towns. In 1948, there were 3,000 refugees living among approximately 9,100 residents in Fürstenberg (Ludwig 2000, 20). One Fürstenberg resident showed me the two small holes in the doors to his kitchen and living room. Entire families had been housed in each room, and nameplates for each family had been nailed to the doors.

In September 1950, work began on temporary workers' housing, called Shanty Town, while construction on the steelworks began a few weeks later. In October 1951, a winterized barrack, the Island Settlement, was built for around five hundred residents, and from 1952 to 1958, barracks also stood on the future sites of Housing Complexes 5 and 6. Some barracks that had been part of Stalag III B were used for workers' housing, though in October 1951 the Builders' Union repurposed them as warehouses. Shanty Town remained the center of social life while the city was under construction, and by 1954 it was home to police and fire stations, a pub called Peace-Steel, communal bathrooms, a snack bar, a food shop, a clothing repair workshop, and a clubhouse (Ludwig 2000, 36–37). Although the construction workforce continued to grow, some workers stayed only temporarily. Nonetheless, this influx of workers from across the country, many displaced from lands ceded to Poland, Hungary, and Czechoslovakia, added to Eisenhüttenstadt's Model City character (Ludwig 2000, 32). An EKO survey found that in 1952, there were around 1,300 residents in EKO Residential City, from 161 hometowns (Ludwig 2000, 35).

In October 1950, the East German Building Ministry appointed architect Franz Ehrlich to design the new city, though his designs, deemed unsatisfactory, have not survived.[10] That same month, the Building Ministry commissioned further designs and chose that of Kurt Junghanns (Durth et al. 1998, 1:362; May 1999, 162). Shortly thereafter, Otto Geiler was asked to revise Junghanns's plan and was given control of the project (May 1999, 163). Though the plans for EKO Residential City would be revised many times, Junghanns and Geiler introduced elements that would end up in the final plan: a monumental factory entrance that acted as the focal point of a central axis, U- and L-shaped apartment buildings, and Housing Complexes, of which their plan had five (Durth et al. 1998, 1:362).

On February 1, 1951, Geiler and fellow architects met in Fürstenberg to discuss his plan for the new city. He later wrote in the meeting's minutes that for the city to have an urban character, it should have a five- or six-story city hall, a main street with four-story apartments and a view of the steel plant, five- or six-story public buildings, and between ten and one hundred meters of room between apartment buildings (Durth et al. 1998, 1:364)—a set of attributes still recognizable in Eisenhüttenstadt's city center. But the following week, architects at a meeting of the Building Academy were critical of Geiler's plan. It lacked courtyards, it insufficiently embodied the Sixteen Principles, and most damning, from Kurt Leucht, it misunderstood "that not a settlement, but rather a city should be created." According to architectural historian Werner Durth, Leucht thereby introduced the city-settlement dichotomy into the Building Academy's debates (Durth et al. 1998, 1:365). Durth writes that over the following year, "a 'settlement' would be a despicable designation, and a 'city' would be held up as a paragon of that which should be striven toward " (Durth et al. 1998, 1:365).

Outside the city center, Geiler's plan consisted of rows of apartment houses, evenly sized along evenly spaced streets, with slim stretches of lawn between them. Architect Thomas Topfstedt called it "hastily constructed factory housing" (May 1999, 164), and Building Minister Lothar Bolz declared that it was a "housing settlement of the earlier style," rather than "a city of a new type" (May 1999, 165). On February 9, 1951, the Building Academy commissioned new plans, ultimately choosing the submission from Kurt Leucht (May 1999, 165–66).

Leucht's plan introduced the self-contained Housing Complexes that were ultimately built, with main streets encircling residential areas that are traversed by foot or bicycle. The Building Academy praised Leucht's plan: the Housing Complexes that fit together into a cohesive whole, Leucht's attention to the Sixteen Principles, the transportation infrastructure's clear orientation, the Central Square at the end of a main avenue, with a grand Culture Palace whose silhouette would be a visual counterpoint to the blast furnaces. The Building Academy also praised the amenities of each Housing Complex, which included schools and shops, day cares, dairies, Young Pioneer houses, laundromats, and barbers (May 1999, 166–67).

Meanwhile, on February 17, 1951, construction had begun for the permanent Residential City, beginning with the first Housing Complex and built according to Geiler's plans (Durth et al. 1998, 1:364–65). In November 1950, the Building Ministry had developed three prototypes for apartment buildings, and those in Eisenhüttenstadt were type 514, four-story buildings with plain stucco exteriors and, inside, two-room apartments and ceilings less than three meters high (Ludwig 2000, 46–47; Keil et al. 1997a, 9). Close to three hundred apartments were built and settled in 1951, and residents were primarily employed in the steelworks, which began operations that September. A year prior, beginning in September 1950, 110 men from across the country had been specially trained for the task (Ludwig 2000, 32). In 1951, construction

FIGURE 25. Memorial Square in a postcard from the 1950s. Courtesy of Ben Kaden.

began on Leucht's plan, and Memorial Square was built to ease the transition between the two architectural plans. The remains of Soviet soldiers were excavated from Camp Stalag III B, cremated, and interred in the square. An obelisk was erected in memoriam, its wording carefully chosen to honor East Germany's alliance with the Soviets while minimizing the fact that the soldiers had died at German hands.

Unadorned Boxes

On January 16, 1952, President Walter Ulbricht visited the city, which then consisted of seven inhabited apartment buildings and three that were under construction (Keil et al. 1997a, 6). He famously disapproved of the bare, functionalist style, calling the apartment buildings "unadorned boxes." He told the Building Ministry, "There should be a greater number of stories in each building, in general at minimum four stories, windows that tip open for better air circulation in the apartments, and an enlivenment of facades . . . through balconies, loggia, bay windows, and an emphasis on entablature" (Durth et al. 1998, 1:373). Ulbricht's sentiment echoes concerns raised during the construction of the Soviet city of Magnitogorsk—that "the proletariat would have *its* attractive buildings" (Kotkin 1997, 119), instilling pride in the socialist project.

After Ulbricht's visit, Eisenhüttenstadt's buildings became increasingly ornate. A 1952 SED decree noted that "the architecture of the city will, in its monumental buildings, express the noble goals of socialism" (quoted in May 1999, 178). Werner Durth calls the reaction to Ulbricht's visit "swift and hectic" (Durth et al. 1998, 1:374). The city would keep Leucht's basic plan, but in three months, the individual apartment buildings were fundamentally redesigned. As construction went on throughout the 1950s, apartments continued to become more elaborate and expensive. The buildings designed in 1951 consisted of one-bedroom apartments, even for families with children, each costing 11,000 Ostmarks (€35,000) to build,[11] with untiled kitchens and bathrooms. On February 6, 1952, following Ulbricht's visit, the Building Academy increased the budget for each apartment building to accommodate wider windows, larger bedrooms, and larger, tiled kitchens and bathrooms (Durth et al. 1998, 1:374); ground floors were raised by half a meter to allow more light into each apartment (May 1999, 181). The 1952 buildings cost 18,000 Ostmarks (€60,000) to build a one-bedroom apartment, though larger apartments were also introduced (Keil et al. 1997a, 9)—55 percent of the apartments planned in 1952 were two-bedroom (May 1999, 182).

In April 1952, Josef Kaiser became chief architect, and he redesigned Leucht's spare buildings. His designs, implemented in Housing Complexes 1 and 2, introduced balconies with corniced roofs, attics with small windows that enlarged the building's silhouettes, recessed windows, decorative cornices, bay windows, and elaborate columned entryways (Durth et al. 1998, 1:392). Apartment size rose alongside costs; the construction of a one-bedroom apartment designed in 1953 cost on average 24,000 Ostmarks to build (around €70,000), more than double its counterpart from two years earlier (Keil et al. 1997a, 10; Durth et al. 1998, 1:400–401).[12] On Lenin Avenue, the Friedrich Wolf Theater was also built. An ornate neoclassical construction, it stood for the next eight years as the central avenue's only building (May 1999, 206).

Housing Complex 1 was built between 1951 and 1955 and housed 5,600 residents. Housing Complex 2 was built between 1953 and 1955 for 7,300 residents (Keil et al. 1997b, 1; 1997c, 1). In December 1954, Nikita Khrushchev gave a pivotal speech in which he promoted prefabricated concrete architecture, explaining, "One should not be pleased with decoration, aesthetic flourishes, and towers attached to buildings for no reason, as if they were sculptures. We are not against beauty, but rather against all forms of excess" (quoted in May 1999, 270). Shortly thereafter, in 1955, the East German Building Ministry introduced the WBS 70, a prefabricated concrete apartment block that would come to typify GDR architecture. By this time, Willy Stamm had become Eisenhüttenstadt's chief architect, and he revised Housing Complex 3 to adhere to shifting political inclinations.

Housing Complex 3 had originally been planned as a reproduction of Housing Complex 2, but in design revisions, its bay windows were replaced with windows of uniform size, and decorative cornices became pitched tile roofs. Many build-ings were also reduced from four to three stories and were heated with coal stoves instead of gas lines to save costs. Neoclassical friezes were replaced with *graffiti*, a more graphic style of bas-relief sculpture that resembles woodcut printing (May 1999, 274–76). It was built between 1955 and 1965 for a population of 3,800 (Keil et al. 1997d, 1).

Housing Complex 4, built between 1957 and 1967 for 5,700 residents, adheres for the most part to the morphology of Leucht's plan, but with freestanding apartment buildings added to two courtyards during the plan's later revisions. Its buildings are three or four stories tall and are made of prefabricated concrete components. In 1959, the city commissioned a special version of the 1W/58 L4 model for Complex 4, with built-in living room cabinets and bedroom ward-robes, radiator covers, curtain frames, and sliding pocket doors, but the project was soon abandoned due to its high cost (Keil et al.1997e, 3). In Complexes 3 and 4, apartments had either one or two bedrooms, though in Complex 4, studio apartments at the attic level were later added to accommodate the growing city (Keil et al. 1997e, 1–2).

Lenin Avenue, with the exception of the Friedrich Wolf Theater, was built beginning in 1961 and is considered part of Housing Complex 4. It was designed by Herbert Härtel, who succeeded Willy Stamm as city architect in 1958. The street is lined with commercial buildings, built at varying distances from the street and tiled in fine Meißen porcelain. Three nine-story apartment buildings with businesses on their ground floors punctuate the horizon and balance the two high-rises, Hotel Lunik and the Magnet Department Store, built to anchor the end of the avenue, which opens onto the empty Central Square (Keil et al. 1997e, 7). The remaining Housing Complexes, 5, 6, and 7, consist primarily of high-rise, prefabricated apartment buildings and are discussed in greater detail in chapter 4. In 1993, a design competition was held to develop plans for Central Square (Klement 1993), though funding fell through before any design could be implemented.

Tensions Between Legacies

East Germans began their study of Soviet urbanism in the early 1950s, when the Soviet Union itself was developing a new constellation of architecture, statecraft, and urban design. The standardized tower-block architecture that came to epito-mize the Eastern Bloc was only just beginning to be developed, but it was not until 1964 that Soviet Premier Nikita Khrushchev would demand its widespread usage. Early Leninist experimentation was giving way to technocratic Stalinism.

FIGURES 26A, 26B, AND 26C. Front doors typify the architectural differences between Housing Complexes: sculptural friezes in Complex 2 (*left*), *graffiti*-style carvings in Complex 3 (*center*), and prefabrication in Complex 4 (*right*), with triple flag holders that were used during public ceremonies in the German Democratic Republic era. 2015. Photographs by the author.

Even the East German media portrayed the disastrous founding of the Soviet city of Magnitogorsk, in 1931, as a counterpoint to Eisenhüttenstadt's modernity and success (Pfannsteil 1977).[13]

City building was made possible by the Soviet Union's distinctive planning logic, reflected in its mechanistic political imagination. Anthropologists and architectural historians have suggested that while socialist cities are not identifiable by a shared architectural style, they were built with a distinctive architectural vision that is inextricably tied to the vertically integrated national economies of the Eastern Bloc (Collier 2011; Hirt 2013; Sammartino 2018; Fox 2020). Human concerns became the concerns of "*urban* administration and planning" (Collier 2011, 81; emphasis in the original) as the social was dissolved into the state's management of synoptic data.

This totalizing outlook allowed East German architects to further the national city-building agenda through a simultaneous embrace of totalitarian planning and modernist principles. Bauhaus practitioners, who conceived of architecture as Gesamtkunstwerke, also rejected a hierarchical relationship between art and design, focusing instead on the totality of a building's atmospherics—no aspect of human experience was too minute to ignore. Jens Beige, an Eisenhüttenstadt architect whose work will be discussed in the next chapter, told me that because he was trained in the socialist era, he considered light and air to be his building materials, as important as the glass, wood, and mortar that would mediate inhabitants' relationship with the outside. The East German architectural emic was evidenced by the fact that every apartment in Eisenhüttenstadt had a view of the sky. "That's one of the beautiful things about the city," he said. "It was something people thought through." Expressing a viewpoint that I would often hear repeated by East German urbanists, Beige told me that the architect's task was to integrate the natural world into a holistic form of urban design, creating a built environment to support residents' physical and psychological health, as well as the health of the body politic.

We did not discuss East Germany's more sinister form of social engineering: its violent, extensive, and oppressive system of political surveillance. Yet it went without saying that after architects designed a building, electricians and other technicians would amend their plans to facilitate access by the Stasi, the East German secret police. Wolf, an elderly friend who lived in a nine-story high-rise, told me that under socialism, each time a private telephone line was installed in his building, neighbors discussed it as a double-edged sword: The line was considered a luxury, but it was assumed to be bugged. Indeed, Wolf thought he could hear a noise inside the walls each time the Stasi's bug turned on.

Thus, the fractal distinction between public and private space that characterized life in the Eastern Bloc (Gal 2002) also enabled the simultaneous existence of different types of attention toward others—regimes of affect and epistemology that that now seem diametrically opposed but that were not always experienced as such. Eastern Bloc socialism's legacy of Stalinist totalitarianism fostered a sense of attention mediated by the constant threat of state-imposed violence. But its legacy of avant-garde utopianism also fostered a sense of attention born of commitments to communitarianism and collective care. During the socialist era, Wolf often socialized with his neighbors, and he fondly recalled their annual New Year's Eve celebrations, where they watched fireworks together on their roof deck. But he also knew who had a private phone line, and he maintained a constant awareness of what could be said, to whom, and how.

The overlapping yet distinct totalizing outlooks that characterized social life in the Eastern Bloc—Stalinist technocracy, avant-garde utopianism—have forced scholars to grapple with opposing perspectives on socialist urbanism. As Collier and others have pointed out, the fantasy of total prescriptive control was indeed responsible for much of the Soviet Union's financial insolvency—technocratic fantasies do not map well onto real-world circumstances. And while "socialism" is all but an empty signifier in contemporary politics, even among scholars it retains a slippery meaning as a failed experiment—in social collectivism (Humphrey 2002a; Berdahl 1999), in nationalized economics (Verdery 2003; Dzenovska 2020), or in totalitarian biopolitical control (Collier 2011). Yet these overlapping perspectives also mean that when contemporary architects draw on the legacy of socialist urbanism, they are able to selectively draw on its component narratives. Thus far the legacy of socialist totalitarianism has dominated in the popular imagination, but the weight of competing historical narratives can change alongside changing circumstances in the present (Trouillot 1997).

Steel and Circulation

Eisenhüttenstadt's development is intimately tied to East German efforts to develop its steel industry. Plans for EKO were finalized on July 27, 1950, two years before plans for the city, and EKO's construction began nearly six months before that of the first provisional apartment buildings (Durth et al. 1998). EKO's origins, meanwhile, can be traced to Gary, Indiana, by way of the Soviet Union. The chain of influence between Gary, the Soviet Union, and Eisenhüttenstadt sheds light on the importance of futurity to the production of urban imaginaries, as well as on the means by which urban ideals are reproduced and circulate.

In 1906, US Steel opened what was at the time the world's largest steel plant in Gary, Indiana. Stalin, upon hearing the news, immediately ordered that a Soviet steelworks be built in order to "catch and overtake" Western industrial productivity, as the Soviet motto dictated. In 1929, the Soviet government hired a Cleveland-based firm to build a copy of Gary's steelworks in the central Caucasus, founding the city that would become Magnitogorsk. The factory produced its first pig iron in 1932 (Kotkin 1997, 42–51).

While the Magnitogorsk steelworks was not an exact copy of Gary's, the two cities remained connected in what may be termed an emulatory genealogy, in which Eisenhüttenstadt would be next in line. The opposing nature of their social and economic systems was eclipsed by a shared belief in the power of steel manufacturing to reflect back onto the urban environment that supported it: Both cities were imagined as forward looking, modern, and responsible for the country's technological developments. Historian Stephen Kotkin (1997, 363) writes, "What Magnitogorsk and Gary shared was a sense that they constituted not merely a single city, however important, but an entire civilization, *and* that their civilization could rightfully lay claim to being the vanguard of progressive humanity."

Construction began on the EKO steelworks on January 1, 1951, and the blast furnace became operational later that year. Its earliest engineers are not named in published histories of the plant (Käthner 1980; Döring 2015; Anton 1999; Nicolaus 2020). In their stead, credit goes to Soviet steel experts brought in from Magnitogorsk. On March 4, 1952, Magnitogorsk's chief metallurgist, Georgi Franzewitsch Michailowitsch, and chief mechanic, Alexander Schulgin, came to EKO to redesign the steelworks. Twenty-five years later, in 1977, the East German national newspaper *Neues Deutschland* commemorated the event (Pfannstiel 1977). Wolf, a retired steelworker, lent me the article, which he had kept tucked in a book for the previous thirty-eight years. He told me he kept the article because he considered it an egregious example of East German propaganda, with its politically minded curation of history and its sycophancy toward the Soviet Union. After Michailowitsch and Schulgin visited, production at EKO immediately increased, and by 1953 the plant was meeting its federally mandated production goal, processing five hundred thousand tons of pig iron per year (Roesler 1997). Postcards were printed with their faces, and Grammar School 10 was named the Alexander Schulgin School (Käthner 1980, 42).

In the early 1990s, Eisenhüttenstadt's mayor, Rainer Werner, took part in the USAA American International Visitors program, which sponsors local leaders from around the world on a four-week trip to the United States. One of the program's goals is to encourage sister-city partnerships, and Werner was eager to have a partnership with a steel manufacturing city such as Eisenhüttenstadt. It is here that accounts vary. Werner claims that he pursued a partnership with Hammond, Indiana, a town that borders both Chicago and Gary and is home to industrial manufacturing, though its steelworks closed in the 1970s. Werner knew from his International Visitors trip that Gary had the highest murder rate in

FIGURE 27. Newspaper clippings from Wolf, a retired steelworker, include a 1977 article comparing Magnitogorsk (*left*) and Eisenhüttenstadt (*right*).

Mein Beruf
Metallurge *Nostalgie*

Seit über drei Jahren erlerne ich im Bandstahlkombinat Eisenhüttenstadt den Beruf des Metallurgen mit der Spezialisierungsrichtung Erzeugung oder, wie es früher hieß Metallurge für Hüttentechnik. In unserer Familie ist dieser Beruf Tradition, mein Vater und mein Bruder arbeiten auch im EKO.

Hier in diesem metallurgischen Zentrum werden 76 Prozent des Roheisens der DDR hergestellt. Ansporn auch für mich als Lehrling, täglich hohe Leistungen in Theorie und Praxis zu vollbringen

FIGURE 28. A newspaper clipping from Wolf that shows an undated article whose headline reads "My Profession: Metallurgy." Underneath the headline, he wrote "Nostalgia."

the United States—it earned that dubious distinction in 1993 (Sloane et al. 1994). Hammond, an adjacent town still part of the same mid-century industrial legacy, was more palatable as a sister city. He told me, however, that after corresponding with Amerika Haus, a transnational organization in Berlin, about setting up a primary school partnership between Eisenhüttenstadt and Hammond, communication ceased and the partnership fizzled, and he was not sure why. A friend of Werner's told me that Werner did pursue a partnership with Gary, but that after finding out through Amerika Haus that Gary was a majority Black city struggling with unemployment and deindustrialization, Werner called the partnership off. But I am inclined to believe Werner. Perhaps he had discussed Gary's crime and racial makeup while still pursuing a partnership with Hammond. Either way, the story illustrates a breakdown in the circulation of industry, ideals, and the right to claim one's place as "the vanguard of progressive humanity" (Kotkin 1997, 363) between Gary (and/or its suburbs), Magnitogorsk, and Eisenhüttenstadt.

For commensuration to take place, certain beliefs and desires must exist that make foreign cultural tropes intelligible, and that propel people to recognize the links between those tropes and aspects of their own culture. In this case, Soviet planners isolated steel production from its capitalist origins and redefined it, in the socialist context, as a technology in service of Soviet goals: the development of industry, city building, and military machinery. East Germans further alienated Magnitogorsk's successful history of steel production from its failures in urban development. Mishaps plagued the city's early years, such that by the late 1930s there were 352 households living in mud huts in the shadow of what was, at the time, the largest steel plant in the world (Kotkin 1997, 136). Kurt Leucht was close friends with Ernst May (Leucht 1991), the German architect who designed the initial plans for Magnitogorsk in 1929, and he would have been familiar with May's Soviet travails. Yet the Alexander Schulgin School prescinds Magnitogorsk's steel from that history.

Iron, as the defining material of modernity, is perhaps uniquely situated to being separated from its social context. In the form of railroads, iron tore through European countrysides, producing new sensory and temporal experiences that had no natural analogue. So, too, in architecture. As Siegfried Giedion (1995) and Walter Benjamin (2002) observed, iron enabled the vast curvatures of cathedral-like arcades and railway stations, signaling the arrival of unprecedented creative and sensory possibilities. Iron also reshaped socioeconomic relationships at a national scale as it enabled new forms of commerce and consumption and remade everyday practices. In the nineteenth century, iron boot scrapers were solemnly used by visitors before entry into the Paris Arcades.

Yet iron's social power lay in its evocation of utopian possibility, an orientation that could not be captured in reproducible urban form. As anthropologists of infrastructure note, "The tensile properties of iron permit it to be drawn into fantastic material formations: high-rises, arcades, and bridges; formations that celebrate a release from the earth and its histories, gesturing instead to a time and space oriented to the future" (Appel et al. 2018, 9). Moreover, the mimetic faculty is always imperfect, producing alterity while reproducing that which is imitated (Taussig 1993). As each city positioned itself as the subsequent iteration of vanguardist modernity, each was shaped by the governmental and economic circumstances specific to its particular iteration, and each was set on a different path.

And as the cities developed over the twentieth century, so, too, did the social connotation of iron. Sabine Rennefanz, a journalist and Eisenhüttenstadt native, told me that the city's name sounded anachronistic "in our glass-and-fiber-optic era." Sociologists hired by the city in 1992 suggested changing its name, under the logic that iron's associations with industry and pollution gave the city an unfavorable image (Schwarz 2004).

Walter Benjamin, who was attuned to obsolescence, saw the mimetic faculty as something whose imprint faded over time. He writes, "The perceptual world of modern man contains only minimal residues of the magical correspondences . . . that were familiar to ancient peoples" (Benjamin [1933] 1999, 721). Perhaps the failure to close the loop on the three cities speaks to the impossibility of recuperating the utopian connotations that iron provoked in the twentieth century. But the efforts to do so speak to the fact that "residues" make it possible to seek out traces of this emulatory genealogy.

RETROFITTING THE HOUSING COMPLEX

The transition to capitalism brought intense disruption and uncertainty to Eisenhüttenstadt as the city adjusted to yet another totalizing sociopolitical system. First came changes to employment. EKO Steel became EKO Steel AG and laid off about three-quarters of its workforce,[1] and as the company struggled to turn a profit in a newly integrated German economy, the number of full-time employees fell from around twelve thousand in 1990 to three thousand in 1993 (Stiglich 2020, 4). Then came changes to the urban landscape, as the newly unemployed left in search of work elsewhere. Since 1989, Eisenhüttenstadt has lost over half its population, which has fallen from a high of just over fifty-two thousand to around twenty-three thousand in 2023 (Stadt Eisenhüttenstadt 2010; Lötsch 2023a). The loss of working-age residents has resulted in a disproportionate number of elderly, changing the character of a city that once had the youngest median age in the nation.

Over the course of the 1990s, social unrest grew alongside economic uncertainty and an increasingly vacant city. In 2004, just over a quarter of Eisenhüttenstadt's working-age population was unemployed, nearly double the national average. That year, Germany introduced the Harz IV welfare reforms, which reduced social support for the unemployed; 1,200 residents blocked traffic on Linden Avenue in protest against the diminished benefits (Stiglich 2020, 305), publicly reflecting the city's reputation as a bastion of East German postindustrial despair, despite the fact that its steelworks continued to operate. The city center was materially decrepit, with boarded-up windows and unpainted plaster facades crumbling to reveal the brick beneath. Around 4,300 apartments were empty,

FIGURE 29. Housing Complex 7 during demolition, 2005. Residents referred to buildings by their decorative elements—for instance, "the Swan" (*shown at right here*) or "the Snail." Photograph by Gabriele Urban. Courtesy of Stadtarchiv Eisenhüttenstadt.

comprising 23 percent of the city's housing stock (Howest 2006, 100–101). In some neighborhoods, most notably the southern portion of Housing Complex 7, vacancy was as high as 59 percent. It was during this period that Eisenhüttenstadt gained the nickname *Schrottgorod*—roughly "Eastern Bloc piece of junk," a combination of *schrott* (junk or scrap) and *-gorod*, the Russian suffix for city, a name that maligned both the city's material state and its cultural legacy.

Against this backdrop, urban renewal programs began in earnest. This chapter examines those efforts, which began in 2002 and have focused on the reconsolidation of the city as it was originally planned. This was made possible by the renovation of the historically protected zone and the demolition of outlying areas built later in the socialist era. I begin this chapter by investigating the reimagination of the socialist Housing Complex, as well as its original design. I then discuss the social world that inhabited the Housing Complex under socialism, defined by what I term a "networked" habitus, as well as contemporary urban renewal efforts and their outcomes.

Such efforts have been aimed not only at lowering urban vacancy but also at reproducing and resuscitating the socialist architectural emic. As city officials discuss the material renovation of the city, they also discuss the recuperation of their city's erstwhile social dynamics—the civic engagement and attunement to others that the socialist architectural emic was intended to bring about. Such efforts represent, in the words of city officials, "a fundamentally new approach to the core substance of historic preservation" (LBV 2016), grounded in the socialist conception of urban space, as the city is reimagined not as a collection of buildings but as a holistically functioning social infrastructure. As they have been carried out, urban renewal projects have largely met with success, reflected in numerous awards and commendations from organizations for architecture and urban planning (BBU 2009, 2013, 2021; DSP 2018; DBP 2015). In 2022, the city's population increased for the first time since reunification (Lötsch 2023a).

I first visited Eisenhüttenstadt in 2010, when demolitions were well underway but renovation projects were still in their earliest phases, and the city had a desolate atmosphere. Boarded-up windows were no longer a common sight, but the facades of unrenovated low-rise apartment buildings in Housing Complexes 1 and 4 were still unpainted, sometimes crumbling, and often streaked with decades of water damage. Along the main streets, flag holders rusted above doorway lintels, no longer used during parades and public holidays. In the high-rise neighborhoods of Housing Complexes 5 and 6, cranes and construction dumpsters were a common sight, as apartments were demolished by the thousands and residents relocated to the "consolidation zones" in Fürstenberg and the city center. The detritus of residents' lives often lay in large piles in front of buildings slated for demolition. Usually this consisted of broken-down pieces of unidentifiable furniture, though I once noticed what appeared to be a bookshelf covered in magazine cutouts of the singer Madonna and ALF the TV alien, traces of a reunification-era childhood that had looked longingly toward the West.

To outsiders, Eisenhüttenstadt was perceived as stagnant and moribund, out of joint with the space-time of contemporary Germany. Max, a social worker in his thirties, commuted to Eisenhüttenstadt from Cottbus, a university city about an hour's drive south. Despite the fact that Cottbus is also part of the former East Germany, Max told me that when he first came to Eisenhüttenstadt in the early 2010s, he felt as if he had entered a "time warp," seeing "all these people with their jean jackets and very old-fashioned jeans—they really looked like they were straight out of the GDR." Anna, also a former East German, who commuted from Berlin, visited Eisenhüttenstadt with her school-age niece around this time. She told me that the girl described the city as being "under a cheese dome [*unter einer Käseglocke*]," a German saying that evokes a social world closed to the reality around it.

But for architects and urban planners, this was a moment of emergent possibility, as long-term plans began to bring a new urban footprint into being. Jens Beige, an architect who has been instrumental in much of the city center's renovation, described the efforts as the natural progression of the city's "cycle

[*Kreislauf*]," which carried a double meaning. In its nonhuman sense, *Kreislauf* refers to transformation through different stages—for example, geologic or mete-orological cycles—but it also refers to the circulation of blood through the human body and is used as a reflection of overall well-being. Cities exist at the nexus of the organic and inorganic, as urban space is constructed through the interplay between human and nonhuman (Lefebvre [1974] 1992). In talking with Beige, I could not help but think of both meanings—that the city's next phase would be defined by the reinvigoration of its vitality. The cheese dome might be removed as Eisenhüttenstadt rejoined the forward historical motion of the nation. Perhaps its socialist legacy could become an asset, rather than an albatross.

It's All Still There

Jens Beige trained as an architect in the 1970s, during the socialist era. When I visited him in his office in 2016, he presented me with a manila folder that con-tained two Wikipedia entries, printed out and stapled separately: one for the Ath-ens Charter and one for the East German Sixteen Principles of Urban Planning. Beige was adamant that I understand the conceptual overlaps between socialist urbanism and early modernism. He was in the midst of developing Generational Living, Affordable Living, and other plans that would ultimately come together as the City Center Development Plan. Close to 38 percent of Housing Complex 1, the city's oldest, was uninhabited (Stadt Eisenhüttenstadt and BBSM 2015, 30). But Beige believed that residents would return to the neighborhood once renova-tions were complete.

Beige described the modernist commitment to holism as a central tenet of socialist urbanism. Under socialism, he said, "there are no empty lots, only empty spaces." He told me that because I was an American, this idea would be com-pletely foreign to me. "Someone from the West thinks of urban planning entirely differently"; in the GDR, "people imagined space." At its core, Beige believed, "urban planning is the management of space." He described the attention he paid to every bench, tree, and path in a building's courtyard. Under socialism, "there were always three dimensions" to be considered, as the perception and experi-ence of citizens were the real object of the architect's imagination. Eisenhütten-stadt was built for a populace without cars, Beige explained, and it was meant to be experienced on foot. He asked me to picture an imagined resident in Housing Complex 1. They might exit their front door; stroll over to Linden Avenue, where they would visit a bakery or meet a friend at a pub; run errands at the post office or City Hall; then relax in a landscaped courtyard before returning home. As he talked, he gesticulated with quiet forcefulness, deliberately tapping the table at each imagined destination. "You have to really go through it," he said. "Every step is carefully thought through." Then he banged on the table with his palms as if to emphasize the totality of the invisible Housing Complex we had imagined before us. "It's all still there. It's ready at hand. It still works. We're coming back to where we started, like on a globe." He seemed to imply that given the proximity of the imagined apartment building to the pub, the bench, and the tree, these urban components needed only to be in sufficiently good condition before they would naturally draw citizens back to the city center—the next stage in the city's "cycle [*Kreislauf*]." Planners in the 1950s had created an urban footprint such that Eisenhüttenstadt's next iteration, decades later, would become inevitable.

East Germans considered urban planning biopolitically, with a totalitarian vision of need fulfillment. Principle 2 of the East German Sixteen Principles of Urban Planning states that "the goal of urban planning is the harmonious fulfillment of the basic rights to employment, housing, culture and recreation" (BpB 2005). Principle 10 then codifies the Housing Complex as the means by which the state would go about fulfilling those rights. The Housing Complex would "comprise a group of apartment houses [*Häuserviertel*] alongside gardens, schools, kindergartens, day cares, and the supplies and services necessary to fulfill the daily needs of the people. Urban traffic may not be permitted within the Housing Complexes, but neither should Housing Complexes and Housing Districts be self-contained, isolated entities.[2] Their structure and planning depend on the structure and demands of the city as a whole" (BpB 2005).

East German Housing Complexes were based on the Soviet city-complex (*gorodskoe khoziaistvo*), the central unit of Stalinist city building (Collier 2011, 82). In both East Germany and the Soviet Union, the role of urban administration was to manage a populace based around the nationalized economy. The number of workers needed in a given city would determine the number of apartments, schools, classrooms, and so on. Yet with its totalizing oversight, the state also became deeply invested in the minutiae of its citizens' lives, estimating how much food or soap would be used by citizens in a given year. Moreover, in the Soviet Union, city building arose alongside Stalinist purges in the 1930s, and its logics became entangled with Soviet efforts to erase so-called bourgeois influences, including that of the nuclear family. As citizens used collective spaces in their apartment buildings and children spent their days in state-run schools and youth groups, the city-complex introduced "a vision of the future that totalized the field of collective life" (5). Stephen Collier (81) points out that the Russian term for a city-complex, *khoziaistvo*, comes from the root *khoz*, meaning "household," and represents a shift wherein daily needs would be fulfilled not by the family but by the state, insofar as the state administration both planned and operated the city-complex. The city-complex was a "nexus of need fulfillment" (83) that could be plugged into an urban plan, reproduced any number of times to accommodate urban growth.

Eisenhüttenstadt's Housing Complexes are some of the few East German examples that closely follow the Soviet model. East German city building was a much smaller enterprise than its Soviet counterpart, and Housing Complexes were implemented only in new construction, which represented a minority of East German housing—in 1971, nearly 80 percent of East Germany's housing stock predated World War II (Ladd 1990, 588). Eisenhüttenstadt was originally planned with four Housing Complexes oriented around Linden Avenue, and Complexes 1, 2, and 3 are some of the only ones in the former East Germany built before the mandated use of prefabricated concrete architecture in 1964. While Housing Complex 4 is less architecturally ornate than Complexes 1, 2, and 3, its proportions follow the urban footprint that was planned before prefabrication, with widely spaced low-rise apartment buildings in L- and U-shaped configurations and housing for around five thousand residents. Housing Complexes built after 1964, such as Eisenhüttenstadt's Housing Complexes 5, 6, and 7, as well as Housing Complexes built in other New Towns, such as Hoyerswerda, Schwedt, and Halle-Neustadt, and in urban satellites such as Berlin-Marzahn, tended to be built in parallel rows of high-rise housing blocks, a style denigrated by East German architects in the 1950s, and housed between ten thousand and twenty thousand residents.

During the GDR era, each of Eisenhüttenstadt's Housing Complexes had its own day care, elementary school, and shops and was designed to serve the economy of movement of able-bodied families with two working parents. Like Beige, architect Herbert Härtel walked me through the movements of an imagined resident. Härtel served as the city's chief architect from 1958 to 1968 and designed much of Lenin Avenue and Housing Complexes 4, 5, and 6. When we met, he took a copy of Leucht's *The First New Town in the German Democratic Republic* from his bookshelf and pointed to a map of Housing Complex 2, explaining how the Housing Complex served residents' daily social and economic needs. Härtel's imagined resident would leave his apartment, drop off his children at day care or elementary school, then bike or catch the bus that would take him to the steelworks. On his way home, he would stop and do some shopping between the bus stop and the school, then pick up his children to bring them home. Older children and teenagers on their way home from school would walk by shops where they could buy treats before congregating with their friends in the courtyards and gardens of the Housing Complex. This ideal resident was imagined so completely—and access to consumer goods controlled so tightly—that, in later decades, residents who moved into the P2 tower blocks in Housing Complex 7 received a booklet with suggested furniture layouts that varied by apartment model and family configuration.

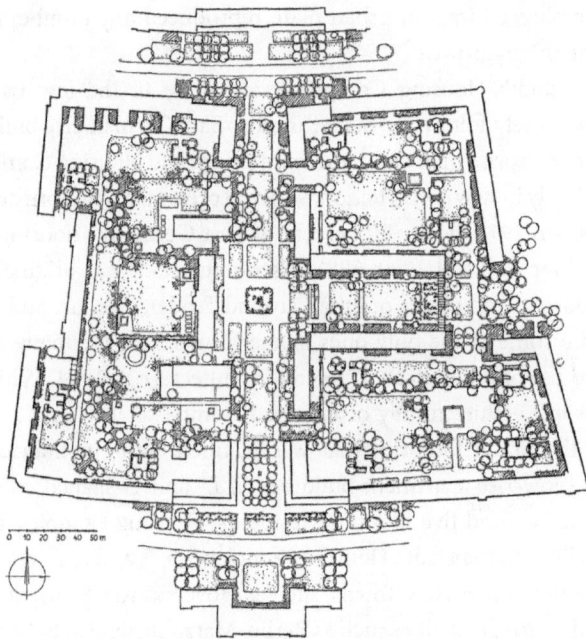

FIGURE 30. The map that Herbert Härtel referenced, depicting a greenery plan for Erich Weinert Avenue in Housing Complex 2, from Kurt W. Leucht, *The First New Town in the German Democratic Republic* (1957). Courtesy of Stadtarchiv Eisenhüttenstadt.

FIGURE 31. A postcard depicts an adjacent courtyard on Pavlov Avenue, 1958. Courtesy of Ben Kaden.

A 1951 report from the East German Building Academy praises the then-unbuilt Housing Complexes of EKO Residential City. The Housing Complexes would provide "all the amenities of urban life," and the report lists schools, day cares, cafeterias, groceries, shops, tradespeople, administrative centers, buildings for social and communal life, cultural facilities such as movie theaters and public bookstores, and green spaces (Bauakademie der DDR 1951, 17–21). Yet the report also notes that Housing Complexes should not be considered in and of themselves. "Their structure and planning depend on the form and needs of the city as a whole!" it declares, with an exclamation point used to underscore the language of the Sixteen Principles (21). The 1951 report further elaborates: Housing Complexes should not be "isolated," "closed off," or built in "elongated shapes," so that "the ways from the apartments to the social, cultural, and societal centers remain short and a clear orientation from the apartment toward such centers is not lost" (20–23). Building on Soviet experiences, and in contrast to "American Housing Cells"—likely referring to suburbs, which were described as having a "uniform and one-note, repetitive homogeneity" (21)—this sense of connectedness to the larger city was seen as essential for warding off provincialism, a lack of community, and a lack of civic engagement. And in contrast to capitalist *Mietkaserne*—rental barracks, a derogatory name for the cramped tenement apartments in which workers tended to live in urban centers—the model city's Housing Complexes would allow their residents ample "air and light" while still providing what "finally once and for all . . . can be identified as an 'urban life'" (18). The Housing Complex represented, according to the Building Academy, "a synthesis between the desire for the best possible sunlight, air, quietness, and proximity to nature on the one hand, and on the other hand the necessity of an appropriate spatial density and proximity to social and cultural establishments" (22).

Moreover, the Building Academy wrote that the model city would be a city of an entirely new kind. Presocialist cities came in different sizes (small, medium, large) or else were categorized by their variations in vibrancy—lively or dull. Instead the model city would offer residents across demographics "all the benefits of urban life, particularly cultural offerings, regardless of the city's size" (Bauakademie der DDR 1951, 37). It would not need a minimum population before it could support concerts, theaters, restaurants, and the like. Workers, normally confined to slums and suburbs, would no longer be cut off from culture—they would "finally be able to recognize that which constitutes urban life" (38). Five years later, in 1956, the Building Academy would declare that the Model City, by then named Stalinstadt, was "a city in the fullest sense of the word . . . the most culturally rich, economically robust, and practical form of settlement proposed or planned" (Leucht 1956, 18).

Herbert Härtel pointed out that Eisenhüttenstadt's Housing Complexes functioned in part because they were serviced by state-run local businesses that provided the city and surrounding region with locally produced provisions: a large industrial bakery, a dairy, municipal greenhouses, and a meat-processing facility. The businesses also drove employment as they grew alongside the city and steelworks. After reunification, the bakery, dairy, and greenhouses were sold off and closed; the meat-processing facility ceased production, but the new owners maintained, on-site, a small shop and café, which my informants still called the meat-processing facility (*Fleischkombinat*), though no meat was processed there. Yet the fact that Housing Complexes were said to "depend on the . . . the city as a whole" was not merely a description of their provisioning or apportionment. Rather, Housing Complexes were intended to guide participation in public life and instill pride in the socialist project. The 1951 report calls the elementary school "the most clearly recognizable crystallization of the Housing Complex" (Bauakademie der DDR 1951, 50) and repeatedly emphasizes the need for cultural offerings for adults; EKO would "play no role in the Residential City" (50). Industry was to be eclipsed by the cultural, political, and domestic life that it enabled.

Kurt Leucht said in an interview that he knew the Housing Complexes had been a success when he saw a little girl petting a bronze statue of a duck; today

FIGURE 32.   Laundry drying in a courtyard in Housing Complex 2, 2016. Clothes dryers are uncommon in Germany. Photograph by the author.

many of Eisenhüttenstadt's bronzes have patches that mark the hands of generations of residents. Leucht had hoped that residents would develop a sense of intimacy *with* the urban landscape as they simultaneously developed intimate relationships *in* the urban landscape. Thus, it was important that Eisenhüttenstadt "have small pubs, not just big restaurants like the HO,[3] but corner pubs, and there were quite a few." Public art would not be "monumental" but would be scattered across the city as "little pieces of cheerfulness" to be encountered in the course of everyday life, fostering encounters with urban space that evinced the state's commitment to the well-being of its citizens.

Indeed, older residents described having a strong emotional investment in their city and an appreciation of the built environment as the manifestation of human labor. When I moved to Eisenhüttenstadt to conduct fieldwork in 2014, I often noticed that my elderly neighbors would shout "Lawn stomper!" (*Rasenlätscher*) at someone who walked across the grass on a street median or in a Housing Complex courtyard. Yet others discussed the term's disappearing usage. When I asked Helga, a neighbor in her early nineties, about this, she explained that "lawn stomper" was deployed by members of the building generation to remind their fellow citizens that the built environment, including landscaping, was not to be taken for granted—an attunement that, in her mind, younger generations lacked. Susi, a preschool teacher in her early twenties, told me that "lawn stomper" was both old-fashioned and childish; she might tell a rowdy child, "Don't be a lawn stomper," but she would never use the term with a peer.

Yet Helga had witnessed the transformation of native pine forest into the landscaped courtyards of the historically protected zone. She described the truckloads of compost brought in to adjust the sandy, acidic soil in which pines thrive. Archival documents attest that in 1958, as city leadership ordered hundreds of seedlings and saplings, it also issued a directive to lay down an inch of compost over what would become the lawns and gardens of Housing Complexes 1 through 4 (Ministerium für Bauwesen 1958). To walk across the grass, Helga said, was to denigrate the monumental effort that went into creating these green spaces.

A few weeks later, a friend in her late sixties told me that she felt that the city had come to express "selfishness" when she saw what urban planners call desire paths (*Trampelpfade*), dirt paths trod diagonally by unrelenting lawn stompers. "People are selfish, they can save some time, and they don't think about whether their actions are disrespectful. Me, I would never do that just to save a minute. I only care about saving valuable [*lebenswertig*] time." I asked her whether there were desire paths in Eisenhüttenstadt during the socialist era. "Yes," she said, "but it wasn't done with the same attitude. We had a name for people who cut diagonally across the lawn: lawn stomper. When someone did that, we would call them a lawn stomper. Now, no one notices." My friend's respect for lawns seemed to stem, in part, from her perception of urban space as the product of the social world that acted on it, and with which she herself was entangled. While she was concerned to some degree with the material condition of her city, she seemed more concerned with the imagined inattention of her fellow residents. No longer attuned to the labor embedded in the built environment, today's "selfish" residents were closed off from the machinations of others, having lost the attentions cultivated during the socialist era.

The Networked Public

My informants often described their city as *verbunden* (connected) or occasionally *angebunden* (tethered, tied together), but they used the terms to describe a web of social and material connectivity that is best translated as "networked." While a tight-knit community may have been described as *eng verbunden* (tightly connected), my informants did not use the term as an analogue of the English term "tight-knit," which implies close or even intimate social ties within a community. Instead, the components being bound together were more abstract, almost technocratic. I first noticed the term in Eisenhüttenstadt when a longtime resident complained about the lack of mailboxes. We were walking to the post office a short distance away when she turned to me and said, "Back then [*damals*]"—when my interlocutors began a sentence with "back then," it went without saying that they referred to the GDR—"you could barely walk a few meters without seeing a mailbox—the city was *that* networked." At the time, I thought she was referring to the bustle of activity that had once defined urban life; I pictured mail carriers rushing around the city, delivering missives from across the Eastern Bloc.

Later, the term came up in conversation with Jens Beige, the architect. During the GDR era, he said, Housing Complex 1 was so "networked" that "you could go shopping in your slippers." To be networked, it seemed, was to have ample provisions and services—he noted that the grocery store received shipments of oranges that would make Berliners jealous—available in such close proximity that you didn't need proper shoes. This usage evoked commercial networks, and indeed many Eisenhüttenstädters noted their city's privileged position in the Eastern Bloc import-export marketplace. But the usage also retained qualities evoked by my friend's complaint about the loss of ubiquitous mailboxes: a sense of having been in constant potential contact with others, a sense that elements from the public sphere could be easily integrated into the home, and vice versa.

A networked habitus relied, in part, on the perception of public space during the GDR era. Eisenhüttenstädters rented their apartments from the GeWi or the

FIGURE 33. Greenhouses visible from Rose Hill, located in front of the high-rise, circa 1965. Photograph by M. Fricke. Courtesy of Stadtarchiv Eisenhüttenstadt.

FIGURE 34. The self-service grocery store in Housing Complex 3, circa 1965. Photograph by M. Fricke. Courtesy of Stadtarchiv Eisenhüttenstadt.

EWG, but their sense of proprietorship extended over the city at large. The communal maintenance of shared space, such as apartment stairwells, was a requirement of tenancy, and civic groups regularly tended to the city's parks. As such, the boundary between public and private space was diffuse and did not map neatly onto the distinction that exists today between public space that is municipally owned and cared for and private space that is owned and cared for by individuals (Fox 2020). With all space owned by the state—or, rather, by the people of East Germany collectively—residents considered both personal space and shared space worthy of their attention and care. One informant described having tended to the gardens on Rose Hill with her work brigade. She particularly loved the cherry blossoms, which were always beautifully maintained. In 2015, she told me, "People thoughtlessly break the branches off as they walk past. Yet those same people will ask you to take your shoes off when you enter their apartment."

Thus, a networked habitus also necessitates training one's attention on the wider urban landscape. Gabriele Haubold (2014, 7–8), in an essay for the city magazine *Colorful and Complex*, described Friedrich Engels Street in Complex 2 as "a lovely little networked street" and urged residents to slow down, take stock of its hawthorn berry bushes, and smile. This notion of networkedness frames residents' perception as the framework through which the natural and built environments are integrated into a cohesive urban landscape (Tsing 2017; Mathews 2018). The resident becomes emotionally invested in their city and its seasonal changes; they smile both at the beauty of the landscaping—perhaps at the labor of past and current residents embodied therein—and at the recognition of networkedness, which joins together a person and their environment in a relationship of mutual concern and shared futurity. While Haubold described the street itself as "networked," the behaviors she encourages suggest that a networked habitus is a learned attunement that both shapes and is shaped by an individual's perspective.

Networkedness, however, has not always been cultivated toward communitarian well-being, as it bears traces of socialism's two faces: communitarian ideals and authoritarian governance. Indeed, the porosity of public and private that existed in the Eastern Bloc stemmed in part from the integration of the surveillance state deep into citizens' private lives (Gal 2002). Gerda, a friend in her late sixties, told me that during the socialist era, the city was "bound together [*verbunden*], like felt," and she mimicked the act of crushing wool with her hands. She had always been somewhat outspoken, she said, and exhibited less fear of the surveillance state than her peers did. (She recalled that at Young Pioneer meetings, her classmates were constantly telling her, "Gerda, I agree with you, but no one says that in the meeting.") As an adult, she worked at a high school cafeteria. She told me, "One day I looked around the cafeteria and noticed every table that had four students at it. I said out loud, 'One person at each of those tables is a Stasi informer.'" After reunification, it would be revealed that roughly one out of every hundred East Germans had informed for the Stasi (Müller-Enbergs 2008), though suspicion and uncertainty made the proportion feel much higher. Gerda's colleagues acted shocked, she said, "but I knew who the informant among them was because she was acting totally shocked. Of course the next day I was called into the school director's office and reprimanded. Afterward I found out that the school director was Stasi too. But that's how it was back then. We were just so bound together, like felt."

Gerda's story illustrates that to be *verbunden(en)*—networked, bound together—requires cultivating certain attunements such that they can inform epistemological regimes. When I spent time with Gerda and her friends, they would occasionally point out a stranger and whisper to me, "He was Stasi" with vitriol that punctuated an otherwise inoffensive scene: An old man walked across a parking lot while we ate bratwurst at a nearby picnic table; a man in a sweater-vest took his seat before an event at the Fürstenberg Museum. Gerda's resigned acceptance of the ubiquity of surveillance in East Germany—"that's how it was back then"—seemed to have marked her cohort with an attunement to the social milieu; they assessed the motivating forces behind an interlocutor's tone or body language and operated under the assumption that others were doing the same. Under these circumstances, for Gerda to "know" that someone was Stasi meant that she had a visceral suspicion based on superficially normal behavior—the coworker who overplayed her shock, or the teenager who spoke too eagerly with a classmate across the lunch table. It was a response to the "unincorporated resid-uum" (James [1890] 1983, 247), or what C. S. Peirce (1931, 24) called "second-ness": conscious thought that relies on the evocation of something visceral rather than logical, as when your blood runs cold when you sense that your colleague is working for the Stasi, even if she revealed as much only through a glance.

But an attunement to the perspective and motivation of others can also be a precondition for care and social sustainability. To cultivate a networked habitus is to recognize one's role as a social agent who both acts and is acted on—who sees while seeing themselves being seen. Yet that same attunement to social embed-dedness can be trained on identifying when a neighbor could use a kind word or a door held open—support given securely in the knowledge that the same would be done for oneself. It remains to be seen whether such attention to others can remain cultivated in the long term, in the absence of a populace raised under a surveillance state that weaponized the observation of everyday life. Urban space, as a living, dynamic thing, must be continually produced, and networked space requires not only particular habits but also particular observations, atten-tions, and conceptions of space (Lefebvre [1974] 1992). While the East German

Building Academy may have subscribed to the modernist belief that "a house is a machine for living in" (Le Corbusier [1931] 1986), Eisenhüttenstadt presents a natural experiment in which the same machinery has come to operate in radically different social contexts.

The Demographic Shift

Eisenhüttenstadt has undergone multiple fundamental shifts—from socialism to capitalism, from horse-drawn carts to cars, from postcards to mobile phones—but one of its most striking is its shift from a young population to an aged one. The explanation most often cited for this shift is the economic collapse that followed reunification: Young people left in search of work, often relocating to the West, where unemployment was markedly lower. Yet the rise in unemployment was not the only factor. Jens Beige told me that by the late 1980s, architects and city officials were already noticing a rapid uptick in retirees. In East Germany, housing for citizens under sixty-five was allocated based on where one had a job or student position. Because Eisenhüttenstadt's original inhabitants were given housing in order to take industrial jobs, the population was artificially young, with the vast majority of residents in their twenties and thirties. In 1951, retirees made up only 3 percent of Eisenhüttenstadt's population, compared with a national average of 15 percent. And that percentage shrank as the city expanded and brought more young people in. By 1960, only 2 percent of the population, close to five hundred residents, was over sixty-five, and the city had the youngest median age in East Germany (Bauakademie der DDR 1960, 2; Ludwig 2000, 75). A 1956 report from the East German Building Academy expresses concern about Eisenhüttenstadt's large proportion of children; 30 percent of the population was under eighteen, which would have rendered Eisenhüttenstadt below average in its percentage of working-age residents were it not for its unusually low percentage of retirees (Bauakademie der DDR 1956, 6–7).

As a result of its demographics, residents often describe the socialist era as something akin to a US college campus. "Back then [damals]," teenagers were constantly running into friends and swinging by the steps of the Friedrich Wolf Theater to see who was hanging out, and young adults spent their free time sharing a beer with neighbors while their children played in the courtyard. Planners in Eisenhüttenstadt told me that in the 1960s, the biggest concern was how to accommodate the baby boom that was projected for the 1970s with sufficient schools, day cares, and two- and three-bedroom apartments.

Yet despite the socialist fixation on technocratic planning and technological progress, the linear increase in life expectancy that took place over the course of the twentieth century seems not to have been accounted for. In 1960, the population aged fifty-five to sixty-five numbered nearly 1,400, yet demographic projections made that year projected only 197 residents aged seventy-five and above by 1980 (Bauakademie der DDR 1960, 11). In other words, among those aged fifty-five to sixty-five in 1960, nearly 80 percent were expected to die before age seventy-five. Yet while life expectancy in 1960 was seventy-one for East German women and sixty-six for men (Statistisches Amt der DDR 1990), the GDR saw a steep increase in the proportion of citizens living past seventy-five between 1950 and 1960, and the proportion of elderly citizens grew consistently over the course of the socialist era (Wiesner 2001, 27–29).[4] As of this writing, life expectancy in Germany is eighty-three for women and seventy-eight for men. In a reversal of twentieth-century demographics, around 30 percent of Eisenhüttenstadt's population is now over age sixty-five (Destatis 2022b; Urbistat 2022).

The capitalist imaginary, like the socialist imaginary before it, tends to idealize youth as the engine of progress and growth. Yet the elderly, too, can become engines of financial profit under certain circumstances: In the United States, retirement communities like the Villages, in central Florida, are regional economic powerhouses with populations well over fifty thousand (US Census Bureau 2020). For a brief moment, it seemed like Eisenhüttenstadt, too, might lean into this model. The city's first "Living Well: Fit for the Future" commendation, in 2009, was awarded for a project in Housing Complex 6 that transformed an abandoned vocational school into two nine-bedroom apartments that served as a full-time care facility for adults with dementia (BBU 2009). The award, overseen by the Brandenburg State government, was developed in 2008 to reward innovation in urban planning that responds to demographic change, climate change, and other contemporary challenges. Eisenhüttenstadt's second Living Well commendation came in 2013 for a similar project on a larger scale. The Chestnut Courtyard (Am Kastanienhof) project converted an abandoned day care in Housing Complex 7 into fifteen apartments for semi-independent elder living, with space dedicated to an on-site nursing service, creating more jobs for builders and health aides in the process (BBU 2013). In 2013, Chestnut Courtyard was folded into a larger redevelopment plan, but the vast majority of land adjacent to the "Senior's Park" was earmarked for the eventual construction of single-family homes (Stadt Eisenhüttenstadt 2013, 4).

Rather than attempt to become Sun City, Germany, Eisenhüttenstadt has centered the elderly in intergenerational living. The pivot was enabled in part by the European Union's 2005 Barcelona Declaration, which introduced the principle of universal design, defined as "the design and composition of an environment so that it may be accessed, understood and used" by the widest possible range of people, including those with varying ability in terms of vision, hearing, mobility, and cognition (CEUDA 2020). In response to the Barcelona Declaration, the Eisenhüttenstadt city government partnered with engineers at the Brandenburg Technical University to develop "Accessible Eisenhüttenstadt." Finalized in 2010, the plan folded universal design principles into the ongoing renovation of municipal buildings—for instance, adding wheelchair ramps and mini-elevators to the lobby in City Hall. As further urban renewal plans are carried out, accessibility continues to be prioritized. The 2014 comprehensive urban development plan notes that accessibility helps lower the city's carbon footprint—people who use strollers or wheelchairs can reduce their reliance on cars—while also improving the city's attractiveness to a wide demographic (Stadt Eisenhüttenstadt and BBSM 2015).

While the development plan is not explicit in its desire to attract families who use both strollers and wheelchairs, the city publicly celebrates its intergenerational families. A 2022 television documentary occasioned by the city's seventieth anniversary portrays Eisenhüttenstadt as a city that young people tend to leave. But then in the last ten minutes, as if to mimic the third-act plot twist that the city hopes is underway, the camera cuts to the sculpture garden in Housing Complex 3 as the narrator describes an intergenerational family who have "stayed"—a formulation that nonetheless assumes that leaving is the default position. "People who are born here, who feel a sense of well-being here, have deep roots in this city," an older woman says, gesturing toward her adult daughter. "Your husband among them." The daughter responds through laughter, "Yeah, he doesn't want to leave. He will not leave." An elderly matriarch joins in, pointing to the older woman as she says, "Anyone who leaves develops a yearning to come back—that I know from you" (Leitz 2022). While many of my informants had adult children who had moved away, others came from families with multiple generations in the city, and those who had moved away temporarily often cited proximity to family as their reason for returning home.

In 2011, the city began its renovation program in earnest when it secured funding for the renovation of Housing Complex 1. Since then, a number of renovation initiatives have been carried out, each with discrete aims. Taken together, their goal has been to diversify Eisenhüttenstadt's age demography, reduce residential vacancy, reduce the city's environmental impacts, and improve a qualitative sense of vitality. And while renovations remain underway as of this writing, the city's initial efforts have proved successful. In 2018, the German National Academy of Urban Planning conferred a special commendation on Eisenhüttenstadt for what it called "Strengthening the City Center: Neighborhoods in Transformation." The commendation highlighted three programs—Generational Living, Affordable Living, and Accessible Living—as well as the renovation of thirteen municipal buildings, including schools and City Hall (DSP 2018). Together with earlier infrastructural renovation efforts, these programs have transformed the city center from one of Eisenhüttenstadt's most decrepit areas to one of its most desirable. Yet Strengthening the City Center is the culmination of decades of large-scale urban redevelopment efforts. And before any of its component projects became possible, vacant apartments elsewhere in the city had to be demolished by the thousands.

Transforming the Urban Landscape

Urban Renewal East (Stadtumbau Ost) has done more than any other contemporary government program to change the urban landscape in Eisenhüttenstadt and, indeed, across the former East Germany, a region also referred to as the "New States."[5] The program launched in 2002. Two years prior, the German parliament published the report by the Lehman-Grube Commission, officially the Expert Commission on Structural Changes to the Housing Industry in the New States. Depopulation and economic decline had been problems for the New States since reunification, and the commission hoped to draw attention to their impacts on the urban landscape. Many apartments had been empty for over a decade and were in a state of disrepair that would make renovations difficult. Older city centers often had not been renovated since before World War II, and newer prefabricated apartment buildings were strongly disfavored as housing trended toward single-family homes and renovated prewar buildings (BUNBR 2016c).

To combat the increasingly decrepit state of their housing stock, many counties in the New States, in the years prior to the Lehman-Grube Commission, had provided tax incentives or grant-based programs to build new housing. Yet the resulting building boom only increased residential vacancy rates, as the population did not increase alongside the new construction (BUNBR 2016c).

In 2001, in response to the commission's report, the German parliament put out a call to counties in the New States for plans to combat the growing vacancy rate. The chosen plan, based on 260 submissions, was Urban Renewal East. Described as a "quality offensive" in urban development, it supported demolitions and renovations (BUNBR 2016c). Later financial documents distinguish between demolitions, infrastructural demolitions, renovations, and a category called "the renovation and securing of prewar buildings, including the purchasing of those buildings by local government," which I will abbreviate here as "prewar buildings" and which includes the funding category Renovation-Protection-Purchase (Sanierung-Sicherung-Erwerb, or SSE), dedicated to helping municipalities purchase and renovate centrally located buildings (BUNBR 2016a).

Urban Renewal funding came from the federal government, and each eligible state applied to the federal government for funding. (Until 2017 only New States were eligible.) City and town governments could then apply to their state for a portion of that funding in one of the four aforementioned categories. Between 2002 and 2016, the federal government spent €5.1 billion on Urban Renewal (BWSB 2024), €286 million of which went to the state of Brandenburg (BUNBR 2016a). In 2009, Brandenburg spent more on demolitions (€5.9 million on demolitions, €5.2 million on infrastructural demolitions) than it did on renovations (€9.8 on appreciations, none on prewar buildings) (BVBS 2009, 2). In 2016, in a move that reflects the program's shifting priorities as larger demolition projects were completed, Brandenburg spent significantly more on renovations (€10 million on appreciations, €3 million on prewar buildings) than on demolitions (€1.9 million on demolitions, €1.1 million on infrastructural demolitions). Between 2002 and 2016, Eisenhüttenstadt received nearly €22 million in federal Urban Renewal funds (BUNBR 2016a, 2).

When Urban Renewal was initiated in 2002, it was projected to last until 2009. During what became Urban Renewal's first phase, the program focused on lowering the vacancy rate in the New States through demolitions. Around three hundred thousand apartments were demolished during this phase, and vacancy in the New States sank from 16.2 percent in 2002 to 8.3 percent in 2010 (Liebmann et al. 2012, 7–9; Stadt Eisenhüttenstadt and BBSM 2022). As the semiabandoned Housing Complexes that had dotted urban peripheries were demolished, Urban Renewal began to increase funding for renovations, as well as for municipalities to purchase and renovate derelict or abandoned prewar buildings in city centers. In 2011, the parliament extended the program through 2025 (Liebmann et al. 2012, 7–9). In 2017, Urban Renewal East merged with a similar program in the former West Germany, Urban Renewal West, which was launched following Urban Renewal East's early success, and the new national program was called simply Urban Renewal. In 2020, the Urban Renewal program was retired and folded into a new national initiative called Growth and Sustainable Renewal (BWSB 2024).

Urban Renewal in Eisenhüttenstadt evolved as the Urban Renewal program itself evolved. The first demolition in Eisenhüttenstadt that followed reunification came in 1998, prior to the Lehman-Grube report. Its object was the Mittelganghaus, a dormitory for steelworkers that had been nicknamed the Bullpen for the young single men who lived there and caused trouble. Its demolition was widely celebrated—it rid the city of the Bullpen while clearing ground for the prosperity that capitalism had promised. As if to emphasize the spectacular entrance of capitalism, the building was demolished with dynamite, and citizens turned out in droves to watch its destruction. But the Bullpen's demolition turned out to be the first step in an ongoing series of demolitions that have been met with significantly less fanfare.

Since Urban Renewal began in 2002, close to 7,000 apartment units have been demolished in Eisenhüttenstadt, lowering the vacancy rate from around 22 percent in 2004 to around 15 percent as of 2020 (Stadt Eisenhüttenstadt and BBSM 2015, 68; Stadt Eisenhüttenstadt and BBSM 2022, 30). But the fates of various Housing Complexes have varied wildly. Housing Complex 7, with a vacancy rate close to 35 percent, was the first to be demolished. In 2003, its southern portion had a vacancy rate of 59 percent, the highest of any neighborhood (Howest 2006, 101–2). Between 2003 and 2005, close to 1,200 apartments were demolished there, covering over seventy thousand square meters (roughly seventeen acres) (BBR 2008, 49). Over the next few years, large swaths of Complexes 5 and 6 were also demolished. Concrete tower blocks, ripped open like dollhouses, became fixtures in the landscape, as sidewalks filled with detritus left by former residents. Yet demolitions could not keep up with the falling population, and the vacancy rate continued to rise. In Housing Complex 1, three apartment buildings were demolished in 2006, despite their location in the historically protected zone (Stadt Eisenhüttenstadt and BBSM 2022; Mann et al. 2015, 25–26).

FIGURE 35. A satirical postcard produced by the Fürstenberger Locals Club reads, "Greetings from Eisenhüttenstadt." 2011. Courtesy of Hendrick P., from the author's collection.

In Fürstenberg, a medieval village subsumed into Eisenhüttenstadt in 1961, residents were particularly outraged by the state of the city. In the early 1980s, a neighborhood on the south side of Fürstenberg was demolished to make way for Housing Complex 7, which rose incongruously against a backdrop of single-family homes and cobblestone streets. The demolition of the Housing Complex decades later only exacerbated residents' outrage. The Fürstenberger Locals Club, a group of longtime village residents, produced a set of satirical postcards where messages like "Blooming Landscape"—a reference to Helmut Kohl's promise that he would make the East German landscape bloom—contrasted with photographs of the ongoing demolitions. A 2012 calendar expanded on the theme, with captions like "Eisenhüttenstadt: half the size of Chicago's cemetery and twice as dead," and sarcastic platitudes like "A city's beauty grows with time," alongside photos of vacant buildings in Housing Complex 7, as well as the cranes, debris, and chain-link fences that had come to characterize the landscape of demolition.

Retrofitting the Housing Complex

The 1990s saw basic renovations in Fürstenberg, on Linden Avenue, and in Complexes 1 through 4, connecting the city's oldest buildings to municipal heat and hot water sources, as well as facade restorations in Housing Complex 2, which won the city its first architectural prize, from the Brandenburg State. Between 2006 and 2013, the city renovated Complexes 2 and 3 using Urban Renewal funds, among other governmental funding streams. But Complex 1, the city's oldest, posed a particular challenge. Between 2002 and 2013, vacancy in Complex 1 rose from 23 percent to 37.7 percent—despite the demolition of close to two hundred housing units (Mann et al. 2015, 26). Complex 1 was home to some of the city's most spare and modest apartments, as well as its oldest, draftiest buildings. By the early 2010s, Complexes 2 and 3's apartment buildings had painted stucco facades adorned with bas-relief friezes. In Complex 1, the paint had faded from facades so long ago that it was impossible to tell what color they had once been. Apartment buildings were a uniform brown, except where pieces of stucco had fallen off to reveal the building materials beneath. Beige, who has worked on numerous Urban Renewal projects, told me he had been frustrated to see Complex 1 grow moribund over the years. His fellow Eisenhüttenstädters failed to appreciate that Complex 1 had what realtors would call "good bones": four-story apartment buildings within walking distance of shops, restaurants, bus stops, and services, and surrounded by landscaped courtyards. Beige could still see East German planners' original vision.

Beige's printouts about the Athens Charter and the Sixteen Principles, which he had given me when we first met, evinced his almost deterministic brand of optimism toward his city's future, seemingly influenced by the mechanistic imagination of socialist modernism. If Complex 1 had renovated buildings, Beige told me, people might repopulate the city center. Given services appropriate for the population, as opposed to the schools and childcare centers that had been there previously, people would embed themselves in the community over the course of everyday life. Then, Beige imagined, they would look out their balconies and admire the landscaping and remark to themselves that the city was nice "again."

Generational Living, which launched as part of Urban Renewal in 2014, aims to accommodate the needs of the disabled, including the elderly, while also inspiring civic commitments among young adults. Between 2014 and 2016, the program transformed twelve apartment buildings, about one-third of Complex 1's housing stock, from uniformly sized two-bedroom apartments into 184 apartments ranging in size from thirty-four to ninety-eight square meters (approximately three hundred to one thousand square feet). While some apartments are intended for parents and children (marketed as Family Living), the majority are best suited for households of one or two adults, either the elderly (Senior Living) or young people looking to move out of their parents' homes (Young Living). (Young Living, which renovated four buildings between 2012 and 2014, was folded into the larger efforts.) Where possible, Generational Living apartments have balconies, wheelchair-accessible doorways and showers, elevators, and renovated hallways and entryways, some with skylights and seating areas, intended to foster daily interaction among neighbors (LBV 2016). The 2015 commendation notes that the project's mix of wheelchair-accessible apartments of various sizes and configurations could appeal to a diverse range of family and household structures (DBP 2015), and Eisenhüttenstadt's comprehensive Urban Renewal Plan cites "social and generational mixing" as one of the primary goals of the renovation (Stadt Eisenhüttenstadt and BBSM 2015, 25–31)—reminiscent of the Housing Complex's original role as a "social condenser" (Murawski and Rendell 2017). Officials in city government told me that by the time Generational Living launched in 2016, all 184 apartments had been rented.

Eisenhüttenstadt's earliest apartment buildings were designed without balconies, following the Soviet city-building tradition aimed at the maximum collectivization of social life. Though Eisenhüttenstadt's apartments were allocated to nuclear families—a far cry from Soviet collectivism—they were nonetheless intended to be places where residents merely ate and slept. This is why Eisenhüttenstadt's high school geography teacher, taking a group of students on a walking tour of Housing Complex 1, explained that what separated a socialist city from a

FIGURES 36A AND 36B. Housing Complex 1, 2010. Top photograph by Gabriele Haubold, courtesy of Stadtverwaltung Eisenhüttenstadt. Bottom photograph by Gabriele Urban, courtesy of Stadtarchiv Eisenhüttenstadt.

FIGURES 37A AND 37B. Housing Complex 1, renovated as part of the Old Shop Street Ensemble, including new balconies, 2023. Photographs by the author.

capitalist one was the socialist city's lack of balconies, as social and leisure activities were to be conducted in communal areas.

When East German President Walter Ulbricht visited Housing Complex 1 in 1952, he denigrated the spare apartment buildings as "unadorned boxes" (Durth et al. 1998, 1:373). Balconies, as well as architectural flourishes such as friezes, cornices, and bay windows, were included in the design of subsequent Housing Complexes, as well as the southern portion of Housing Complex 1, built after Ulbricht's visit. But while they were initially perceived as a concession to bourgeois sensibilities, balconies soon became places of heightened sociality. Residents could observe the surrounding area and forge bonds with their neighbors from a space of semiprivacy. Beige explained that in the high-rise towers of Housing Complex 7, balconies had been particularly close together, which was instrumental for fostering relationships between neighbors—though residents saw that closeness as a bug, not a feature.

Nonetheless, the balconies that were built during the renovation of Housing Complex 1 represent a recuperation of the Housing Complex's original aims, refracted through a modern sensibility. The idea that a lack of balconies would lead to greater socialization outside the home assumes an able-bodied populace able to easily access local gardens and pubs. The renovated apartments are similarly intended to facilitate residents' daily social interactions, but they do so for a more expansively imagined urban public, including those with limited mobility. For those residents, balconies offer an essential engagement with public space. Buildings renovated as part of Generational Living, in 2015, have interior balconies, essentially semiprivate overhangs overlooking the buildings' stairwells, that residents can use in winter or in inclement weather. Buildings also have exterior balconies, though the county historic preservation board mandated that they be visually recognizable as a contemporary retrofit. As such, the balconies, constructed from locally produced steel and glass, appear incongruous, affixed to the exteriors of low-rise buildings with pitched roofs. Yet the juxtaposition is the point, an indication of ongoing investments in the urban landscape. Project managers write that balconies should appear to fracture building's facades; in doing so, "the 'breaking' and 'reforming' of building components" is intended to "holistically [gestaltlich] represent both the new usage and the new users themselves. 'Old and new,' 'past, present, and future,' will become legible in the urban landscape" (LBV 2011).

Housing Complex 1 was also home to the Old Shop Street (Alte Ladenstrasse), renamed, following reunification, for the city's first grocery store, which opened there in 1953. In 2015, Generational Living was folded into a larger project, the Old Shop Street Ensemble, as the long-abandoned shop was transformed into the centerpiece of the neighborhood, home to a café and multipurpose community space, a physical therapy center, and the local headquarters of People's Solidarity, an East German nonprofit that provides a wide range of social services, including Meals on Wheels and a twenty-four-hour nursing and healthcare service. In 2015, the Old Shop Street Ensemble won the German Real Estate Developers' Award in Modernization, granted by a consortium of nationwide associations in architecture and urban planning. Project leadership highlighted the importance of revitalizing the communitarian ethos that once defined Housing Complex 1, writing that "the realization of the project the Old Shop Street Ensemble represents a fundamentally new approach to the core substance of historic preservation. Historic preservation can no longer be about the 1:1 historical restoration of the buildings, but rather the reactivation and revitalization of the neighborhood for older and mobility-impaired residents" (LBV 2016). Variations on this statement are repeated in other Urban Renewal documents, which consistently cite the Housing Complex's "reactivation and revitalization" (BWSB 2021a) through the social atmosphere cultivated therein.

In folding Generational Living into the Old Shop Street Ensemble and highlighting the renovated grocery store as the "key feature of the ensemble" (BWSB 2021a), planners have elevated an image of care as an essential component of contemporary urbanism in Eisenhüttenstadt. Perhaps in the absence of enumerated principles, this centerpiece will act as a reminder that ability and economic productivity are not preconditions for participation in public life—nor, by extension, are they preconditions for having value as a person and citizen. As anthropologists have observed, care work can take on weighty cultural value, particularly in places where economically mediated notions of value have failed to provide the social uplift they once promised (Muehlebach 2012). And as residents repopulate Housing Complex 1, each encounter with the built environment becomes an opportunity to summon an expansive imagination of civic belonging (Fennell 2015, 7),[6] set off by the visceral recognition of shared subjectivity among residents who are invited to consider the full humanity of their neighbors.

Since its opening in 2016, the Old Shop Street Ensemble has been the site of numerous meetings and community events, including candidate forums for city council and collaborations with the nearby Pestalozzi School, an alternative school for mentally disabled students. The Pestalozzi student catering group provided cakes for the ensemble's inaugural coffee klatsch, which the local newspaper celebrated as a "white tablecloth" event and an overwhelmingly successful "experiment" (Lötsch 2019). And as it revitalizes the neighborhood, the ensemble has also become a place to celebrate mid-century socialist culture. Recent offerings include a documentary film screening about Dean Reed, an American folk singer who defected to East Germany in 1973, and an exhibition on

Tamara Bunke, an Eisenhüttenstadt native better known as Tania the Guerrilla, who died fighting alongside Che Guevera in Bolivia in 1967. While both events were modest in scale, they reflect a populace eager to embrace the various facets of Eisenhüttenstadt's socialist legacy and, perhaps, a refusal to accept "failure" (Appadurai and Alexander 2020; Ojani 2023) as the necessary result of market-driven obsolescence.

The Hangout

When I visited Housing Complex 1 in 2023, I found a materially transformed urban landscape. Apartment buildings that were derelict and uninhabited in 2015 were now resurfaced and freshly painted, with new windows, balconies, and wheelchair-accessible entryways. Neat landscaping stood where unkempt hedges once climbed up the back side of apartment buildings. Parents and children went by on bicycles, heading home from the nearby Pestalozzi School and Astrid Lindgren Elementary. Balloons tied to a balcony indicated that someone was throwing a ninetieth birthday party. At the center of the complex, near Linden Avenue, I found the eponymous Old Shop. The community room had been renamed the GeWi Hangout (Gewi-Treff) and was operated jointly by the GeWi and People's Solidarity. A sign on the door explained as much, describing the Hangout as an "open meeting place for all the city's citizens," where neighbors could socialize, drink coffee, play games, and attend events. "You are heartily invited," the sign read in bold, and as I did not see any operating hours listed, I pushed the building's door open.

Inside, I was greeted warmly by a woman whom I had previously come to know as Heidi the Witch (Hexe Heidi), so named because she ran a community garden on Leisure Time Island called the Herbal Witch's Association (Kräuterhexeverein). Heidi had organized educational and community events, including botany workshops for the local schools and a New Year's Eve disco for mentally disabled adults. I attended a free class that she taught, where a group of retirees and I learned how to make butter and decorate it with edible flowers. Now she was the manager of the GeWi Hangout. We had not seen each other since 2016, and she immediately offered me lunch on the house, though the price would otherwise have been modest.

That day's offering was an Arabic meal, she explained, prepared by the three women who worked behind the counter at the Hangout's café—two asylees from Syria and one from Afghanistan who had settled in Eisenhüttenstadt. The Hangout served lunch three times a week: Tuesdays were Arabic, Wednesdays were German, and Thursdays were African, though Heidi was quick to point

FIGURE 38. The Aktivist in an undated photograph. Courtesy of Ben Kaden.

out that the kitchen staff also included Germans—she considered the mutual influence between Germans and foreigners to be essential for migrants' social incorporation.[7] A younger man came in, and Heidi told me that he worked next door, at the People's Solidarity headquarters. "Meal-time [Mahlzeit]!" he said, greeting the room, before taking his seat at a long table where about a dozen elderly Germans sat clustered in small groups. It was a habit I had observed in the city cafeteria, and informants told me that the greeting was common in school lunchrooms and factory canteens. But the city cafeteria, located inside a derelict office building, had struggled financially, cut back its hours, and shut down in 2016.

Over lunch, Heidi told me about her work organizing events at the Hangout—coffee klatsches, game nights, craft nights—and proudly showed me that she stored her crafting supplies in a chafing dish taken from Hotel Lunik, its origins indicated in large red lettering. Anthropologists note that salvage often transforms noncapitalist goods into commodities (Tsing 2015, 43), but the chafing dish had resisted this trajectory. It was salvaged from the ruined hotel not to "unlock" its future exchange value (Khatchadourian 2022, 319) but to keep it out of the hands of people who might. Heidi, a proud Eisenhüttenstädter and chair of the local chapter of the Left party,[8] valued the chafing dish for its "sensuous" qualities (Oushakine 2014) and the affective response it might provoke. Like the facades retrofitted with balconies, which had been "broken" and "reformed" to make visible the union of old and new, the former centerpiece of Eisenhütten-stadt's cityscape had been reconstituted as part of this new imagination of palaces for the people—a reminder of the city's origins contained within its current developments.

As we spoke, Heidi explained that her favorite events were the dances, which were held every two weeks. "Can you imagine people in their eighties having a dance party?" she said. "But the ladies get dressed up, they do their hair—it's one of the most popular events." The café served refreshments, and its adjoining multipurpose room had ample space for a dance floor. I was reminded of one of my first visits to Eisenhüttenstadt in 2010. The Aktivist, a beloved restaurant and dance hall that had closed following reunification, was in the process of being restored and transformed into offices for the EWG. Gabriele Haubold, then the director of Urban Renewal, told me that when she began the restoration of the Aktivist a few years prior, she had received pushback from members of the public who resisted the dance hall's conversion into office space. But the agitators were mostly elderly and unlikely to use a dance hall. "They wanted to return to a time when they were young," she said, but the restoration of the historic building could only do so much.

When I first heard this story, I thought it was a poignant reflection on time's arrow. But since then, I've wondered whether there was another layer to the agitation. Consider the project summary for Young Living, the program aimed at helping young adults move into their first homes, which notes that for members of the "building generation," it would be "incredibly meaningful" to see the renovated neighborhood "reestablished as an entry point for a third generation of residents" (LBV 2011)—their "entry" would be into lifelong civic commitments. Looking back, perhaps the people who wanted to restore the Aktivist's dance hall merely wanted reassurance that the city as they knew it might endure—reassurance that appropriate social infrastructures would be maintained such that expansive civic commitments might grow in a new generation of residents. The dance parties that Heidi described were hardly engines of economic revitalization, nor did they include the young people that Urban Renewal projects aimed to attract. But nearly two decades after plans for the Aktivist's renovation began, a new generation of elderly residents had proved that unexpected liveliness can in fact emerge, given appropriate space, care, and social circumstances.

3

HISTORY IN THE URBAN LANDSCAPE

Following the collapse of Eastern Bloc socialism, the duality of the city as a simultaneously material and abstract entity became apparent, as the same material conditions came to house radically altered social worlds and urban imaginations (Boym 2008; Huyssen 2003). Berlin, the capital of East Germany, became the seat of government for reunified Germany in 1990. That year, the East German parliament building, which had stood alongside the city's opera house and cathedral since 1976, was demolished under the guise of asbestos eradication. The Reichstag, still damaged from the 1933 fire that gave rise to Hitler's reign, was famously "wrapped" by artists Christo and Jean-Claude in 1995—the fabric was weighed down with steel from Eisenhüttenstadt's facility (Nicolaus 2000, 63)—then restored with a modern dome crafted by architect Norman Foster. It reopened in 1999. Groundbreaking for the adjacent Memorial to the Murdered Jews of Europe soon followed (Young 2000, 222); the now-iconic groupings of granite stele opened in 2004. Urban space was rapidly becoming the domain in which socialist history was lived and contested—and, indeed, it was the place where shameful events in German history were broadly worked through.

In Eisenhüttenstadt, the loss of the socialist emic was felt particularly acutely. As discussed elsewhere, Eisenhüttenstadt was imagined as having no prewar past. While other East German cities, such as Leipzig and Weimar, could fold the socialist period into a longer history, Eisenhüttenstadt was understood as belonging entirely to an epoch that was suddenly considered shameful. Nearly overnight, the city was transformed from a showpiece at the center of the Eastern Bloc to a post-city at the periphery of Western Europe.

In the process, citizens grappled with the production of history in real time. The German language distinguishes between *Geschichte*, history as it is codified— more literally, history as it is laid down stratigraphically, in layers (*Schichte*)— and *Vergangenheit*, the past, or that which has been. As socialism went from being a mark of distinction to a mark of shame, citizens had to reevaluate their understanding of Vergangenheit in light of reunified Germany's Geschichte— the fact that their lived experience of the past forty years might be at odds with accepted narratives of East German repression and worthlessness. Meanwhile, the city's material and semiotic landscape shifted as the new nation-state—and the absence of its predecessor—was made manifest in the texture of everyday life, transforming everything from currency to license plates to, as will be examined here, street names, which forced residents to navigate sociopolitical rupture at the same time as they navigated familiar urban space.

This chapter examines the transformation of Eisenhüttenstadt's street names as a lens through which residents understood their shifting position vis-à-vis the nation and its history. Eisenhüttenstadt's leadership in the 1990s took as a foregone conclusion that socialism would be scrubbed from the urban landscape. Yet residents nonetheless recognized the multiple, layered aspects of socialism embodied in the tightly knit (*verbundenen*) city—the competing faces of

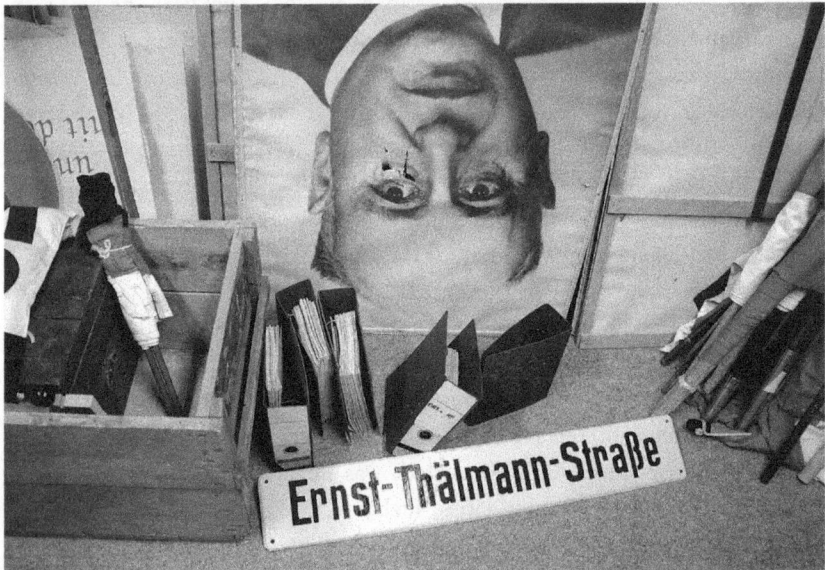

FIGURE 39. Items from the archive of the Museum of Utopia and the Everyday, including a street sign from the socialist era, 2023. Photograph by the author.

utopianism and authoritarianism—and grappled with the reduction in meaning that inevitably takes place as Vergangenheit is distilled into Geschichte (Trouillot 1997). City officials now publicly celebrate the building generation and its communitarianism ethos. But in the 1990s, uncertainty over socialism's legacy prevailed. Despite the city's material durability, it was unclear whether anything of its sociopolitical origins would remain apparent to those who encountered it. In examining historical documents, I show how the transition to capitalism was experienced in real time, as residents came to consider the legibility of history within the urban landscape through debates over street renaming. I then examine the shifts in meaning that new names have undergone, and their shifting role within the historically preserved city.

Possibilities and Poetics of Street Renaming

Streets exist as an essential component of urban life, acting as both conduits and gathering places. But they are also the primary organizing principle for urban planning and administration, and, as such, the names assigned to them become an essential component of the urban imaginary. Moreover, like all infrastructures, streets exist as a promise (Appel et al. 2018), built to shape movements and affects that may signal or cultivate certain sensibilities in those who encounter them. Anthropologist Rudolf Mrázek (2002, 8) points out that in Indonesia, European colonists considered modernity and progress to be embodied by the smooth black asphalt they laid down over the countryside as they, quite literally, made inroads into the country. But in Eisenhüttenstadt, poetics were ascribed less to streets themselves than to their names, a key site through which the priorities of the state become enmeshed in the everyday. And following the collapse of socialism, socialist names embedded in the landscape served to reiterate the sudden imposition of historical rupture that had recently taken place.

Across the former East Germany in the early 1990s, major cities changed the names of streets associated with socialism: In Berlin, Lenin Avenue became Landsberger Avenue; in Leipzig, Lenin Street became Prager Street; in Dresden, Lenin Square became Vienna Square (Raatz 2011). The decisions were made at the local level, but the directives tended to come from above. In Eisenhüttenstadt, the national parliamentary representative for Oder-Spree County, Jörg Ganschow, proposed a parliamentary initiative to rename the streets in Eisenhüttenstadt; a proposal was then sent to Eisenhüttenstadt's mayor requesting that he create a street-renaming task force. The justification for renaming, Ganschow wrote, in a paragraph that was often repeated in task force documents, was that many street names "make manifest the city's role as the first socialist [city]. This must come to an end. Not only are there anachronisms, but there are unfortunately some names that in today's times could be seen as a mockery of the victims [of socialism] and are therefore unacceptable" (Ganschow 1990; Fromm 2002a).

The task force's chair, Günther Fromm, told me that Eisenhüttenstadt's residents felt singled out. The perception was that, having been a model of socialism, Eisenhüttenstadt was to be scrubbed of its socialist vestiges more aggressively than its neighbors, though one might imagine that residents of Karl Marx Stadt, renamed Chemnitz, or Leipzig, where five hundred streets were renamed (Raatz 2011), felt the same. Nevertheless, renaming occurred unevenly nationwide. In Berlin, streets whose analogues were renamed in Eisenhüttenstadt, such as John Schehr Street and Ernst Thälmann Square, remain to this day, complete with additional signage that offers a brief biography of their respective namesakes.

The Eisenhüttenstadt city government approved Ganschow's measure on November 14, 1990 (Fromm 2002a) and put out a call for volunteers for the street-renaming task force, ultimately selecting ten members. The task force held four town hall meetings between January and March 1991. In May of that year, it sent the mayor two proposals for street renaming, which they referred to as the minimal and maximal variations. As was common practice in local government reports, each task force member signed the proposal with his or her name and street address (Arbeitsgruppe "Straßennamen" 1991). Months of public debate continued, both in the town halls and in local media. On October 23, 1991, the mayor approved a selection of the task force's proposed changes (Der Oberbürgermeister 1992; Fromm 2002b).

The decision to provide two options stemmed from both ideological and financial concerns. Fromm, the task force chair, told me that both variations were based on the idea that names associated with "power" should be eliminated from the landscape. But the task force struggled to define power, as some of socialism's most influential figures—Karl Marx, Friedrich Engels, Rosa Luxemburg—died before the founding of the East German state. As a resident named Köhlner noted in a letter to the local newspaper, such figures should not necessarily be lumped in with the legacy of East German authoritarianism. Besides, Köhlner suggested, why should Karl Marx be associated solely with Eastern Bloc socialism when he was the author not only of *The Communist Manifesto* but also of *Capital*, a key primer for the new era (Köhlner 1991)?

Curiously, neither Friedrich Engels Street nor Karl Marx Street was included in the minimal and maximal variations, though Marx-Engels Square, which would be changed to Market Square, was included in both. This was most likely because Marx-Engels Square was in Fürstenberg and therefore had a presocialist name—Market Square—to which it could return; the task force saw "back-naming" (*Rückbenennung*), the restoration of presocialist or pre-Nazi names, as a separate task from "renaming" (*Umbennenung*), although both were overseen by the same task force. Other cities, such as Dresden and Leipzig, also distinguished between renaming and back-naming and ceded to back-naming where possible (Kliesch 2024; Raatz 2011). One wonders what the lived experience of the former East Germany might have been had back-naming not been so widely accepted. Socialist cities were modular, after all, as the Soviet television program *Irony of Fate* illustrates (Yurchak [2005] 2013, 36),[1] and the same cast of characters from East German history was honored throughout the country. Yet back-naming reifies a capitalist interpretation of the built environment, naturalizing the union of certain streets and certain names as if the socialist period were merely a temporary disruption to the proper order.

In a decision with heavy Foucauldian overtones, the minimal variation suggested eliminating the names of people who had "wielded power" in political office in the Eastern Bloc: Wilhelm Pieck Street, Lenin Avenue, Klement Gottwald Street, Georgi Dimitroff Street, Walter Ulbricht Station, and Otto Grotewohl Ring, as well as street names associated with defunct political movements, such as Street of the Konsomol, named after the Soviet youth organization. The maximal variation, by contrast, included any names associated with socialism, adding to the minimal variation Helmut Just Street, John Schehr Street, Thälmann Street, and Fritz Heckert Street (Arbeitsgruppe "Straßennamen" 1991; Stadt Eisenhüttenstadt, Der Stadtverordnetenvorsteher 1992).[2] In both variations, every name that was to be replaced was listed alongside its replacement. For some streets, the task force suggested two or three replacement names.

Each name change—whether to change a name at all and, if so, which name to choose—was decided by a vote in a closed meeting of the fifty-two city council members. Fromm remembered the meeting as contentious, and its transcript ends with the line, "I beg of you, quiet!" (Stadt Eisenhüttenstadt, Der Stadtverordnetenvorsteher 1992, 12). The residents opposed to renaming were relatively small in number, but vocal. In addition to the many letters that the city council received, a group of 245 residents circulated a petition against the "undemocratic process of renaming." Yet much to their disappointment, a further 3,994 residents signed in support of the measure (Boehme 1992).[3] Proponents of renaming saw the process as necessary and "undemocratic," the cry of a sore loser. An op-ed in the local newspaper criticized the opposition's reluctance to accept their loss. In describing the disappointment of residents who had voted against renaming, the columnist wrote, "That too is democracy" (Käthner 1991).

The task force was additionally concerned with the costs associated with street renaming. If streets were to be renamed, street signs would have to be replaced and wages paid to the people who replaced them. The city's Bureau of Civil Engineering estimated the costs to be around 60,000 Deutschmarks (around €90,000) for the maximal variation and 34,000 Deutschmarks (€80,000) for the minimal variation (Haupt- und Finanzausschuß 1991). Thus, what initially seemed in Ganschow's proposal like a purely political decision quickly became a material and, by extension, financial one. In the end, eighteen streets were renamed—the maximal variation minus Fritz Heckert Street, whose residents had petitioned against its renaming, and whose name change was subsequently rejected in the city council vote. But the final costs were much higher than even those of the maximal variation. East German street signage had been white with black lettering; reunified German signage was blue with white lettering. In order to ensure a unified urban landscape, every street sign in the city was replaced (Fromm 2002a).

Between Loss and Disappearance

The residents who wrote letters to the city council tended to fall into one of two camps: those who were categorically against renaming, and those who accepted it, sometimes reluctantly, and suggested replacement names. Both camps were unified in the belief that they should save future generations from the pain and upheaval that accompanied the current scrutiny and reevaluation of the past. But the ones who rejected renaming altogether evinced a sense of personal injury at the prospect. They bristled at what they saw as the erasure of East German history, rather than its integration into the history of the newly reunified nation.

Heinz Schmidt of Fritz Heckert Street told a local paper, "We should be proud of what we, in these forty years, faithfully honored and championed. We will surely not, in the writing of history, take offense at it" (*Schlaubejournal* 1991). H. Köhlner, who questioned Marx's legacy, wrote, "We were, after all, proud for forty years of the truly brave daughters and sons of our nation. . . . [With renaming], we suppress history without dealing with it" (Köhlner 1991). Gerhard Zimmermann told the local newspaper, "He who strikes out historiographically controversial names takes over history. Names should be eliminated only after a working-through of history has been achieved" (MOZ Redakteure 1991). Renate Schwartz asked, "Do we not erase, with the change to a street . . . also a bit of our city's history? Were we not once proud of 'Eisenhüttenstadt,' the first socialist city in the former GDR?" (*Schlaubejournal* 1991). The Lonzek family, who lived at Fritz Heckert Street 26, summed up the sentiment in a letter to the city council: "This is not the right way to process the past. . . . To fit Georgi Dimitroff Street with the name Street of Unity is, for us, an impossible thing. It could well be that people in the future will be ashamed of that portion of our history [reunification]. Do we want then to once again rename the street, or is it not better to keep the current names, accept our past, and in the future not commit the same mistakes?" (Lonzek 1991).

The mistakes in question, it seemed, were the erasures of "historiographical controversial names." In addition to concerns over erasure, letter writers urged the city council to remember how, with time, charged names lose their potency. Dr. M. Pudack (1992), in a long, typewritten letter, wrote that "just as one must learn to live with a King Street or a Wilhelm Street, others [must learn to live with] an Ernst Thälmann, John Schehr, or a Helmut Just Street, respectively." Erika Olsen asked a local newspaper, "Must we categorically change the names that streets and plazas have had until now? [In the future] will we want to once again renounce the past, as if it had never been? . . . Lenin is still a historical figure who effected serious change in the world. After decades, that historical image will be recognized differently, and will continue to change. In 50 years, one will once again think differently from today, and today's 'great men' will perhaps be judged completely differently" (*Schlaubejournal* 1991).

The erasures of the maximal variation were overt and unambiguous, blunt manifestations of regime change. To some degree, residents were responding to the fact that the internal contradiction embodied in our vernacular use of the term "history"—our belief that history is what happened, and our knowledge that it is not—which is normally concealed in sociopolitical discourse, had suddenly become apparent (Trouillot 1997, 49). But residents were also responding to an understanding of the East German past that was dominated by the need to pay respect to the victims of East German authoritarianism, as decades of crimes committed by the East German secret police were, at the time, on the brink of being brought to light. As the East German government collapsed in late 1989 and early 1990, citizens stormed and occupied the Stasi archives in Erfurt, Leipzig, and Berlin, where agents had been in the process of destroying documents. In 1995, a federal project began to reconstruct shredded documents; this is still ongoing. Shortly after reunification, in 1991, the German parliament appointed Joachim Gauck, who later served as president, as commissioner of the Stasi Records Agency, a newly formed government division that would oversee evidence of Stasi crimes (Hermann 2021). Thus, East German history became subject to a "working through of the past" (*Vergangenheitsbewältigung*) (Adorno 1959), a process understood as analogous to West German denazification. Scholars still cite the reunification period as *Vergangenheitsbewaltigung*'s muted second chapter (Schulz 2022).[4] And in the 1990s, as Ganschow's letter explains and as the warring petitions evince—3,994 for street renaming, 245 against—it was considered disgraceful to prioritize one's attachment to the socialist era over the need to pay respects to the victims of the socialist regime.

Yet the Stasi archives themselves illustrate the fact that injustice is most read-ily remediated when there is evidence of its having occurred. Perhaps some letter writers feared that any erasure of the historical record would be an injustice to future generations, limiting the potential for future, unforeseen needs for reme-diation. The letter writers seemed most concerned with a distinction that politi-cal philosopher Adi Ophir makes between loss and disappearance. He observes that sociopolitical remediation is most difficult when loss slips into disappear-ance. When something is lost, it remains retrievable, even if only in the minds of those who mourn it. "To lose is to remember," Ophir (2005, 91) writes, and that which is remembered may be conveyed to an interlocutor—the first step toward remediation. Western cultures construct monuments and cultivate col-lective memory precisely because such acts diffuse memories of loss into the larger social body (Halbwachs [1925] 1992; Augé 2004). Yet when the burden of memory lies solely with an individual, loss risks slipping into disappearance. And when that occurs—when the lost thing cannot be conjured in the interlocutor's mind—then the possibility for remediation is foreclosed.

Disappearance, therefore, exists when only the thing's loss can be conjured. In perceiving a disappearance, one can never know the disappeared thing itself, but rather "the traces of the disappeared, and the traces of the disappearance" (Ophir 2005, 57)—similar to what Dawdy (2016, 25) describes as an evocation of "past-ness," which occludes a detailed accounting of past events. Disappearance signals the possibility of loss while also acting as a reminder of the inaccessibility of that which now sits in the "bottomless silence" of forgetting (Trouillot 1997, 30). "In disappearance," Ophir (2005, 45) writes, "what is there emerges as temporary, and temporariness emerges as something that is there." Disappearance, in signal-ing loss while refusing a full accounting of that loss, can act as a reminder that the world as we know it is potentially fragile and subject to historical disjuncture.

While the residents of Fritz Heckert Street may have successfully petitioned against their street name's change, today the street's name no longer signifies, first and foremost, the man Fritz Heckert, though it keeps his memory available for those who wish to pursue it. Rather, it signals the existence of an erstwhile East German lifeworld. Alongside more ambiguous namesakes like "Wilhelm" and "Rose," absent a socialist lifeworld—or a world in which socialism is integrated into unified German history—"Fritz Heckert" is a stand-in for any number of historical figures, a signifier simply of pastness.

Still, it seems fitting that the residents of Fritz Heckert Street were successful in their petition. Born in 1884, Heckert was a relatively well-known German Communist during the first part of the twentieth century. He was a member of the Spartacus League alongside Rosa Luxemburg, and a founding member of the German Communist Party (KPD),[5] where he served on the Central Committee with Walter Ulbricht. In 1932, as anti-Communist violence escalated in Germany, Heckert fled to Moscow, where he continued to serve the KPD in exile; he was publicly stripped of his German citizenship the following year and died shortly thereafter, in 1936 (BASD 2008).

Many of Eisenhüttenstadt's street names honor members of the Spartacus League and the early KPD. Despite their disfavor under Stalin, who rejected any association with the internationalists, these figures—Clara Zeltkin, Julian Marchelski, Karl Liebknecht, Franz Mehring—often had no association with authoritarian governance and therefore were not included in the maximal variation. But Heckert's name had been particularly prominent in East Germany; it was held up alongside Ernst Thälmann as a fallen comrade of the country's leadership and a victim of Nazi violence against German Communists. There was a Fritz Heckert Street in Berlin (renamed in 1991) and a Fritz Heckert Housing District in Chemnitz (then Karl Marx City) with a population of ninety-two thousand (Richter and Engst 2024); the Fritz Heckert Medal was awarded by the East German Federation of Unions; and the *Fritz Heckert* was East Germany's only luxury cruise liner, with two swimming pools, restaurants, and room for around three thousand passengers. (After an initial investment from the state, the ship's funding came mostly from individual donations.) (TV:Schwerin 2019).

FIGURE 40. Wolf's collection of letters addressed to Stalinstadt show an enduring interest in shifting names in the urban landscape, 2015. Photograph by the author.

Today Fritz Heckert Street is a reminder of Fritz Heckert the man but also of the other Fritz Heckerts—the streets, schools, ships, and soccer clubs—that have not persisted into the present.

Historical Practices

Other letter writers were concerned less with the street names themselves than with the impact the name changes would have on the course of everyday life. Unlike the people who wrote about history and remembrance, who were concerned with future generations' understanding of history, these letter writers were concerned primarily with their own experience of history, which they encountered in mundane actions that constituted the "unmaking" of socialist life (Humphrey 2002b, xvii). Residents would have to re-register their new address with the city's registration office, as well as other organizations: their bank, their insurance company, and so on. With the volume of street name changes, wait times at the registration office, previously negligible, were now up to an hour. Marion Kauschke (1991), of Fritz Heckert Street, wrote that "standing in line is, like before, our free-time activity"—a refutation of the belief that capitalism would bring an end to the queues that had characterized life in the Eastern Bloc in response to material shortage.

Many residents wrote about the burden of having to order new stationery, or the expense of having to mail letters to family and friends, insurance companies, and magazines notifying them of the new address. Karl Heinz Manz (1991), under the heading "Name Change to Street of the Konsomol!,"[6] listed the things for which he would have to pay: "Personal identity card, insurance, bank account, stamps, return address stamp, personalized writing paper and envelopes, newspaper account, package-sending account. . . . And many more things." The Brandenburg Interior Ministry addressed these complaints in an announcement on August 22, 1991. The post office would deliver mail to old addresses for six months after the change. Citizens who had already paid for Federal Republic identity documents would have their fees waived for any additional documents—passports, drivers licenses, and personal identity cards—reissued with the new address. The registration office would work to minimize wait times. And, as one would expect in a free-market economy, all commercial expenses—new letterhead, business cards, signage, and so on—would be borne by individual business owners (Muth 1991).

The letter writers' focus on the material consequences of political change evinces a sympathetic symbolic order (Fennell 2015), one in which the material world is a minefield of potentially painful encounters. Ordering new stationery is usually a benign process, but for the residents for whom it was not, the simple act of filling out an order form forced them to encounter the loss of their identity as GDR citizens. The letter or the stamp or the insurance card, inherently inert, was imbued with meaning, its unfamiliar name signaling the arrival of a totalizing culture that took its own superiority for granted. Residents today still bristle at small administrative tasks they associate with the tedium of capitalist overreach (Fox 2020, 647).

Street names are, to the state, an instrument of synoptic data, but to the individual, an address exists as one point in an endless series of dyads. The loss of familiar street names was not only the loss of a postal address but the loss of a relational system—a web of dyadic relationships in which one can envision the connection between oneself and one's family member, friend, or even insurance representative, always a connection between two entities. As Georg Simmel (1972, 123) points out, a dyad is the most fundamental grouping in the social order, but it is also the most fragile—dyads lack a "super-personal life" and cannot survive the death of one participant. Although a letter may still be delivered to a new address, the dyadic relationship between, say, Lenin Avenue 18 and Street of the Konsomol 20 would be dissolved with the change in name and replaced with analogues from a new web of relationships. And the loss of a dyadic relationship means the loss of an aspect of one's own identity. Residents might struggle to be recognized when the grid by which they knew each other was suddenly erased.

The rapidity of change contributed to the intensity of residents' pain and confusion. Heinz Bundach (1991) complained of the "express-train tempo" of street name changes. A resident interviewed in the local newspaper suggested waiting three to four years before any changes were made: "We should give it a little time. It seems to me that [right now] the whole thing is too emotionally charged" (MOZ Redakteure 1991). The GDR ended in a sudden and unexpected way: The federal government had promised freedom of travel between East and West Germany, and residents flocked to the Berlin Wall's checkpoints in anticipation of a change in policy. When functionary Günther Schabowski was asked during a televised press conference when this open travel would begin, he replied, without a direct order from above, "Effective immediately." People at the Berlin Wall overwhelmed the border checkpoints, and thus began the dissolution of the country. Now, in a similarly sudden and unexpected way, that country's historical legacy was being erased in a manner at odds with the measured passage of experiential time.

Street renaming made historiography, and its effect on the experience of temporality, transparent. Not only was the construction of Geschichte from Vergangenheit made apparent—and thus revealed as a political process marked by human foibles (Trouillot 1997)—but its rapid codification shifted understandings of history that had theretofore been experienced as fixed. The letter writer Dr. M. Pudack, sensing this judgment and disjuncture, decried being made to feel ashamed of Ernst Thälmann, "who did not, like many others, emigrate to Stalin in the Soviet Union, and who was held in a fascist prison and a concentration camp." He asked, "Who would allow [Thälmann] to stand in a row with Hitler and Stalin?" (Pudack 1992). In fact, Thälmann had been closely allied with Stalin, who personally intervened to instate him as chair of the Hamburg KPD in 1928 (Cuevas-Wolf 2017). But in East Germany, that history—the so-called Wittorf Affair—was thoroughly suppressed; Thälmann, who was murdered at Buchenwald in 1944, was glorified as a martyr in the nation's origin myth.

Residents like Pudack thus had a viewpoint similar to that of Klee's Angel of History, the figure who watches as experience rushes into the past. As the past piles up and Thälmann, the man in whom he had such pride, comes to fall on top of Hitler and Stalin, whose names, too shameful to live with, had already been wiped from the landscape, Pudack sees the falseness in calling these events "progress" (Benjamin 1968, 258). Yet Walter Benjamin's critique is twofold: that we designate historical progress arbitrarily, but also that we consider progress inevitable. The Western conception of history, Marxism included, reifies the unity of time and progress as a natural fact. Benjamin goes on to say that "by dint of a secret heliotropism, the past strives to turn toward that sun which is rising in the sky of history" (255). He is critiquing not whom we choose to remember, but that we portray history as something that is constituted alongside the passage of time.

Eisenhüttenstadt's streets now transmit different sociopolitical memories than the ones with which they were originally planned, their history now situated within that of the Federal Republic. Yet they continue to foster a lived experience whose coming-into-being was motivated by the socialist project. As practical streets, they are material traces of the labor required to bring a socialist lifeworld into being, a rebuke to historical materialism and its imagination of progress as an invisible hand. But as "poetic" streets (Larkin 2013), they are a testament to the "heliotropism" of the past, portraying a sanitized version of socialist history that has been thoroughly and properly "worked through" (Benjamin 1968; Adorno 1959).

An Eternal Regime

The letter writers who suggested new names evinced a sense of urgency. Progress meant adopting capitalist norms, and the stakes of having obsolete street names were different in the capitalist era. If, under socialism, city leadership had refused the directive to change the city's name from Stalinstadt to Eisenhüttenstadt, the result would likely have been a violent interrogation by the secret police. But under capitalism, refusal would result in the slow, entrenched decline of a city marked by obsolescence. Indeed, even with extensive name changes, Eisenhüttenstadt experienced decades of urban decline, and name changes did little to stem the outmigration of the early 1990s.

Yet the name changes reflect a more fundamental shift in the city's sociopolitical landscape: the transformation of housing from a social good into a commodity. As such, street names remained an essential component of sociospatial formation, but they took on an important secondary role: the cultivation of desire. Under socialism, Eisenhüttenstädters looking to move house would submit a request for a housing swap to their real estate company, the GeWi or the EWG, which maintained lists of residents looking to move within the city.[7] For instance, a family expecting a child might swap with empty nesters; one resident told me about undergoing a housing swap after her divorce. But under capitalism, the urban landscape is a "phantasmagoria" of choice in which the "auratic" effects of commodities call out to us, transmitting imaginative possibilities (Benjamin 2002, 7, 119). Through street names, real estate could speak directly to consumers, and the suggestive value of socialist names had real socioeconomic stakes in the context of a capitalist real estate market. No city would want to drive away potential tenants by clinging to names that had been publicly called "anachronistic" and "mocking" to the victims of socialism (Ganschow 1990).

Letter writers like Pudack reluctantly embraced the "creative destruction" that would be necessary for Eisenhüttenstadt to thrive in the new era (Harvey 2006). Pudack (1992) suggested Sycamore Avenue, Brushwood Street, Maple Way, Birch Way, and Pine Way, noting that streets named for trees would be particularly apt to replace those named for defunct preindustrial trades such as Glassblowing Street and Basket Weaving Ring. Other letter writers, too, suggested names that were associated with nature. H. Krüger (1991) advocated against "names by the dozen" and instead wanted Mountain Street for Fritz Heckert Street, near Diehlo Mountain, and On the Green for Helmut Just Street, since it was near a village green. R. Rockstroh (1991), from Fritz Heckert Street 38, railed against a suggestion to use numbers, as they use in the United States, citing the undue influence of English on the German language and the fact that numbers are "cold." He continued, "How would it be, if we indeed stayed 'neutral,' and our streets were named after animals, plants, planets . . . and so on? Wouldn't that be nicer, and most notably, warmer? . . . Wouldn't it be better, more honest, more permanent, and more durable than names of politicians and statesmen?"[8]

His suggestion was that names that were "warm" and "nice" would also be names that were "honest" and "permanent" in their apoliticism, existing outside historical time and its attendant sociopolitical circumstances. As such, the cultivation of desire—the efforts taken to make Eisenhüttenstadt's real estate attractive to potential consumers—is portrayed as politically neutral. Yet even allegedly apolitical street names interpolate political subjects. The names Sycamore Avenue and Maple Way are metaphors for an invented past, replacing the socialist story of a city violently inserted into its landscape via human intervention—pine forests razed, industrial processes induced—with an origin myth drawn from capitalist urbanism: A city grows organically as the result of increased storage capacities and the subsequent division of labor (M. Smith 2020; Graeber and Wengrow 2021). Names that are "warm" and "durable" evoke an eternal, extrahuman past that naturalizes the city's existence. The letter writer Rockstroh (1991) goes so far as to suggest that such names should be chosen as a rebuke to human activity, citing the damages wrought by recent human leaders as evidence that human beings are "far from the most clever, highly developed, best life form in the world." Yet street names that decenter humans also exist for a strictly human audience. Capitalism hides its destructive forces through its embrace of the new, and as the capitalist landscape has come to erase traces of political upheaval, so, too, has it aligned the city with an imagined history made palatable for the new era.

Many of the city's new street names evoke nature, rurality, and preindustrial life. Lenin Avenue, the city's main artery, became Linden Avenue, so named because the street is lined with linden trees. Philipp Müller Street became Chestnut Street; Red Square became Rose Square. Other names reinforced this pastoral image and situated the city in reunified German culture: Wilhelm Pieck Street became King Street, and Phillip Müller Street became Wilhelm Street. Klement Gottwald Street became the Old Shop Street. Cement Street became Oderland Street, a reference to the region around the Oder River. Thälmann Street became Beeskower Street, named for a nearby medieval village, and Georgi Dimitroff Street became Eichendorff Street, named for a nineteenth-century Romantic poet. Yet, as discussed elsewhere, Eisenhüttenstadt's lindens and roses were an integral component of socialist city building, intended to evoke pride in the state's ability to provide opulent landscapes for working people. To consider the natural world as fundamentally permanent and apolitical, as the letter writers suggest, is to erase this history. Between 1955 and 1958, the Stalinstadt city government spent close to seventy-seven thousand Ostmarks on landscaping for the city center (Rat der Stadt Stalinstadt 1955; Ministerium für Bauwesen 1958), roughly €100,000. The greenery plan for Complex 1 alone calls for four different species of maple tree, all native to North America and Asia.[9] For Complexes 2 and 3, there are orders for hundreds of barberry, honeysuckle, and spirea plants and 355 *rosa rugosa* roses; herbaceous perennials are named down to the subspecies variety, such as September Snow panicle phlox (Rat der Stadt Stalinstadt 1955; Ministerium für Bauwesen 1958).

Such attention, care, and expense lavished on landscaping lent significance to the city's greenery, whose slow maturation materialized the incremental "building" of the "building generation." Hence older residents, as discussed earlier, now watch for "lawn stompers" who fail to appreciate the labor embodied in the urban landscape. Other informants showed me photographs from the 1950s and 1960s and marveled over the spindly saplings and garden beds dotted with immature plants that had yet to fill in. The young plants were considered appropriate for the young city. Some told me that the city was replete with public art precisely because it would otherwise have felt barren in the decades before the vegetation matured.

Once while we were walking in the hills overlooking the city, two elderly informants pointed out the site of what was once their favorite pub. It had burned down some years earlier—they suspected arson and insurance fraud—but they told me it had the best view in the whole city. There was no trace of that view now, a white-haired woman named Elke said, explaining that back then (*damals*) when she had visited the pub, the trees in the city were young. Now the trees were mature and blocked the view. We were walking through a forest near a nature preserve, but from the hilltop where the pub had stood, a visitor would have been able to look down at the city below. My companions seemed disappointed as we stood for a few minutes, peering at rooftops that were visible through bare winter trees. If the pub were to come back, it could offer only a diminished version of its former self. The time of young trees had been a brief, finite moment—a time when the natural landscape conformed to the imaginative needs of socialist city building. Now, mature trees subsumed the city into a homogenized landscape, no longer capable of evincing a distinction between new socialist trees and those that predated the city. But the view seemed fitting in an urban landscape in which land was abstracted into units of comparable exchange value, alienated from the material qualities that had lent it sociocultural significance. And the time of mature trees could be expected to endure indefinitely.

East Germans had just experienced the collapse of a regime that proclaimed itself eternal; they may have been skeptical of capitalism's similar claims. But names in the urban landscape create an imagination of "unbound seriality" (Chatterjee 2006, 6) that speaks to the inherent futurity of infrastructural projects (Appel et al. 2018). Street signs stand ready to address an infinite series of potential interlocutors. Moreover, as scholars have established, names take on a social life that exceeds any single individual, triangulating between the named thing, speakers of the name, and the name itself (Humphrey 2006; Butler 1997). Streets have no internal sense of self that can exceed the subject interpellated by naming. A street's subjecthood is coterminous with the connotative force of its name.

As such, street names are perceived as "eternal" even when recent history refutes such unbounded temporal imaginations. In considering the options offered for the renaming of Lenin Avenue, a resident named Heinz Bundach wrote that he approved of changing the name to Linden Avenue but protested, "Absolutely not Federal Avenue [Bundesallee], because the Federal Republic has powerfully disappointed us, and we don't want to be reminded of this for all eternity." Federal Avenue was not a particularly popular choice; the local newspaper conducted nine person-on-the-street interviews about renaming Lenin Avenue, and the only person even remotely positive about Federal Avenue was a visitor from Aachen, in West Germany, who said, "For Lenin Avenue, I'd make the case for Federal Avenue" (MOZ Redakteure 1991). Fromm, the task force chair, had suggested the name Federal Avenue, he told me, because it seemed only right to honor the new regime as vocally as he had the old—a reproduction of a belief in centralized power that, for others, was now a painful reminder of how seamlessly one purportedly eternal republic had been swapped for another.

Shifts in Meaning

Decades have passed since the name changes were implemented. Shifting social circumstances have changed their meanings, and the letter writers who predicted such changes proved prescient. In 2016, I was walking along Saarlouiser Street with Karsten, a high school geography teacher, when he told me that the street had been named for Saarlouis, a West German city with which Eisenhüttenstadt formed a sister-city partnership in 1986—Karsten and others called the arrangement "the first German-German city partnership." Saarlouiser Street is one of Eisenhüttenstadt's longest boulevards, a tree-lined street that gently curves through Housing Complexes 2 and 3, along buildings with pastel facades and ornate architectural details, including wrought-iron window work and decorative friezes. Karsten was not directly involved with the renaming process, but he was deeply invested in local history and active in Eisenhüttenstadt's historic preservation circles. He told me that in the early 1990s, Eisenhüttenstadt was proud of this partnership—in retrospect, naively so—and so named one of its most beautiful boulevards after Saarlouis. During the socialist era, this was the Street of the Konsomol.

Karsten had heard that after the renaming, Saarlouis reciprocated and named one of its streets Eisenhüttenstädter Avenue. A few years earlier, he had found himself in Saarlouis, near the German-French border, and decided to visit his hometown's namesake street. He was excited, he said, but when he found Eisen-hüttenstädter Avenue, it was in a gray, forgotten corner of the city, a tiny stretch of poorly traveled industrial road. His traveling companion saw his disappoint-ment and insisted that the spot had been specially chosen because Eisenhütten-stadt, being an industrial city, should have a namesake in an industrial area. But Karsten remained unconvinced. Though he loved and admired Saarlouiser Street in lived experience, the name now evoked for him the unreciprocated admiration the East had for the West, and the derision the West had for the East.

Even streets that were not renamed have come to exist within a universe of signification that is new and different from the one in which they originated. It is a central tenet of semiotics that signs gain their meaning in their differ-ence from other signs—the alternatives with which they may be compared or exchanged (Saussure 1959). Yet scholars, most notably anthropologists Susan Gal and Judith Irvine, have also established that the "axes of differentiation" along which difference may be perceived are culturally and historically contingent (Gal and Irvine 2019, 112). Changing circumstances can both reproduce and block the reproduction of existing binaries, changing the qualities associated with a given signified. The perception of meaning is thus deeply contingent not only on an individual's ability to perceive difference but also on their imagination of possible alternatives.

In 2015, I was driving through Eisenhüttenstadt with two acquaintances from Berlin, one an Eisenhüttenstadt native and one visiting for the first time. The visi-tor was enthralled by the traces of socialist kitsch; he laughed as we came to a stop at the corner of Karl Marx Street and Street of the Republic. "Which republic?" he asked, pointing to the street sign. "Was it renamed after reunification?"

"Actually no," the native said, sounding puzzled, as if she had never considered the question before. "Now it refers to the Federal Republic, but back then [dam-als] it would have referred to the GDR"—the German Democratic Republic, or East Germany. Street of the Republic had survived because its signification was imagined as seamlessly moving from the German Democratic Republic to the Federal Republic of Germany. After all, if names associated with "power" were to be eradicated from the urban landscape, the East German state would have been first in line. But considered as a linguistic sign, the "republic" derived its meaning from the system of value in which it operated. And in this instance, one system of value had been erased by and replaced with another whose vocabulary was mostly shared but whose divergences, though few, were radical.

The republic's layered meaning was not immediately apparent to all who encountered Street of the Republic. It took relatively deep knowledge for the visi-tor to ask about the street sign—the knowledge not only that Eisenhüttenstadt had been part of East Germany but that streets were renamed after reunification, and that the country often referred to as East Germany was in fact the German Democratic Republic. I lived one block over from Street of the Republic while conducting research about street renaming and had never thought to ask the visitor's question. But a West German would call their country the Bundesrepublik, as "federal-republic" is a compound word. Thus, for someone raised in the Federal Republic, the stand-alone "republic" would have a socialist connotation. Street of the Republic was an East German miscalculation of how best to conform to capitalist norms.

Idling at the red light, I understood that for some, the lost East German street name—the name that signified the German Democratic Republic—had fallen into the "bottomless silence" of historical erasure (Trouillot 1997, 30), eclipsed by the new republic for which the same signifier now stood. But for the visitor, the name had an entirely different significance, also radically altered from the original, and serving as a trace of the rocky transition from socialism to capitalism. Meaning, too, like East German citizens, could "move without moving house" (*umziehen ohne umzug*).

The Aha Moment

The aforementioned efforts to erase socialist history from the urban landscape are at odds with the mandate to protect the city as a federally designated historic site. Perhaps, given the decision to eliminate street names associated with "power," historic preservation can be interpreted as preserving an image of socialism stripped of its authoritarian history, and the daily movements made possible by Housing Complexes can thus be reimagined as resuscitating only the communitarian aspects of a "networked" habitus. In this new imagination of socialist history, a full reckoning with authoritarian legacies is occluded as East Germany teeters between loss and disappearance (Ophir 2005, 87). Visual reminders situate Eisenhüttenstadt as a late socialist space—the Soviet and East German flags in the five-story mural on Linden Avenue, names like Karl Marx and Rosa Luxemburg Streets—but the full reality of socialist daily life and its deep entanglement with an authoritarian police state is not immediately legible. What is instead preserved is a rose-colored image of socialist urbanism that conforms to contemporary imaginations of urban thriving.

On July 19, 1975, the East German parliament passed the Law on the Preservation of Monuments of the German Democratic Republic, which created a national registry of historic sites. Counties were then tasked with submitting sites that would be appropriate for the registry. At the time, Eisenhüttenstadt operated as its own county (Kreisfreie Stadt), and in April 1977, the Cultural Division of the Eisenhüttenstadt City Council submitted its historic preservation list, which included German-Soviet Friendship Square (now Memorial Square), where the cremated remains of over four thousand Soviet POWs from Stalag III B were buried; Lenin Avenue (now Linden Avenue); and a church in Fürstenberg that dated to around 1400 (Rat der Stadt 1977, 2). In 1984, the city council updated its contributions to the registry with the designation of Housing Complexes 1, 2, and 3 as historic sites (Fromm, n.d. [late 1980s], 15).

Johannes Remenz, then the chair of the Eisenhüttenstadt County committee for historic preservation, wrote that the decision stemmed from the fact that, although Housing Complexes 1, 2, and 3 had been built only a few decades earlier, the kind of building projects they represented "were now part of history, and unrepeatable" (Remenz, n.d. [late 1980s], 11). A 1984 report from the city council further cited the "historical singularity [*Einmaligkeit*] at the city's foundation," historically located between the founding of East Germany and the implementation of *Plattenbau* architecture (Rat der Stadt 1984, 2). Architect Gabriele Haubold (1999, 192) wrote that by the time Housing Complexes 5, 6, and 7 were built, "the dream of a creative, industrial architecture was dreamed out." The historically protected zone thus represents the last gasp of modernist experimentation in East German urbanism.

On July 22, 1991, as part of the reunification process, the Brandenburg State government passed a law that transferred its historic preservation sites to the historic preservation list of unified Germany. Eisenhüttenstadt's historically preserved city center, at ninety-four hectares, became the largest historically protected site in Germany (Pehnert 2016), and it remains the largest in Europe (Stadt Eisenhüttenstadt 2021). But without appropriate funding for maintenance, the city's historic preservation status had had little material consequence, and Eisenhüttenstadt's city center was in severe disrepair. Marina Wehlisch, who served as the chair of historic preservation in Oder-Spree County, was born in Eisenhüttenstadt in 1960. It was not until she began working for the county preservation authority in 1992 that she even learned about her city's historic preservation status. In 1995, restoration efforts began in Housing Complex 2. Oder-Spree County had prioritized the renovation of its largest historic holding and helped the city acquire funding from the Brandenburg State. Facades were refinished and their sculptural details restored; insulation was also added throughout the buildings; insulating doors, double-paned windows, and utility systems were put in; and heating was converted from coal stoves (*Ofenheizung*) to natural gas (Haubold 2000, 84–90).[10] The restoration efforts won the city its first architectural prize, the Brandenburg State's Brandenburg Builder's Prize (Brandenburgischer Bauherrenpreis), in 1996 (Haubold 2000, 102).

When the colors were restored to facades, it was an "aha moment," Wehlisch said. "It was astonishing. I lived there as a young woman and I would never have said that there were ever these contrasting colors, never blue, yellow, or red. I never saw that. But it was so." I, too, was surprised when I looked at color photographs from the 1950s and saw that buildings in Housing Complex 2 were painted in pink and yellow. I had assumed that the colors were a modern invention, given that unrestored buildings in Housing Complex 1 showed no trace of ever having been painted. Even Tom Hanks, in his conversation with David Letterman, claimed that "when it was called Stalinstadt, none of the buildings had paint" and showed a selfie he had taken in front of an unpainted, decrepit building. But the preservation authority had worked with Eisenhüttenstadt's surviving architects and with restorers specializing in color restoration to paint building exteriors as they had originally been designed. Eberhard Harz, the former GeWi chair, told me that Kurt Leucht's inspiration had been colors found in nature: sandy yellows, clay reds, and muted pinks and blues. Architectural details are often highlighted in contrasting colors.

Longtime residents were unable to tell me when the city's buildings transformed from colorful pastels to a uniform brown. Wehlisch suggested that because of the pollution from the steel plant, a gray dust would have disguised the paint within three years of a building's construction. If Wehlisch's estimation is accurate, then there was likely never a time when Eisenhüttenstadt looked the way it does today. By the time Housing Complex 3 was finished in 1965, Housing Complex 1, finished a decade earlier, would have already begun to discolor. In their simultaneous state of restoration, the Housing Complexes in the city center present not the city as it was, but an idealized version of Eisenhüttenstadt that might have developed from the same foundations.

Trouble on Linden Avenue

Amid these tensions between preservation and erasure, residents evince a desire for historical narratives and material histories to be made legible in the urban landscape. For example, the meter-long granite slabs that pave the sidewalks along Linden Avenue were mined by prisoners of the Ravensbrück prison camp and intended for use in the new world capital Germania—the Nazi reimagining of Berlin—where they would have been used to build the Soldier's Hall Pantheon. During World War II, the granite was stored in a warehouse at Stalag III B, the Nazi prison camp in Fürstenberg. At the war's end, ten thousand cubic meters of granite remained in Stalag III B; it was seized by the victorious Red Army and used, in part, to build the Soviet Victory Monument in Berlin. The rest was later used for other Soviet monuments in Berlin, as well as in East Germany's model socialist city (Drieschner and Schulz 2002, 2004).

Günther Fromm, who served as chair of the street-renaming task force, told me to look closely at the paving stones along Linden Avenue—he said I would see numbers etched into the corner of each stone to indicate where it was to be installed in the Soldier's Hall Pantheon. I walked down Linden Avenue, examining the sidewalk closely, but I never found a trace of any numbers. I asked around; an acquaintance had also looked, unsuccessfully, for etched numbers along Linden Avenue. When I asked him why he had tried to do so, he told me it was because of Fromm. I asked Axel Drieschner, the curator at what is now the Museum of Utopia and the Everyday. He, too, had spoken to Fromm and looked for the etched numbers. But Drieschner was trained as a historian and had researched Stalag III B. He told me that any markings on the granite were likely to have been in builder's chalk, and archival photos of the site did not show any at all.

In 2021, however, the sidewalk's history began to surface, pushed forward by the linden trees for which the street had been renamed. The trees had matured to the point that their roots were now displacing the paving stones above, making the sidewalk along Linden Avenue dangerously uneven. Gunther Fromm told the local newspaper that this presented "a treacherous situation," and Michael Reichl, director of the city's planning department, said, "There's no easy solution" (Lötsch 2021).

Asked for comment, Drieschner told the paper that replacing the granite with asphalt would be out of the question. "This is no dull, monotonous paving," he said. "If you notice, you can really see the craftsmanship [*gestalterische Qualität*] in it." The hand-hewn stone evoked the human labor that had contributed to its construction, imparting an "aura" across time and space, considered rare in the industrial era (Benjamin [1935] 2008, 22). But the granite had been finished only on one side after it was salvaged from the prison camp. Reichl noted that this made it particularly difficult to manage, as an irregularity of even a few centimeters on a paving stone's underside could interfere with a linden tree's root zone and result in a dangerous displacement. Just as ruins are unevenly temporally sedimented (Stoler 2016, 13), so, too, are histories unevenly recuperated, thrust forth by something that grows while the ruins settle above. Fromm had wanted the history of the paving stones to be apparent to users of the built environment. But that history had slipped from a state of loss to one of disappearance (Ophir 2005). Rather than numbers etched in stone, which would have signaled the existence of erstwhile plans, there were only the unsteady footsteps of passersby to indicate that the paving stones had been imprecisely repurposed.

FIGURE 41. Young linden trees along Linden Avenue, then Lenin Avenue, 1960s. Photograph by M. Fricke. Courtesy of Stadtarchiv Eisenhüttenstadt.

FIGURE 42. Linden Avenue, 2023. Photograph by the author.

Meanwhile, the city was caught between its mandate for historic preservation and its obligation to preserve the mature trees, now under environmental protection, as well as the pragmatic need to move pedestrians safely through its streets. In 2021, a plan to replace mature lindens with younger ones was rejected by city leadership (Lötsch 2021). When I asked the mayor, Frank Balzer, about this in 2023, he told me it was an ongoing issue, but he seemed genuinely shocked by the suggestion that a different tree variety—perhaps one with a less expansive root system—might be used to line the sidewalk. It seemed that on Linden Avenue, other trees would not be considered. The qualities in the name that had theretofore seemed merely connotative had become materially implicated in the street itself. Over twenty years after the renaming, the arbitrary relationship between signifier and signified had come to seem like a natural one. The moment of flexibility, a liminal moment between regimes, had passed, and while connotations might change, the name, imbricated in a web of meaning, was perceived as permanent.

HOUSING FOR THE SOCIAL REALM

In March 1990, shortly after the fall of the Berlin Wall, the East German parliament created the Treuhandanstalt Trust. At the time, Treuhand was the world's largest holding company, tasked with selling roughly twelve thousand of East Germany's state-owned businesses (*Volkseigener Betriebe*, or VEB) to investors who would, ostensibly, help them transition to a market economy (Roesler 1994). That month, local leaders in Eisenhüttenstadt administratively transformed VEB EKO Stahl into an organization of joint stock companies, EKO Stahl AG and subsidiaries, in order to enable its sale by the Treuhand. Substantial investments would be needed to modernize the steelworks such that it could remain economically competitive in the European market, and Western ownership—by a company willing to make those investments—was seen as essential to EKO's continued operation. Local political leaders vocally lobbied the Treuhand to approve EKO's restructuring plan, which ultimately resulted in its sale to the Belgian company Cockerill-Sambre in 1994 (Döring 2015; Nicolaus 2020).[1]

But with Germany's monetary union in July 1990 came massive social and political upheaval. The Ostmark, which had been traded with the Deutschmark at a rate of five to one, would now be exchanged at a rate of one to one. East German businesses saw profits shrink as costs soared.[2] Treuhand liquidated its assets in what *The Washington Post* called "Eastern Germany's bargain basement" (Atkinson 1993). By the time the Treuhand ceased operations in 1994, it had sold 70 percent of its holdings at a loss of around 200 million Deutschmarks. Unemployment in the former East Germany rose from effectively zero to approximately 15 percent as unprofitable firms were downsized and closed

FIGURE 43.   Housing Complex 6, undated photograph circa 1960s. Courtesy of Detlef Juckel.

by their new Western owners. In 1991, the president of the Treuhand, Detlev Karsten Rohwedder, was assassinated, shot through his bedroom window in a murder that remains unsolved, though police have long suspected the far-left Red Army Faction (Kellermann 2021), which is thought to have carried out the killing as retaliation for the Treuhand's social and economic damage.

Eberhard Harz served as chair of the GeWi during this period, and he sought to keep its assets out of the hands of the Treuhand. March 1990 saw the first meeting of Eisenhüttenstadt's city council as part of reunified Germany, which Harz described to me as a "solemn" affair. Representatives played the national anthem of the Federal Republic before putting forth their new agenda items—chief among them the transformation of the GeWi from a state-owned business (VEB) to a corporation (GmbH). Shortly thereafter, in May 1990, the city council held a special session in which it voted to approve the GeWi's incorporation, though the city government was and remains the only shareholder. The GeWi's organization and management remained unchanged, but the move would prevent the Treuhand from selling the ownership rights to what had theretofore been municipally held real estate (SVV 1990). Harz and others in Eisenhüttenstadt told me that the GeWi's incorporation also enabled it to become the only real estate company in Brandenburg that retained its East German management team into the 1990s. Though no comprehensive data exist against which I might verify the claim, it speaks to the self-perception of Eisenhüttenstadt as uniquely and directly inheriting the outlook and organizational structure of socialist urbanism.

Harz told me that his decision to pursue incorporation was motivated by both practical and ideological concerns. He oversaw 260 employees whose jobs he sought to safeguard—firms that were sold by the Treuhand saw their staffs reduced by an average of 72 percent (Roesler 1994, 509). But his "main reason," he said, was "to rescue housing for the city and for the social realm and not allow it to fall under the control of the Treuhand." Harz described himself as a true believer in socialism who nonetheless accepted the reality of reunification. As such, he sought to use the administrative tactics of the new system to exercise what he saw as responsible civic leadership. "My problem was that housing is a social concern [*soziale Frage*]," he explained, an outlook shared by the majority of city council representatives but not by Western real estate speculators. To them, the city would be perceived as an investment—an abstracted, legalistic form of ownership, precluding usage (Strathern [2002] 2022, 86)—rather than as a material entity that shaped lived experience.

This chapter discusses how Eisenhüttenstadt's real estate companies, the GeWi and the EWG, have creatively navigated the tensions between housing's facets as a social good and as a commodity, which became apparent upon the transition to capitalism and ultimately arrived at the cooperation agreement that enabled the transformation of the city center. Such efforts reflect the preservation of structures of governance that allow leaders to act on lived experience through holistic urban design. I examine the origins of this tension, as well as the development of the EWG and Housing Complexes 5 through 7. I then discuss the challenges presented by the East German real estate sector's "old debt," and the recent developments that have helped resolve some of those challenges.

The Homunculus

The collectivization of property made real the essential foundation for Communism, as laid out in the *Communist Manifesto*—"The theory of the Communists may be summed up in the single sentence: abolition of private property" (Marx and Engels [1848] 1978, 485). In this context, historian Kimberley Zarecor (2018, 97) suggests that city building was made possible by a "socialist scaffold": the integrated organization of state agencies that oversaw everything from finance to construction to transportation and that governed cities with an eye toward their role in a nationalized economy.[3] Following the transition to capitalism, this "scaffold" was systematically dismantled across the Eastern Bloc as new proprietorial arrangements were implemented alongside changes in governance. But in keeping the GeWi intact, Harz managed to preserve the proprietorial simplicity of socialism, which was understood as essential to the holistic management of urban space—and thus to the "socialist scaffold." Socialist planners celebrated the indivisibility of urban space, which they credited with enabling cohesive urban management and design. After all, while capitalist cities reflected the competing interests of individual property owners, socialist cities were understood as representing the single, cohesive vision of a collectivized nation.

Later in life, Kurt Leucht would reflect on his efforts to design the Model Socialist City. In an interview that he gave in 1993, at age eighty, he singled out the first of East Germany's Sixteen Principles as the most important. It states that "the city as a form of settlement did not arise by chance" (BpB 2005). This principle reflects the Marxist doctrine that urban forms are the expression of socioeconomic forces. But it also denaturalizes the built environment, emphasizing the immense effort behind urban design, often reified as the backdrop to life's unfolding, and exposing what Foucault (2009, 21) called the "artificial" nature of the human milieu. Leucht insisted that Principle 1 applied to all types of urban development, not only to socialist New Towns. Yet he was also quick to distinguish between settlements, which offered merely housing, and cities, which offered interconnected spaces for housing, work, culture, and recreation. As discussed in chapter 1, settlements were not considered respectable output for urban planners, and Leucht considered them wholly distinct from his discussions of the urban. He explained that for many in the GDR, urban space was considered a "homunculus," something that, in its most ideal form, emerged fully mature, like Athena from the head of Zeus (Leucht 1991).

Eisenhüttenstadt's design "was certainly from another time," Leucht said. "I would like to design an entire city today, not just a worker's settlement. But that's what was so special about that era: at the same time that the first five hundred apartments were being built, so, too, was a new theater, which stood at first in a green meadow." Photos show the Friedrich Wolf Theater in the middle of a construction site, but memory is fallible, and for its first eight years the theater was the only building on the street. Leucht explained that building a theater for a city of less than one thousand residents would be impossible under capitalism— no theater could turn a financial profit with such a small population. "If there were an investor in the steelworks [today], you would only be allowed to build apartments," he said. But socialist architects developed their cities in the service of social outcomes, and Leucht believed that cities required spaces for leisure and public gatherings—essential instruments for the development of community (Leucht 1991).

Contemporary scholars may be inclined to counter Leucht's claim. After all, capitalism has no shortage of amenity-rich residential neighborhoods and unprofitable theaters. But perhaps Leucht was simply speaking in broad strokes. He conflates the material city—a configuration of buildings that may well be reproduced elsewhere—with its socialist emic, which would not necessarily be reproduced alongside another iteration of the city's architectural plans. And perhaps, too, schizmogenesis—the process by which identity forms in opposition to a binary point of comparison (Bateson [1936] 1958; Graeber and Wengrow 2021)—is in play. Leucht's imagination of capitalism was based primarily on everything that socialism was not.

But even while housing was broadly conceived as a public good, its potential status as a commodity was never far from hand. Take, for instance, an essay by city architect Herbert Härtel celebrating the decision to build Housing Complex 5. "With the fall of the old social order and in contrast with the capitalist era," Härtel (n.d., 12) writes, "private property ownership is no longer a deciding factor for the urban design [stadtebaukunstlerischen Gestaltung] of the neighborhood, which allows us to design large-scale projects that reflect the construction of the city for no other purpose than its usage to future residents." Härtel describes the Housing Complex in a blend of positive and negative terms common to East German rhetoric, wherein capitalism pervades as a ghostly counterfactual: Housing Complex 5 would have not only housing (as would be expected under capitalism) but also schools and shops to fulfill daily needs; it would not be socially isolating (as expected under capitalism) but would be connected to the city center and able to be traversed on foot (12). The complex was to be understood as facilitating socialist social life—and materializing a mindset in which socialist outlooks were paramount—despite the fact that, like the rest of the city, it outwardly resembled a potentially capitalist urban landscape.

Jens Beige expressed a similar sentiment when he told me that an American could never have designed Eisenhüttenstadt. Under capitalism, he said, Eisenhüttenstadt would be "unthinkable." East and West Germans approached urban design from diametrically opposed starting points [Ansatzpunkte], he explained: "Back then [damals], colleagues from West Berlin, they were always attentive to cost [Zahl]; that's how they saw the cities of the Old States. That's what architects there were responsible for"—designing buildings that would eventually turn a profit. East German architects, in contrast, constructed urban space, not individual buildings, and the success of urban space cannot be easily quantified. While capitalists tended to tout the metrics of particular buildings—Beige used the height of a skyscraper as a hypothetical—no single metric could predict the type of success that East German architects sought. Besides, he said, a vibrant, well-used urban space would naturally engender capitalist-style metrics of urban success, such as high property value and low vacancy rates. "An architect in America would think entirely differently—they have an obligation to think differently" from East Germans, he told me. In order to understand the city, I could not merely study its urban design. Rather, he said, I had to "contemplate that which stood behind the built environment" and understand the emic that motivated its coming into being.

Leucht, Härtel, and Beige evince that there are two cities in play: the material city and the abstract city, the city as a stage for lived experience and the city as an expression of sociocultural outlooks. Such duality is inherent to urban planning and administration, which relies on abstractions, overlaid onto lived experience, in order to operate (Scott 1999; Abram and Weszkelnys 2013). As such, conceiving of the city in its material-cultural duality is de rigueur in the domain of experts. Yet when the lived experience of citizens is taken into account, there is always tension between the city as material entity and the city as conceptual object (Rabinow [1989] 1995; Holston 1989), particularly given the individual nature of semiotic perceptions in the urban landscape. From an individual's perspective, the perception of signs is always "bundled"—an apple's redness cannot be perceived apart from its roundness, and so on (Keane 2003). When considering the multiple, layered meanings inherent to urban infrastructure (Appel et al. 2018), one finds that its various facets are always dimly present, but different facets come to the fore under different circumstances and for different interlocutors. Housing in East Germany was experienced as shelter, as a public good, as a manifestation of state power, and as an exemplar of the limits of state provisioning, among other facets. But it also maintained a double life as a commodity.

East Germany adhered to the trappings of capitalism when it came to real estate, and housing operated in large part according to capitalist logics that predated the socialist state.[4] Each local government maintained a *Grundbuch* property directory, a German tradition that became widespread in the nineteenth century. While *Grundbücher* from the East German era document the expropriation of individual landowners, they nonetheless conceptualize land in terms of the "parcellized sovereignty" inherent to capitalism (Wood 2002, 44)—and, indeed, *Grundbücher* were essential for the restitution of property following reunification (Brückweh 2019). Furthermore, in a "fractal" iteration of this transactional relationship (Gal and Irvine 2019), within the scale of the apartment building, landlords took money from tenants in exchange for the tenants' right to exclusive occupancy.

Anthropologists hold that property is first and foremost a social relationship, triangulating between people, things, and the social collective (Strathern [2002] 2022).[5] As such, personal property was an essential component of social life in the Eastern Bloc (Verdery 2003), even in the absence of capitalist private property. But under socialism, personal ownership was conceived as a responsibility of care, rather than by an abstract set of rights that could be instantiated even in the absence of the thing in question (Humphrey 2002b; Cherkaev 2023). In East Germany, money was exchanged for the right to occupy an apartment, but the act of exchange had significantly greater social consequences than the capital in play. Paying rent in East Germany was a performative reproduction of capitalist practices, as rents were decoupled from any notion of property value. For the duration of the East German era, rents for prewar apartments were calculated according to market costs in 1936 (although that law had little effect in Eisenhüttenstadt), and rents remained stable for the duration of a tenant's contract, making every apartment effectively rent-controlled. In 1989, East Germans spent, on average, 2.4 percent of their incomes on housing (Zitelman 2021).

Moreover, the GeWi and the EWG took out loans from the East German Central Bank (Staatsbank) in order to carry out their building projects, but East German housing debt existed in something of a closed system. The East German government controlled where its citizens could live and could therefore also guarantee that the housing it developed, via governmental banks and real estate companies, would be fully inhabited. Thus, real estate companies could be guaranteed a steady stream of income that would underwrite their operating costs. But tenant rents were not priced to enable real estate companies to pay off their loans. Loans would be paid back to the East German Central Bank over an unspecified time period, reflecting the longevity of the socialist project.

Reunification, however, represented a shift wherein housing's role as a commodity, which until then had been insignificant and performative, suddenly took on effectual force. East German real estate companies found themselves saddled with astronomical debts on which payments were unexpectedly due. And as real estate companies passed those costs on to consumers, the East German state reemerged in a phantasmic form, its debt transforming apartments into spaces that now demanded a substantial portion of one's income. Tenant contracts were renegotiated nationwide in 1991 as part of the reunification process, and many East Germans saw their rents rise to around 20 percent of their incomes between 1991 and 1993; low-income East Germans saw theirs take up between 28 percent and 43 percent (Schaefer 1993, 7). And as citizens struggled with this new financial burden, real estate companies looked ahead to years of insolvency. The solution that Eisenhüttenstadt's leadership found to these inter-connected challenges stemmed from the city's development during the latter part of the GDR era.

Building the EWG

The development of Eisenhüttenstadt's real estate market was closely tied to the development of its steelworks, as was the nature of Soviet-style city building. Six blast furnaces were built at EKO between 1950 and 1953, but they produced only pig iron, a metallurgic precursor to refined steel. Mid-1953, however, saw grow-ing unrest across East Germany as workers began to organize against increas-ingly strenuous demands on their labor. On June 9, 1953, in an effort to quell the growing protest movement, the East German Politburo issued a directive to slow industrial construction, including a directive to halt the construction of new blast furnaces in Eisenhüttenstadt. Plans for two blast furnaces and a steel refin-ing facility were put on hold and did not resume until 1964, following pressure and funding from the Soviet Union (Fromm 1999, 139; Nicolaus 2020, 24–30).

Eisenhüttenstadt's first four Housing Complexes were built between 1951 and 1967, and the city came to expand as the metallurgical process expanded, ultimately leading to the construction of Housing Complexes 5, 6, and 7 and the planned construction of 8. Already in 1958, provisional plans were put in place for Eisenhüttenstadt's future expansion, should construction on the steel plant resume. In tandem with the 1964 decision to invest in the construction of a refinery in Eisenhüttenstadt, the East German government authorized the construction of a new Housing Complex, adjacent to Complex 2, to house the first tranche of new employees who would be brought to work in the new facility. Housing Complex 5 represented the first expansion beyond the city's original urban boundary, as well as the first use of prefabricated concrete architecture. Rows of four-story apartment buildings built in 1959 gave way to twelve-story P2 tower blocks built in the early 1960s; by 1964, the complex was complete, with approximately 6,500 residents (Keil et al. 1997f).[6]

Housing Complex 6 signaled the arrival of an entirely new neighborhood typology. Separated from the city center by the Oder–Spree Canal, Complex 6 was built for a population of around sixteen thousand and was composed entirely of prefabricated concrete architecture (Keil et al. 1997g). Its northern section, built between 1966 and 1969, was constructed primarily of Q6 apartment blocks, the distinctive "butterfly roofs" that are said to look like outstretched wings. Like those in Complex 5, the apartments are aligned in rows, with five- and six-story apartment buildings punctuated by nine- or twelve-story high-rises. The southern section, built between 1972 and 1978, consisted primarily of the iconic P2 *Plattenbauten* that became common across East Germany; the area has since been nearly entirely demolished. When Complex 7 began to rise even further afield from the city center, cut off by railroad tracks and dominated by P2 high-rises, it continued the trend toward high-density, high-rise, concrete construction.

Architect Gabriele Haubold, in an essay titled "Modern Times, or The End of Coziness," describes looking at GDR-era photos of Complex 6 in 1999, when the complex's vacancy was around 21 percent (Howest 2006, 102). "It was all so modern back then [*damals*]—the butterfly roofs along neat rows of apartment houses, sandboxes and playgrounds, balcony balustrades with a waffle pattern, mushroom lights, organized stands of trees, lawns, fountains, ornamental concrete fences. Backless benches, planters with roses and creeping jenny. Everything fit together" (Haubold 1999, 191). Haubold describes the development of that emic in which she takes the urban whole into account, but she also takes seriously the feeling it cultivated, the imagination of a "sympathetic" public that emerges out of the subjective experience of urban space (Fennell 2015). Indeed, she does not mince her words: "In my professional engagement with the material construction of the past and future, it has become clear to me that [Housing Complex] 6 had a distinctive meaning for the people who planned and constructed it: Believe in the possibilities of industrial building practices, maintain hope in the creative possibilities of new technologies, and optimism that we might move forward" (Haubold 1999, 191).

The decision to expand Eisenhüttenstadt with a seventh housing complex was approved by local authorities in 1965, but its construction was tied to that of the steel refinery, which would turn out to be decades in the making. Construction of the northern section of Complex 7 was first scheduled to begin in December 1968, then May 1972, and it finally began in March 1983. Ground broke on the southern section in 1985, and construction was completed by 1987 (Keil et al. 1997h, 2–3). Meanwhile at EKO, a cold rolling mill was completed in 1968. But the steel it produced was outsourced for further refinement, including by nonsocialist European neighbors; products were shipped to a French company, which was contracted to produce anticorrosive zinc coatings (Nicolaus 2020, 32). In 1979, the GDR announced efforts to decrease its reliance on steel refined outside the Eastern Bloc. Between 1981 and 1984, the federal government partnered with the Austrian corporation VOEST-Alpine AG to build a new converter steel facility at EKO (Nicolaus 2020; Howest 2006, 71).[7] Housing Complex 7 was built between 1983 and 1987 for 7,750 residents (Keil et al. 1997h, 2), many of whom moved to Eisenhüttenstadt to take jobs in the converter steel factory.

Although housing and employment were, officially, available to all GDR citizens, individuals often struggled to find housing and employment in the same

FIGURE 44. A 1975 booklet for P2 residents in Eisenhüttenstadt, published by the regional planning office in Frankfurt Oder, shows the P2 apartment tower. Courtesy of Thomas and Bettina.

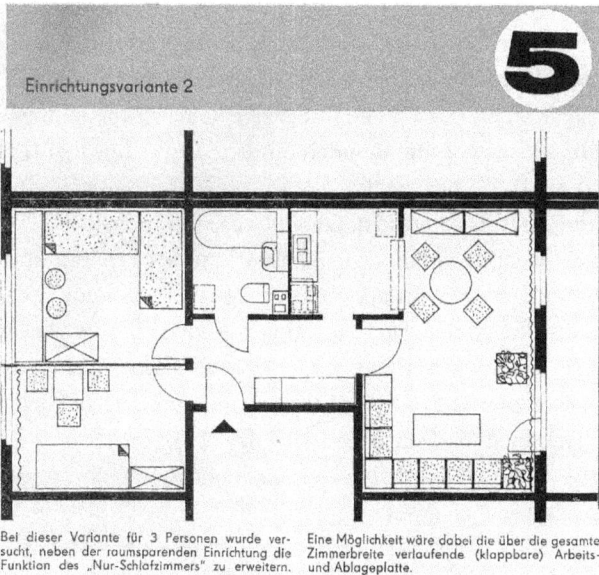

Einrichtungsvariante 2

Bei dieser Variante für 3 Personen wurde versucht, neben der raumsparenden Einrichtung die Funktion des „Nur-Schlafzimmers" zu erweitern.

Eine Möglichkeit wäre dabei die über die gesamte Zimmerbreite verlaufende (klappbare) Arbeits- und Ablageplatte.

FIGURE 45. A 1975 booklet for P2 residents in Eisenhüttenstadt shows the suggested layout for a five-room apartment for a parent and two children. Courtesy of Thomas and Bettina.

location. Gabriele Haubold's personal experience is an illustrative example. Newly graduated from architecture school, Haubold and her husband were excited to both find work in Magdeburg. But there were no apartments available in Magdeburg; the local housing authority assigned Haubold and her husband to separate rooms in gender-segregated dormitories. She estimated that they would have had to wait at least five years for an apartment. Rather than live apart, she inquired about employment for architects in Eisenhüttenstadt, ultimately taking a job at the Frankfurt Oder office of urban planning, which oversaw the region. Although she has a deep appreciation for Eisenhüttenstadt, she was reluctant to move back home at that point in her life, preferring the intellectual atmosphere of a university town. But she also knew that she and her husband could join the EWG and quickly become eligible for an apartment in the ever-expanding city. They moved into a two-bedroom apartment in Housing Complex 6 in the 1970s. Other residents told me similar stories; in a small country like East Germany, nowhere was too far from home, and young couples looking to put down roots often sought out cities where they could find both housing and employment. Married couples were given priority housing assignments, and young couples could expect to move quickly up waiting lists—at least in the places where people moved up waiting lists. Eisenhüttenstadt's abundant housing in Complexes 5, 6, and 7 was built and operated by the EWG, which was then called the AWG (Arbeiterwohnungsbaugenossenschaft, or Workers' Housing Cooperative), a real estate cooperative that also emerged out of the political unrest of 1953.

During the early 1950s, pressure to increase production quotas without increased resources had been particularly intense in the construction trade. One Eisenhüttenstädter described going hungry while being forced to work for two weeks straight after laying the foundation for the city's hospital (Fromm 1999, 139). On June 16, 1953, construction workers went on strike in Berlin. By the following day, the unrest had spread nationwide. In Eisenhüttenstadt, workers at the EKO steel plant went on strike, save the blast furnace operators—blast furnaces in steel factories must remain continuously operational—and 1,800 protesters demonstrated in the streets, later storming the socialist party headquarters in Fürstenberg. Witnesses described mayhem, with shots fired and typewriters thrown from windows (140). Ninety-five people were arrested and thirty were ultimately imprisoned for their actions that day (143).

In response to the June uprising and ongoing national unrest, on December 10, 1953, the East German government issued Executive Order 129, "On the Further Improvement of Workers' Working and Living Conditions and the Rights of Unions [Gewerkschaften]." The government promised that wages would be increased for most workers while the cost of living would decrease ("Gesetzblatt der DDR" 1953). Crucially, as part of the government's steps to address a nationwide housing shortage, citizens would be authorized to form building cooperatives: "According to the wishes and needs of the workers, it is necessary to form workers' housing cooperatives and to fund them with state aid. The Ministry of Construction will be instructed, in cooperation with the Ministry of Finance and in agreement with the trade unions, to draw up a model statute for these workers' housing cooperatives within three months. These will include provisions for financial lending with favorable terms, and the preparation of people's property [*volkeigenen Grund und Boden*] for free (*unentgeltlichen*) and indefinite use, with material and technical assistance from industry" ("Gesetzblatt der DDR" 1953).

In March 1954, around two hundred Eisenhüttenstädters met to discuss the founding of a building cooperative with city leadership. By April, the city had offered the collective a loan of 500,000 Ostmarks, around €700,000. The Eisenhüttenstadt AWG was officially founded in July, and the city granted it permission to build in Schönfließ, a village adjacent to Eisenhüttenstadt (Gericke 2004, 13–15). Between 1955 and 1956, the AWG built sixteen attached two-story single-family homes, which they sold to members for 2,500 Ostmarks, roughly €1,500, to be paid back over five years; the AWG would collectively own all real estate. The first residents moved in on December 21, 1954—Stalin's birthday, still an auspicious day (21), as de-Stalinization would not be instituted until the 1960s. The AWG houses were built by hand, by volunteer labor, after work hours. Much of the construction material was left over from other sites in the area. The homes lacked connections to public utilities, and residents described using energy from construction sites to power their electric lights (23).

Historian Andreas Ludwig (2004, 88) suggests that the development of workers' housing collectives was a success in part because it enabled the preexisting Western cultural desire for homeownership and entrepreneurship to be made legible under the guise of socialist collectivities. But with success came co-optation by the state. Over the course of the 1960s, Eisenhüttenstadt's AWG transformed from an ad hoc volunteer organization building single-family homes into a professional real estate cooperative. In 1959, it began construction on its second site, which would become Housing Complex 5, building four-story apartment buildings that already more closely resembled the unadorned apartment blocks of Housing Complexes 4 and 1 than the hand-hewn cottages built a few years prior. The organization developed a professional staff and, in 1963, contracted with the city to erect industrially produced apartment buildings in Housing Complex 5, which it financed with loans from the East German Central Bank, a trend reflected nationwide. By 1957, there were 560 AWGs with sixty thousand members across East Germany. By 1961, AWGs were responsible for 66 percent of all new construction (Ludwig 2004, 89). In Eisenhüttenstadt's AWG, residents

FIGURE 46. Postcard depicting the AWG houses, 1959. Courtesy of Ben Kaden.

FIGURE 47. Housing Complex 5, early 1960s. Photograph by M. Fricke. Courtesy of Stadtarchiv Eisenhüttenstadt.

paid entry fees and donated their skills and labor; as at the GeWi, tenants were required to contribute to the collective upkeep of their apartment buildings, with responsibilities outlined in each rental contract.

The EWG's growth in Eisenhüttenstadt was also propelled by the fact that the city center was considered increasingly unlivable as the socialist era wore on. Many apartments were heated with coal stoves, and residents had to haul coal from their basements, dispose of the ashes, and continually stoke fires in winter. Hot water was in constant short supply. Architects and urban planners recall little if any funding being allocated for the maintenance of apartment buildings during the socialist era. The prevailing attitude seemed to be that decrepit buildings should be demolished and replaced with modern tower blocks. Architects in Eisenhüttenstadt pointed to the Nikolaiviertal in Berlin's Mitte district as precedent; there, in the 1980s, medieval buildings were demolished and replaced with tower blocks. Wolfgang Perske, a former city official who, in the GDR era, oversaw the construction of concrete building components, told me that he and his colleagues once looked optimistically toward the eventual demolition of Fürstenberg's main street. The medieval village, now under historic preservation, was to be replaced with tower blocks as part of Housing Complex 8. Gabriele Haubold told me to imagine a city center comprising tower blocks through East German eyes: Tower blocks were associated with vibrant, well-populated districts. In 1989, 274 apartments were uninhabited due to disrepair, and 228 of them were within the GeWi's city center holdings (Rat der Stadt et al. 1990a, 1990b).[8] Residents had not yet come to associate tower blocks with an unfulfilled, abandoned future. "When I think of the city center, I don't know what I would have done," Haubold told me—such was the degree of disrepair and the difficult of securing funds for renovation.

Old Debt

Following reunification, many East German housing cooperatives found themselves in dire financial circumstances. As discussed, real estate companies—AWGs and municipal organizations like the GeWi—had funded their construction projects with loans from the East German Central Bank. But those loans had not been taken out with any expectation that the housing complexes would be profitable enough, through rental income, for the loans to be paid back in the foreseeable future. As part of the reunification process, 72 billion Ostmarks in real estate debts were transferred to West German banks. Upon Germany's monetary union, East German real estate cooperatives collectively owed 36 billion Deutschmarks, referred to as old debt (*Altschulden*). But with depopulation across the former East Germany, rental income was rapidly drying up (Wiede-mer 2004). In 1993, the federal government attempted to forestall the growing crisis in the East German real estate sector with the Old Debt Assistance Law (Altschuldenhilfegesetz). Any former East German real estate company could have up to half its old debt forgiven, up to a remainder of 150 Deutschmarks per square meter (around €200), if they sold 15 percent of their housing stock and used the profits to pay down the remaining old debt (Volksstimme 2011). But the law did little to alleviate the growing burden of old debt. Some real estate com-panies eager to sell could not find buyers, others were reluctant to enter into the restrictive deals dictated by the Old Debt Assistance Law, and many saw mainte-nance, repairs, and staff salaries as higher financial priorities. Yet leveraged with old debt, real estate companies were unable to fund the maintenance and repairs that would enable them to retain their tenants (Wiedemer 2004).

When Urban Renewal East was announced in 2000, many in Eisenhüttenstadt and across the former East Germany saw the program as an essential lifeline for struggling East German real estate companies. The program would offer debt forgiveness without the obligation to sell real estate assets—a concession for which the Brandenburg State government had advocated since 1998 (Allendorf 1998). Municipalities could apply for funding, which would be allocated to real estate companies, for the demolition of residential buildings that were at least 15 percent vacant; demolished buildings would have their associated old debt forgiven, up to seventy Deutschmarks (roughly one hundred euros) per square meter. Between 2000 and 2008, 80 percent of the buildings demolished as part of Urban Renewal East received old debt relief (Liebmann et al. 2012, 44).

In 2009, Urban Renewal initiated a further round of demolitions and debt forgiveness, funded through 2013 (Liebmann et al. 2012, 44). But Urban Renewal was never imagined as purely a demolition program; its goals were to "reduce the functional loss of urban space and create sustainable urban structures" in the former East Germany (1). And as vacancy in the East German real estate market began to stabilize in the early 2010s, dropping from 16.2 percent in 2002 to 8.3 percent in 2010 (8), funding was allocated away from demolitions and toward renovations. More importantly, buildings demolished with Urban Renewal fund-ing after 2013 would not have their associated old debt relieved.

In 2019, the Brandenburg finance minister, Christian Görke, noted that old debts were still of great concern to his constituents. Across the former East Ger-many, old debts amounted to €2.1 billion; in Brandenburg alone, former state-run companies such as the GeWi held €312 million in old debt, and former AWGs held €189 million. "It was a mistake from the start, in the implementation of the Reunification Treaty, to retrospectively assign debts to [East German real estate companies], in connection to their creation of housing [Wohnraum] in the GDR.

This process was unique and has no comparable counterpart in West Germany," Görke said at a press conference (MDFE 2019).

Oliver Funke, the chair of the GeWi, told me that neither he nor his colleagues anticipated that the old debt relief would expire in 2013. Urban Renewal would continue to fund demolitions after 2013, but they would not be accompanied by old debt relief. The 2015 Urban Renewal Plan projected the demolition of 959 apartments between 2015 and 2020, and 283 apartments between 2021 and 2025 (Stadt Eisenhüttenstadt and BBSM 2015, 73). While the demolitions would help reconsolidate the city's population in the city center, they also diminished the pool of potential tenants without relieving any old debt. GeWi leaders voiced concerns about their ability to stay in business, as did leaders of the EWG. But the companies were at a crossroads. After demolishing much of Complexes 5, 6, and 7, the EWG had very little vacancy, but its holdings were in areas slated for demolition. In 2010, the EWG's vacancy rate was 3 percent. If demolitions progressed as planned, the company would lose the tenants it displaced, as it would be unable to find them comparable apartments elsewhere among its holdings (Stadt Eisenhüttenstadt and BBSM 2015, 21).

At the same time, the city center, owned primarily by the GeWi, was becoming increasingly vacant. Between 1995 and 1999, the city government received 116 million Deutschmarks (roughly €70 million) for renovations in the city center (Haubold 2000, 3)—what historic preservation official Marina Wehlisch described as her aha moment. But while facades had been restored in Housing Complexes 2 and 3, much of Housing Complexes 1 and 4 remained unrenovated. In the 2010s, a handful of buildings were demolished in Complex 1, with the reluctant approval of the historic preservation board, in response to the area's increasing vacancy.

In 2014, leadership at the GeWi, the EWG, and city hall negotiated a plan with the Brandenburg State Interior Ministry aimed at forestalling the demolition of the city center and maintaining the financial solvency of both realtors. The state would oversee and help fund the sale of nine buildings in Housing Complex 4 from the GeWi to the EWG. The GeWi would use the income toward renovations in Housing Complexes 1 and 3. The EWG would renovate its new holdings with Urban Renewal funding. When it eventually demolished more apartments in Housing Complex 6, the EWG could offer its tenants relocation to the city center (Stadt Eisenhüttenstadt and BBSM 2015, 60). Because of the burdens of old debt, East German real estate companies are restricted in their ability to take out loans. Thus, the EWG's purchase relied on unconventional funding sources[9]—namely, a subset of Urban Renewal funds (Sanierung-Sicherung-Erwerb, or SSE funding) earmarked for East German cities to buy centrally located historic buildings (Stadt Eisenhüttenstadt and BBSM 2015, 6). The plan's success rested on the city's ability to secure the necessary funding, which in turn rested on the strength of its 2014 Comprehensive Development Plan and 2015 Urban Renewal Plan. Urban planning in Germany is governed by development plans that are submitted by local governments to higher authorities; there is no presumptive right to develop, as exists in the United States (Hirt 2013). As a result, local governments are positioned to play a relatively active role in urban development, provided they can secure the cooperation of local landlords and state governments.

In 2015, the Brandenburg State government allocated €36 million in Urban Renewal funding to Eisenhüttenstadt, nearly half its total of €76 million in Urban Renewal spending between 2015 and 2018 (BBU Verband 2015). Part of the funding would go toward the EWG's purchase of nine buildings from the GeWi, prompting the front-page headline "Now the City Can Become More Attractive: Cooperation Agreement Secures Urban Renewal" (*Märkischer Sonntag* 2015). Many of the city officials with whom I spoke credited the plan's success to the collaboration between the city government, the GeWi, and the EWG, which enabled large-scale projects not seen elsewhere in the region—hence Eisenhüttenstadt's receiving half the state's funding over a three-year period. In conversation, city officials called the cooperation between the GeWi, EWG, and city government "exemplary" and "entirely unique." Harz called the city's lack of proprietary complexity an "incidental gift from the socialist era."

The funding thus set in motion plans that have since been carried out, earning the city a series of Living Well awards from the Berlin-Brandenburg Housing Association (BBU). The awards, established in 2008, are granted to real estate companies in Berlin and Brandenburg that respond innovatively to demographic and climate change. In 2021, the GeWi won for its "Lighthouse" project, which used €2.1 million in self-funding to transform a four-story apartment building on Linden Avenue into a group home for intellectually disabled adults, including those with dementia. Two- and three-bedroom apartments were transformed into seven-to-nine-bedroom group homes with enlarged kitchens and balconies; the ground floor has a day facility overseen by the charity Workers' Wellness (Arbeiterwohlfahrt), which manages various assisted living facilities throughout the region (Lötsch 2022b). In 2022, the EWG won a Living Well award for its renovation of the nine buildings in Housing Complex 4, which it named the Peaceful Path Quarter (Quartier Friedensweg). The Living Well announcement highlights the neighborhood's suitability for various age groups, as well as its energy efficiency: Renovations connected Housing Complex 4 with heat and hot water powered by off-gas from the steelworks, and buildings were retrofitted with improved insulation (BBU Verband 2022).

Verena Rühr-Bach, chair of the EWG, described the cooperative deal as an obvious solution to the two real estate companies' geographic and financial constraints,[10] but also something that depended on the commitments of the city's leadership. She explained in an interview in 2016 that she had floated the idea to the GeWi chair who preceded Oliver Funke, but he was unenthusiastic, and nothing materialized. Although the scale of the project was relatively modest, at nine buildings, Rühr-Bach saw it as essential to securing the longevity of the EWG and as a public gesture of cooperation. It materialized the fact that as the city's transformation was underway, the relationship between tenants and land-lord had to be reconfigured to accommodate the changing material conditions of the city—the demolition of areas outside consolidation zones—making visible the fact that apartments were a commodity that, while providing essential shelter, also provided for the well-being of a large proportion of the city's economy.

The Peaceful Path Quarter has also addressed some of the city's concerns over its demographic changes. As long as ArcelorMittal kept the steelworks open, there would likely be well-paying jobs. But the city was seeing a grow-ing portion of its workforce commute from elsewhere: Just under five thousand workers commuted in 2005, and just under six thousand did so in 2011. City leadership expressed concern over the large proportion of commuters that were under thirty years old, which exacerbated the city's lack of children and projected future shrinkage (Stadt Eisenhüttenstadt and BBSM 2015, 11). At the same time, according to interviews, officials were concerned about the rising cost of housing and feared pricing out elderly residents. Many of the city's newly retired residents had been unemployed since reunification, and their incomes were meager. The Peaceful Path Quarter responded to both groups.

Between 2015 and 2023, the EWG renovated its nine buildings in Housing Complex 4 with around €32 million in Urban Renewal funding. The project transformed 305 standardized apartments into 248 apartments of various con-figurations that range from 43 to 109 square meters (approximately 500 to 1,200 square feet), including three- and four-bedroom layouts for families with chil-dren (Lötsch 2022c). The buildings are wheelchair accessible, but Beige, who worked on the project, explained that to keep down costs that might be passed on to renters, elevator access is not available on every floor. The ceremonial first tenant, presented with a large cardboard key, was an elderly wheelchair user. But as if to underscore the city's emphasis on generational mixing, a YouTube video about the renovations also shows a young firefighter putting his bicycle in the elevator as he comes home from work. The firefighter goes on to describe how pleased he is to be able to live within biking distance of the firehouse and walking distance of his daughter's preschool, echoing the movements of Härtel's imagined tenant (EWG eG 2019).

When the project opened in 2022, the average leaseholder was fifty-six years old, but ages ranged between twenty-two and ninety-one; all apartments had been rented out, even before renovations were complete (Lötsch 2022c). Rents were priced between €4.9 and €6.5 per square meter (BBU Verband 2022), well below the national average of €11.8 per square meter (BWSB 2022), and one-quarter of the apartments are reserved for low-income renters (Lötsch 2022c).[11] The EWG received 450 rental inquiries, though there were only 248 apartments, and Rühr-Bach noted that she was particularly proud of the fact that ninety-seven tenants were new to the city. Many of them were families with children, representing a successful resolution to the commuter problem raised years earlier (Lötsch 2022b). Moreover, the project earned the EWG its fifth Living Well award, making it the first real estate company in Brandenburg to garner the distinction (BBU Verband 2022).

Urban planning always produces a present absence; we choose to build one thing and not another. Thus it is notable that the redevelopment of Complex 4, which lies outside the historically protected zone, nonetheless retains the morphology of a socialist Housing Complex: The proportion and placement of buildings are unchanged, and the project has prioritized accessibility, affordability, and social diversity. The Peaceful Path Quarter is named for the pedestrian and bicycle path that cuts across Complex 4, a hallmark of early Housing Complex design. And the 2014 development plan highlights the walkability of Housing Complexes 1 through 4 as grounds for marketing Eisenhüttenstadt as "the city of short distances," which appeals equally to mobility-impaired residents, busy working parents, and people looking to reduce their reliance on cars (Stadt Eisenhüttenstadt and BBSM 2015, 27–31). Perhaps the residents who have repopulated the city center might look out their windows and notice not only the presence of green—the renovations included plans for new gardens and playgrounds—but also the presence of human-scale, human-centered urban design rather than that of socialist obsolescence.

As in Housing Complex 1, when I visited Housing Complex 4 in 2023, I found an urban landscape that had been significantly transformed. The stained, unpainted facades along Street of the Republic were resurfaced and painted in soft tones of blue and gray, and the rusting balconies had been replaced with new models. Stepping into a courtyard where I could access the Peaceful Path Quarter, I found wide covered balconies and spacious new entryways, accessed by freshly paved paths. Nearby, buildings that were modernized as part of Affordable Living had also been renovated with new facades, windows, and balconies. As of this writing, the renovation of Housing Complex 4 is still underway, and the renovated buildings contrast sharply with their unrenovated neighbors. The tidy buildings of Affordable Living, with their pitched red roofs and metal balconies, are mirrored by those across the street that still have aging slate roofs and chipped plaster balconies. Yet ubiquitous construction equipment and scaffolding also signal the neighborhood's ongoing transformation, heralding positive change.

FIGURES 48A AND 48B. Street of the Republic in Housing Complexes 3 and 4, 2015. Photographs by the author.

FIGURES 49A AND 49B. Street of the Republic in Housing Complexes 3 and 4, renovated as part of the cooperation agreement, 2023. Photographs by the author.

In the Peaceful Path Quarter, four-story apartment buildings were once tightly packed. But as demolitions have continued, expansive courtyards have emerged—in some cases, over one hundred yards separate facing buildings. Michael Reh, who succeeded Gabriele Haubold as the director of Urban Renewal in 2019, told me that the city continues to struggle with high vacancy rates, and that buildings in the interior courtyards of Housing Complex 4—those that are not along the street edge—are a priority for demolition. These buildings, he explained, were added later, to meet increasing demand for housing as the socialist era wore on.[12] As such, they are a paean to late socialist expediency, rather than to early socialist utopianism, and their demolition has enabled the city's original urban footprint to reemerge. Reverence for the city's origins is pervasive among both planners and residents, and Reh told me that demolishing the buildings along courtyard perimeters, laid out in the early 1950s, was out of the question. To do so "would have been a sacrilege," Reh said, "and no one wanted that."

Indeed, city leaders repeatedly cited the spacious proportions of the city center as one of the most notable inheritances of socialist urbanism. Complexes 1 through 4 had been designed before East Germany began demanding that its planners build "cheaper, better, faster," in the words of the Soviet slogan,[13] and immense credence had been given to residents' need for access to light and air. The high-density tower blocks of outlying Housing Complexes, city leaders explained, had therefore been the first apartments to be demolished.

At the same time, we must not reify the city center's renovation as a natural inevitability. Architect Jens Beige compared the reactivation of the Housing Complex to the rotation of the earth, as if it were the natural order that Eisenhüttenstadt emerge from its dark period. But it is a policy choice to reinvest federal money into financially struggling cities. In Eisenhüttenstadt, the GeWi and EWG feel like entities that are too big to fail. But their collapse would be negligible to the larger German economy, and their continued operation is no guarantee. Programs that have kept real estate companies solvent, including Urban Renewal, rely on a fragile alignment of local, state, and national priorities. Plans must be proposed at the local level and must reflect cooperation between the city governments and landlords, but they are ultimately enabled by the federal funding that is earmarked for the benefit of struggling communities and that is responsibly administered by states. As in the 1950s, Eisenhüttenstadt continues to represent national concerns made manifest at the local level—and its urban landscape continues to be made possible through both locally driven activity and generous federal funding.

TABLE 1 Vacancy, 2003–24

HOUSING COMPLEX	UNITS 2003	VACANCY 2003	UNITS 2013	VACANCY 2013	UNITS 2024	VACANCY 2024
1	1,512	23%	1,341	38%	1,254	19%
2	1,964	24%	1,997	9%	1,971	6%
3	1,003	24%	1,064	15%	998	2%
4	2,047	12%	1,792	17%	1,614	26%
5	1,699	8%	1,158	3%	1,031	7%
6 North	704	22%	3,273	9%	3,041	8%
6 South	3,888	14%	0	-	0	-
7 North	2,000	30%	366	11%	155	1%
7 South	1,149	59%	0	-	0	-

Sources: Mann et al. 2015, 25–26; Howest 2006, 102; Stadt Eisenhüttenstadt and BBSM 2015, 48; Stadtverwaltung Eisenhüttenstadt, Abteilung Stadtentwicklung/Stadtumbau 2024.

Lunik as Counterfactual

It is not difficult to imagine what might have happened to Eisenhüttenstadt had city leadership not "rescued" housing for the "social realm," as the former GeWi chair Eberhard Harz described. Across the city, buildings that are privately owned stand out as "eyesores" (*Schandflecke*), as informants repeatedly called them. Even people uninterested in urban planning could tell me offhand which buildings were privately owned—they were abandoned and in severe disrepair, often missing most of their windows and covered in graffiti. There were two high-rise dormitories and an office building in Housing Complex 6 and a boarded-up grocery store in Housing Complex 5. Most notably, at the end of Linden Avenue across from City Hall, there was Hotel Lunik.

Lunik was once an opulent hotel. It hosted international guests, such as the Austrian steelworkers who helped design the converter steelworks, and had an Intershop that accepted foreign currency, sold imported goods, and, according to one informant, made the hallways smell like expensive perfume. The East German leader Erich Honecker ate there when he visited Eisenhüttenstadt (Neiser 2022a). Journalist Janet Neiser described learning a song in school as a child in the 1980s: "In Lunik rings the telephone! Delegation, delegation. A swarm of bees around Reception. The world comes together in our young city" (Neiser 2022b). Lunik continued to operate as a hotel until 2000, but it lost its allure in the capitalist era. A rotating series of businesses occupied its first floor, including a drugstore and a Greek restaurant, but none proved economically viable. In 2006, the building was sold at forced auction to a Hamburg-based real estate developer named Ulrich Marseille. But it soon became clear that to Marseille,

FIGURE 50. Hotel Lunik, 2015. Photograph by the author.

FIGURE 51. Hotel Lunik's rooftop dining room, 2023. Photograph by the author.

the investment existed only on paper. He boarded up the building and seemed to simply walk away.[14] Lunik loomed over Linden Avenue, the barbed wire and plywood installed around its entryway doing little to deter vandals.

In the early 2020s, residents and city leadership began to increase pressure on Marseille. Over the years, various leaders had attempted to negotiate with him without success (Neiser 2019), and at quarterly town hall meetings, residents asked why the city could not simply expropriate the landlord (Rada 2023). In 2019, Marseille applied for and received individual historic status for Lunik, outside of its status as part of the historically protected zone, yet he continued to leave the building untouched. In 2020, a fire on the upper floors damaged the building's roof. In early 2023, the county historic preservation board announced that it had no choice but to repair the structural damage and bill Marseille €500,000 for the job; the debt would limit his ability to sell the hotel to a buyer willing to make further repairs (Rada 2023). Around the same time, the citizens of Eisenhütten-stadt began their own campaign. Ilona Weser, a retired county administrator, collected over two thousand signatures for an open letter that she sent to Marseille's home in Hamburg and published in Eisenhüttenstadt's daily newspaper (Neiser 2023a); signatories included prominent Eisenhüttenstädters such as the former city architect Herbert Härtel and the former EKO chair Karl Döring.

The letter described Eisenhüttenstadt as "Germany's first model socialist city… an expression of a bygone social vision that today is a first-class architectural ensemble renovated to the standards of historic preservation" and noted its interest to "researchers, architects, urban planners, artists and creative people [including] two-time Academy Award winner Tom Hanks" as well as the editors of *Geo Saison*, a high-end travel magazine, which put Eisenhüttenstadt on its January 2023 cover as one of twenty-three cities to visit that year. "This fills us with great pride and great joy," Weser wrote. But Lunik stood out in a "highly visible portion of the historic area." The undersigned beseeched Marseille to invest in the upkeep of his holdings and "fulfill [his] obligations as the property owner" (Neiser 2023a).

Residents understood that to Marseille, Lunik was first and foremost a commodity, while from their perspective it was an integral material component of the urban landscape. As anthropologists have noted, such opposing "frameworks" (Goffman 1974) come into play when essential urban infrastructures are traded as commodities (K. Phillips 2023). Moreover, as discussed, the ownership of capitalist real estate is an abstracted relationship (Humphrey 2002b; Strathern [2002] 2022), comprising, after Roman precedent, the rights to dispose of (*abusus*), manage (*usus*), and benefit from (*fructus*) (Cherkaev 2023). While the letter referred to Marseille's "obligations as the property owner," those obligations were determined primarily by the property's historic status: Under Brandenburg state law, the owner of a historic property has an obligation to protect the material integrity of their holdings (Land Brandenburg 2004). But the letter seemed to have purposely elided this obligation and the more general obligations of ownership, suggesting that *abusus* was prohibited by virtue of Marseille's ownership, rather than because of the building's historic status.

Such wishful thinking was widespread among residents. One day in 2015, I was walking past Lunik with Otto, a retired steel engineer and nearly lifelong Eisenhüttenstädter, when he began to tell me a familiar story: The hotel was an "eyesore" and a "trace of capitalism." City leadership, overexcited by their newfound access to free enterprise, had sold off valuable assets without fully realizing the consequences of their actions. Now Lunik was in the hands of someone who had likely never visited the city, and who did not seem to care about its material degradation. Otto and I had both recently seen an exhibition about Lunik at the nearby Documentation Center for Everyday Culture in East Germany (now the Museum of Utopia and the Everyday), which commemorated the site as a sort of permanent ruin. Portraits of people who once worked at Lunik were displayed alongside photographs of the building taken in 2005, ten years prior, when the hotel's interior was already covered with rust, mold, and peeling paint.

Then Otto told me that he wished that the city had a chance to do it all over again, carefully considering the stakes of who owned what land, selling to buyers who were invested in the well-being of the community instead of to the highest bidder. I asked whether Lunik might yet be sold to such an owner, but he brushed the question off. Otto was concerned less with Lunik itself than with what it evoked—the initial frenzy of privatization, which was a historical event unlikely to be repeated, he noted, as capitalism had already saturated the former Eastern Bloc. "Maybe in Cuba or North Korea they'll do it better," he said, implying that Lunik's problem lay in the hasty imposition of a social order that made space for the individual ownership of civic goods without a prohibition against *abusus*.

Walter Benjamin (1968) observed that the urban landscape is composed of ruins, discarded things whose material histories speak to the constant novelty that capitalism demands. For Benjamin, the ruins of modernity were things that had lost their commodity status. Removed from the possibility of exchange, ruins evoked a "sideways" nostalgia (Boym 2007) that signaled that "newness and progress were not exactly an illusion, but they were certainly a gross simplification of the dialectical spiral of history" (Dawdy 2010, 762). In doing so, ruins stood out against an urban landscape that concealed its alternative histories behind modernist narratives of unrelenting progress (Benjamin 1968). Yet even as scholars have attended to the modern ubiquity of ruins (Stoler 2013; Edensor 2005; Dawdy 2010), ruination has nonetheless been considered as resulting from the withdrawal of capitalism, which leads to emptiness (Dzenovska 2020), abjection (Navaro-Yashin 2009), and material decay (Pérez Fernández 2023).[15]

Lunik, in contrast, was a ruin precisely because of its role as a commodity. Had it belonged to the "social realm," as did housing, city leadership would have invested in its material well-being. But it instead belonged to a financialized system of ownership that imposed constraints on the city's authority. Anthropologist Xenia Cherkaev (2023, 78) suggests that the Soviet conception of ownership was *usufruct*, comprising the rights to manage (*usus*) and benefit from (*fructus*), with *abusus* curtailed by the Soviet Union's harsh punishment of damage to state property. Similarly, Eisenhüttenstadt's leaders seem to have taken seriously their obligations to manage and benefit from urban space without considering that they might also dispose of it (*abusus*). But Marseille's deployment of his right to *abusus* was enabled by the opposing framework with which he approached his ownership—as the exclusive right to the profits of a financial instrument that was, incidentally, tied to the material reality of a historic East German hotel. In a reversal of Benjamin's urban landscape, Lunik, the ruin, was a commodity alienated from its social context, and it contrasted with a "first-class architectural ensemble" (Neiser 2023a) that thrived because of the social relationships embodied therein.

Harz, the former GeWi chair, also contrasted Lunik with the Aktivist, which was restored in the early 2000s and transformed into offices for the EWG. The Aktivist was a restaurant, dance hall, and center of social life during the socialist era. Its ornate design featured wood paneling, stained glass, chandeliers, and brass flourishes. But the Aktivist had been run by the Organization for Commerce (Handelsorganization), whose holdings, which also included Lunik, were put up for auction by Treuhand in May 1991. From this point, the buildings' histories diverged. Lunik sold right away, but by 1996, there were no buyers for the Aktivist, and the building lay empty and unused.

Harz explained that as city leaders came together to discuss plans for the Aktivist, they looked to the GeWi as a model, as the organization had recently begun renovations in the city center after wresting control of its holdings from Treuhand. In 1996, through a collaborative agreement that also included the GeWi and EKO Stahl, the city oversaw the transfer of the Aktivist from Treuhand to the EWG.[16] Designating a new landlord in the *Grundbuch* would be the first step toward securing funds for renovation, and the EWG was considered the most suitable landlord among various municipal stakeholders. At the time, Verena Rühr-Bach explained, the EWG's offices were located in Housing Complex 5, and the organization was looking to move closer to the city center. Inhabiting the Aktivist, in Housing Complex 2, would ensure the building's future use at a time when the commercial success of a large restaurant was uncertain. But by 1998, plans to fund the renovation through EKO fell through. In 2003, the EWG convened its own working group on the Aktivist, led by former EKO chair Karl Döring, which liaised with the city government to generate an urban development plan based on preserving East German culture. Through the development plan, the city managed to secure state funding for the founding of the Documentation Center for Everyday Culture in East Germany, repurposing the defunct Kindergarten 2 as a museum, and the renovation of the Aktivist (Gericke 2004, 83–84).

The EWG carried out the renovation between 2007 and 2011, to great acclaim. Upon its completion, the renovation won the city its second architectural prize, the Brandenburg Building Culture (Baukultur) Prize for historic preservation. At the awards ceremony, Brandenburg State leadership noted the energy-efficient infrastructures and skilled restoration, which reconciled an attention to local history with contemporary needs (BBU Verband 2011). The community room, with decorative columns and brass chandeliers, was restored as an open-plan office, with glass cubicles that preserved the feel of the space. The adjacent bar still operates as a pub, serving classic German foods, its dark wood booths lending it an intimate, club-like atmosphere. I've found it to be a place where people go when they have time to enjoy their surroundings, more luxurious and slightly more expensive than a bakery or café. In 2022, a fifteen-year-old intern at the EWG made a short web-based project about the Aktivist that drew on municipal publications (EWG 2022a). The project's subtitle, "Not Without the Akki," spoke to the intimacy and fierce attachment with which residents approached their city—and to the consequences of treating real estate first and foremost as a material entity, placing control with local stakeholders who are invested in its social effects.

In June 2023, city leadership shocked residents with the announcement that they had purchased the Hotel Lunik from its derelict landlord. "Hotel Lunik and Dormitories Now Belong to the City" read the headline of a press release, though the city did not release details on the cost of the real estate or on the deal's financing. The press release explained that the buildings would be owned by the GeWi, though the dormitories would soon be demolished—Marseille owned all three buildings and had insisted on selling them as a package deal. Together with Oder-Spree County leadership and the historic preservation board, the GeWi and city government had created the Lunik Company (Lunik AG), which would seek funding for Lunik's restoration. The press release also noted that it was necessary to "repeatedly correct" media reports that falsely called the deal a "buyback"— the city had never owned Lunik or the dormitories (Stadtverwaltung Eisenhüttenstadt 2023). Their ownership had transferred directly from the Organization for Commerce to Treuhand, and the city's acquisition of them represented an unprecedented development, as well as the triumph of urban space conceived as a public good.

INFRASTRUCTURES OF SOLIDARITY

"Social infrastructures" are a slippery subject to social scientists, referring alternately to material and immaterial structures, as well as the social relationships that undergird them. In sociology, scholars such as Eric Klinenberg define social infrastructures as the urban spaces in which certain forms of sociality are cultivated, thereby contributing to the collective good: libraries, schools, parks, and so on (Klinenberg 2018). But anthropologists have long considered such social infrastructures to be necessarily embedded in the social, which both enables and reproduces them (Star 1999). Taken together with anthropologists who consider infrastructure the site of political mediation (Larkin 2013; Appel et al. 2018), as well as those who examine how people feel, both sensorily and affectively, with relation to an urban public (Fennell 2015; Berlant 1997), one finds that the collapse of socialism offered a natural experiment in the entanglement between the various components of "social infrastructure," its social and material natures, and its reliance on immaterial infrastructures, habits, and state apparatuses. Moreover, as established by scholars of ruination (Stoler 2013; Daniel 2013), people trained in and by social infrastructures to inhabit certain forms of sociality do not lose those attunements with the loss of their regime.

In Kurt Leucht's 1994 interview, the interviewer asks him what aspects of the city still have meaning today, and he answers with a complaint about the absence of community. He explains, "Community [*Gemeinwesen*] must be brought together in social facilities. Community [*Nachbarschaft*] cannot be left to its own devices, rather it must be combined with a central point in the city." Leucht does not address the fact that the social infrastructures that brought people together

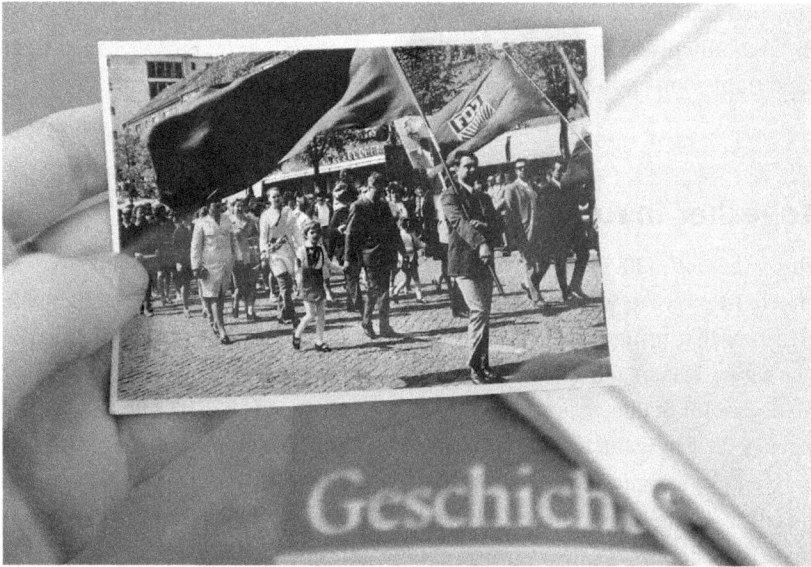

FIGURE 52. An informant shares a photo of a Young Pioneers parade from the 1980s, along with his old schoolbooks, 2015. Photograph by the author.

have, for the most part, disappeared. But for him it seems beside the point. Even if such groups did exist, they would need a built environment that supported them—the built environment creates the necessary conditions for community cohesion. Leucht goes on to say, "This is what I, to this day, criticize about Eisenhüttenstadt: the Central Square is certainly there, but there is only a single house on it [since demolished]. It lacks community-building facilities." A grand Culture Palace had originally been planned for Central Square, but nothing was ever built. During the socialist era, shacks were set up as workspaces for craftspeople, but the area is currently used as a parking lot for City Hall.

Here, I consider social infrastructures as these congealed forces of social and material networks. As Shannon Lee Dawdy shows in her work on social stratigraphy, if we dig in the places where the material world hints at buried histories, we also find that the social falls into those same "grooves" (Dawdy 2016, 45). This chapter examines contemporary social life in order to understand how past iterations of urban experience are embedded in social infrastructures, both socially and materially. I examine the durability of Eisenhüttenstadt's socialist-era communitarianism, as well as the durability of cultural practices that are entangled with the cultivation of solidarity. I then describe how the binary distinction between housing as a commodity and housing as a social good has been "fractally" reproduced (Gal 2002, 79; Gal and Irvine 2019, 19) in different iterations of urban experience. I further show how, as asylum seekers began to be housed in Eisenhüttenstadt in 2015, this distinction bore on the rights of asylees as their legal rights came into conflict with their rights to the city (Harvey 2013).

Together Instead of Alone

Since the early 2000s, the Eisenhüttenstadt city government has invested in efforts to improve what it calls "soft factors" in urban renewal: the intangible elements that bring vibrancy to urban life. The centerpiece of this plan is the Place for a Forum and Information in the City Center (Ort für Foren und Informationen im Stadtzentrum, or OFFIS), which opened in 2008 and houses the Agency for Engagement. The agency has two full-time employees and two part-time employees and hosts a range of activities that support social services and socialization: rides for the elderly and disabled, classes where individuals can share their knowledge on a variety of subjects (I attended classes on butter making and edible plants, and a driver's education refresher course), outdoor chess in the summer, photo contests, and the publication of a quarterly magazine, *Colorful and Complex*, which features local news, essays about the city, and interviews with residents. Regular columns include "Streets and Their People," which chronicles place-based histories, and "Portraits from Linden Avenue," which includes interviews with people who work along the street. In 2014, I was new to Eisenhüttenstadt and eager to connect with people. One day at the local library, after I explained as much, a librarian directed me to OFFIS. There I met Angela, then the director, who introduced me to Gerda, who brought me to the Group.

On the first Tuesday of every month, I met with the Group. I rode my bike from my apartment in Housing Complex 1 over the bridge that crossed the railroad tracks and across the vacant fields where Housing Complex 7 once stood. There I reached the Blockhouses at Chestnut Courtyard, tower blocks of eighty-five apartments at what had been Complex 7's southern tip. When the rest of Complex 7 was still standing, the Blockhouses had stood apart; they were custom-built for the site and therefore considered higher-quality construction than the neighboring P2 *Plattenbauten* (Härtel, n.d.). They also had, in 2015, some of the only remaining community rooms in the city.

On the ground floor of one apartment building was a kitchen where the Group made coffee and washed dishes, as well as a large meeting room whose bookshelves indicated its use for addiction and support groups. A small office next door was sometimes occupied by a woman from the EWG who oversaw the use of the communal spaces. The Group met in Complex 7 monthly to celebrate members' birthdays over coffee and cake, and to make a plan for the following

FIGURES 53A AND 53B. Excursions with the Group, 2015–16. Photographs by the author.

weeks: Thursdays were for bike rides and walks, no matter the weather, preferably with a pub en route. Saturdays were for mini golf or bowling. Every few weeks there would be something special: an excursion to Potsdam to ride bikes around Wannsee, or a barbecue in the backyard of someone who lived in Fürstenberg or Schönfließ. One day, Group members asked me to give a presentation about life in the United States. One member set up a projector in the meeting room so that I could share photos, and I brought peanut butter and jelly sandwiches, which most of the members politely declined—chicken and schmalz was often the sandwich of choice. Shortly before I left Eisenhüttenstadt, the Group presented me with a photo album commemorating my time with them, and one member read Goethe's "Coptic Song," often read at graduations—its closing line, "Be the anvil or the hammer," is intended to set young people on a decisive life course.

The Group began in 2007 when Andreas, one of the younger members, a native Eisenhüttenstädter then in his forties, put an ad in the local paper looking for hiking and biking companions. Later members joined by word of mouth. When I participated, the Group had about twenty members, all Germans in their fifties or older, in a wide range of socioeconomic positions, from people who had been on public assistance for years to retired engineers who lived in well-appointed homes. Yet because of their age, all members shared habits and cultural attunements from the socialist era. When we held a white-elephant gift exchange at Christmas, members shouted, "Open it slowly, like a *Westpaket*," referring to the packages of Western goods that East Germans were sent by friends and relatives abroad. When we walked and biked throughout the area, Group members pointed out the sites of the greenhouses and dairy that used to provide groceries to the region and recalled clearing trails with their brigades or Pioneer groups. Once, as we were leaving a nature preserve in the late afternoon, a middle-aged woman told me that she never would have worried about staying in the woods after dark "back then" (*damals*). In such a communitarian society, there was no conception that walking alone at night was a dangerous activity, even for a teenage girl. Later, an elderly acquaintance echoed the sentiment. Miming an elbow jab, she told me that she could no longer walk alone at night in today's "elbow society"—a derogatory term for the pervasive self-interest of the capitalist era.

Members referred to the Group as "the Group" in conversation and in written correspondence. But one day, while members were getting their coats on at the end of a gathering in Complex 7, the woman in the EWG office mentioned that she was organizing the schedule for the next month and needed to write down a name for the group. Someone shouted, "Together Instead of Alone." Everyone laughed, as the phrase rhymes in German: "Gemeinsam statt Einsam." The woman wrote it down.

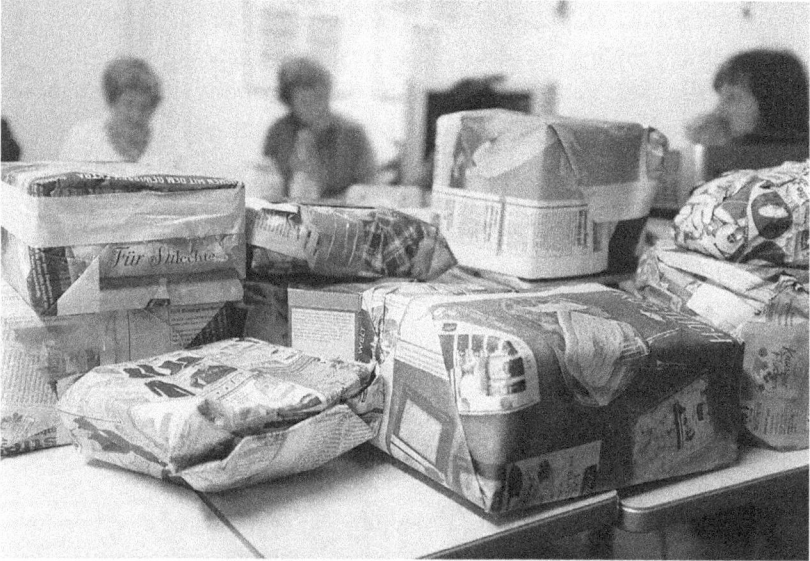

FIGURES 54A AND 54B. Christmas party with the Group in Housing Complex 7, 2015. Photographs by the author.

The House Society

I told this story to friends in Berlin, and one former West German said, affectionately, "That's so *Ossi* [East German]." Group life had been an essential part of East German culture, and social affects are not automatically retrained alongside regime change. Geographic or institutional proximity, rather than mutual interest or shared identity characteristics, was often the basis on which bonds were imagined. Children were pressured to join the local chapter of the Young Pioneers and often spent time after school with their Pioneer groups. A friend who gave me a tour of his elementary school picked me up at my apartment and walked me there because that's what his Young Pioneer group leader had done on his first day of school.[1] Workplaces were organized into brigades, which often engaged in community service after hours. Many informants told me that their brigades had been primary social units, where young adults made friends and occasionally met spouses. And tenants belonged to "House Societies" (*Hausgemeinschäfte*), units of social organization and informal political organs organized around the apartment building.[2]

Apartment rental contracts in Eisenhüttenstadt stipulated a certain number of workdays that residents were expected to provide for their landlord; one informant shared a GeWi contract from 1986 that mandated three workdays per month. Each apartment building also had a designated House Society leader (*Hausgemeinschaftleiter*) who organized periodic cleanings, enabling residents to fulfill their work obligations. One elderly Eisenhüttenstädter fondly described the socialist era as a time when people "didn't turn their noses up" at the prospect of signing up for chores and spending time with neighbors on collective labor. He told me that the GeWi often purchased cases of beer to incentivize participation in spring and fall cleanups, where residents cleaned stairwells and performed small acts of maintenance such as repainting doors and hallways. The man described a scene that was often evoked when informants described the socialist era, in which one neighbor tended to a barbeque while another swept the entryway, and another kept an eye on the children playing in the courtyard. Each House Society also signed a contract with its landlord that outlined its compensation for the maintenance of outdoor spaces, including raking leaves from the lawn, trimming hedges, caring for trees and flower beds, and maintaining fountains, sandboxes, and play areas. Another informant shared a contract from 1989 that showed that her House Society, for its outdoor maintenance, earned 344 Ostmarks (€125) annually, which it spent on its social events, including parties, picnics, and excursions.

Little scholarship on House Societies exists, but one study comparing two apartment buildings in Dresden notes that during the socialist era, House Societies offered a network through which citizens could navigate their economy's constant material shortages—researchers found it difficult to disentangle private feelings of neighborly care from practical matters of mutual reliance (Günther and Nestmann 2000). While some of my informants saw their House Societies as a perfunctory form of state participation or an exploitive source of manual labor, others saw them as an essential form of social collectivism that disappeared rapidly following reunification.

Helga Boehm, who passed away in 2023 at the age of ninety-five, had been her building's House Society leader. She maintained a list of every resident's birthday and made sure that no birthday passed without conveying good wishes; residents came to expect that on their birthdays, neighbors would stop by for coffee and cake. Helga lived in one of the high-rises along Linden Avenue, then Lenin Avenue, and she felt lucky that the residents bonded so well. The building had thirty-three apartments, most of them one-bedrooms, and the residents were mostly single people or couples without children. At first, Helga was put off by what she saw as a claustrophobic, small-town nosiness. Visitors had to register in a House Book, and as ardent socialist she was embarrassed that her neighbors would find out that she saw relatives from West Berlin. But she soon came to find the concern that neighbors had for one another comforting. House Societies set an expectation of community in which the development of trust was contingent on mere proximity, foregrounding the communitarian aspects of the socialist networked habitus.

After reunification, things began to shift for Helga. Sitting at a blonde wood card table in her cozy living room, Helga and I went through a list of residents from 1989 as she told me about how all but two had either died or moved away. She had tried to continue organizing events for the building over the years, and she showed me the desk drawer where she had stored thirty euros, gathered around five years prior and set aside to buy beer and snacks. But she was then in her late eighties, and she had trouble getting to know her neighbors. She told me that she had tried to maintain a GDR-style birthday list, but new neighbors had cited concerns over data privacy and declined to share their personal information. Shortly before we met in the winter of 2015, Helga had seen a moving company bringing things into the building, and she asked one of the moving men about the people moving in. She had always made an effort to greet moving vans with the goal of making new neighbors feel welcome. But the man barked at her, "Why do you want to know? What are you, from the Stasi?" Helga told me that she was "totally horrified" and dropped her efforts to get to know the new neighbors.

FIGURES 55A AND 55B. Scenes from Helga Boehm's photo album depict communal lawn care and residents gathered before an excursion. Courtesy of Helga Boehm.

But when I asked Helga what the most consequential change had been for her following reunification, she told me it was the loss of the communal washing machines. The top floor of her building, off the roof terrace and party room, had had two washing machines and a rudimentary dryer (*Schleduermaschine*) that were shared among the building's residents. After reunification, "in the blink of an eye," the washing machines and dryer were taken away. It was a real shame, she said, because when you have to share that kind of thing, that's where relationships are. She knew it was a small component of relationships, but when you had a list in the laundry room where every one of the thirty-three households signed up to use the machines, you knew, "OK, now Frau Schultz is doing her laundry," to use Helga's example, and you could go up and chat when she was done and it was your turn. You had small, serendipitous interactions, and you kept other people in mind. Helga and her neighbors protested the removal of the washing machines. The GeWi, which owns the building, told them that the machines had to be removed because they used too much electricity, and residents would have to buy washing machines to install in their own apartments. Helga and her neighbors offered to set up a collection to offset the electricity costs, but it was no use.

Helga had believed that there was something special in the socialist city. Born shortly before World War II, she felt she had no choice but to participate in a social movement that strove for a different kind of world than the one that had produced the violence of her early childhood. But the loss of the laundry machines revealed to her the ease with which that world could disappear. GDR planners worked to figure out the ideal window placement for ventilation and calculated how long it would take to walk between points in the city. But no amount of careful architectural planning could replace an instrument of social engineering as integral as a washing machine.

Kurt Leucht, in a 1990 letter to Gabriele Haubold, wrote that although a city can have a Communist unity of work, housing, and leisure, "there is no such thing as a socialist city and can never be, any more so than there can be a socialist bratwurst" (Leucht 1990). The debates in the GDR Building Academy about how to avoid the pitfalls of capitalist cities—their sprawl, their monotony, their overcrowded slums—were ultimately about how to build the ideal city. When that city functioned under a socialist regime, it was a socialist city. Haubold explained to me that Leucht was proud of the city he had designed, but his letter expressed his belief that while a city may reflect socialist ideals and embody a socialist planning process, it ultimately cannot be socialist in form. Just as it was ridiculous to think that a bratwurst could be socialist, so, too, was it ridiculous to think that a city could express a political orientation outside the regime that operated within it.

FIGURES 56A, 56B, AND 56C. Pages from Helga's scrapbook include an announcement for the building's thirtieth anniversary party and an excursion to Müggel Lake (*left*), a sign-up sheet for an excursion to view the Niederfinow boat locks (*center*), and an invitation to autumn cleaning (*right*). Courtesy of Helga Boehm.

Attention to Origins

The layered nature of urban space as both a material and social entity has long been manifested in the city's many publications, which foster an urban imaginary that circulates alongside their images and articles about urban development. In addition to *Colorful and Complex*, the OFFIS publication that is distributed for free throughout the city, there are also glossy, full-color quarterly newsletters published by the GeWi, the EWG, and the municipal utility provider, with photographs and articles describing their ongoing projects. There is the municipal publication *City Mirror*, a quarterly magazine that has been published since the socialist era, and *The Märker*, a daily newspaper that tenants of the GeWi and EWG receive as part of their apartment rentals. The *Märkische Oder Newspaper* (*Märkische Oder Zeitung*, or MOZ), a regional newspaper, has offices in Eisenhüttenstadt and is the city's most widely read daily paper. As Urban Renewal East and other plans were carried out over the course of my fieldwork, it was impossible to avoid the many headlines and photographs about the projects that showed up in my mailbox, on my doorstep, in municipal buildings, and in the newsstands along Linden Avenue. This tendency to report on and document urban developments reinforces the self-conception of Eisenhüttenstadt as a notable city, despite the abandoned buildings and diminished population that might point toward the contrary. One informant, not an Eisenhüttenstadt native, laughed as she told me about her neighbors' self-contradictory attachments to their hometown. "They love it, but they hate it," she said. "They gripe about it constantly, but they also think it's the center of the universe."

As I was an anthropologist studying urban development, my presence in the Group offered an outlet for members to share their interest in the city's history, as well as their many back issues of city publications. (GeWi tenant newsletters from the 1990s include repeated calls for volunteers to tend to public green spaces, a role vacated by the loss of House Societies and now the responsibility of professional landscapers, the cost of which is prorated across tenants.) Group members also shared municipal publications from the 2000s that highlight the city's public art, as well as publications from the socialist era that celebrated the city's history. Many owned copies of *Eisenhüttenstadt and Its Environment* (Gansleweit 1986) and *30 Years Eisenhüttenstadt* (Käthner 1980). Rarer but still popular was the expensive hardcover publication *Stalinstadt: New Lives, New People* (Colditz and Lücke 1958).

The publications offered an opportunity for Group members to cultivate collective memories of their city. When one member brought a copy of *30 Years Eisenhüttenstadt* to Saturday mini golf, the members in attendance squeezed two small tables together so that everyone could see the book, leaning over one another's shoulders. Scrutinizing the black-and-white photographs, members collectively identified local landmarks—one debate centered on distinguishing the interior of the Aktivist from that of City Hall, which was decided based on the position of the doors—and discussed personal recollections of the depicted places: who had lived in the city's various dormitories, how little they had paid, who had worked with hot slag in the steel factory, whose brigade had tended to the outdoor bowling (*kegeln*) area on Leisure Time Island (now overgrown), what was sold on each floor of the Magnet department store, a five-story building across the street from Hotel Lunik.

My presence as an outsider also offered Group members the opportunity to reinhabit some of the historical attunements of the socialist era, when citizens had been inculcated with pride in a sanitized version of their city's history. Members took great pleasure in quizzing me about the story in which Building Minister Selbmann felled a pine tree as the symbolic start to the city's construction—though they occasionally argued about details, with some insisting that President Wilhelm Pieck had wielded the ax. The topic came up when we were walking near a stand of pine trees behind the hospital; I was told it resembled the uncultivated forest that once extended across the region. Mostly, though, it came up when Group members asked me abruptly over coffee or beer, "How many hits of the ax?" Twenty-seven, I learned, because the pine was young and flexible and perhaps someone had dulled the ax—for every swing, the building minister had promised onlookers a case of beer.

None of these informants had been present at the ax swing, as they called the event, but they were invested in cultivating the memory of their city's originating moment. Like the planners and architects seeking to reactivate the urban core, Group members looked to the building generation as exemplary Eisenhüttenstädters. Many shared family photographs that depicted the city under construction in the early 1950s, with smiling groups of men and women in work clothes gathered on the stoops of unfinished apartment buildings. Others, however, highlighted the short-lived nature of the utopian "construction period" (*Aufbauzeit*) and the difficulty of its reproduction. Nearly all the city's first residents had been working-age adults and their school-age children, but by the later decades of the socialist era, Eisenhüttenstadt no longer had such demographic uniformity. Many informants told me that when Housing Complex 7 opened in the early 1980s, it had a large proportion of older residents moving out of the city center, where they maintained social networks, and that the fabled cohesion of House Societies felt like an urban myth.[3]

In January 2016, I found myself chatting with two county-level politicians at the reception following the mayor's New Year's address. We were in the grand lobby of the Friedrich Wolf Theater, and the mayor had just announced plans to build an old age home in Central Square. The audience in the theater had gasped in disappointment. One of the politicians said, "My father was from here and he was really attached to the city. He felt like he built it up himself."

"Utopia!" replied the other. "It was in people's hearts, this society that they hoped for, even as the progress of the city got bleaker and bleaker. You go from these big courtyards with lots of greenery to the tightly packed buildings in Complexes 5, 6, and 7. You can really see how they ran out of money and out of ideas."

Sunlight Deficits and Human Beings

Herbert Härtel, the former chief architect, told me that while he spent much of his career under mounting pressure to cut costs, he was free from pressure to consider the financial profitability of the buildings he designed. When I visited his apartment in Housing Complex 2, he pointed to the greenery outside, describing how the landscaped courtyard lent the complex a parklike atmosphere. He also told me to pay attention to the relatively low population density, which reflected the fact that the city center was built with maximal concern for residents' quality of life. Later Housing Complexes were constrained by the obligation to construct *Plattenbauten*, while capitalist neighborhoods, Härtel explained, were constrained by the architect's need to provide a return on investment. Neither resembled Eisenhüttenstadt's city center.

He described further aspects of the socialist emic implemented in the city's design: the fact that main streets have a gentle curve to avoid visual monotony and that residential buildings were arranged with attention to cardinal and wind direction, which, in addition to adequate spacing, allows for maximal sunlight and air circulation. "No one sees this, no one knows this," he said, referring to the environmental and experiential considerations that went into the design of the city center. But "architecture's impacts are in the social well-being of residents." He compared the mindset of a capitalist architect, who would be concerned about profit, with the socialist architect, who was concerned with residents' economy of time. Härtel seemed to imply that the full personhood at the center of the architect's imagination might not be perceptible to residents as such but was perhaps felt as they inhabited the Housing Complex in the course of everyday life.

As much as infrastructures manage the circulation of resources, they also define resources as such, creating boundaries between an ecological environment and the technologies perceived as being embedded within it (Scott 1999, 13). Christina Schwenkel (2018, 113) notes that in Vinh, Vietnam, a city designed in large part by East German architects and planners, "the ecological was positioned as symbiotic with the infrastructural, rather than external to it." Schwenkel credits this to "a trend in Vietnamese urbanism to view the elemental forces of nature as integral to and constitutive of the city, rather than as rural or green matter out of place." But perhaps it also reflects the tendency of East German planners to harness natural forces as instruments of human well-being—the free gift (Bataille [1967] 1989, 28) of renewable resources.

Härtel, in an essay about designing Housing Complex 5, writes that as per a 1960 decision by the federal government, the city would be obligated to build tower blocks in the new Housing Complex. At the time, the area had four-story apartments built by the EWG. It would soon have rows of twelve-story P2s—but it would not be a barren monotony. Härtel writes of the design of Complex 5, "Some elements of urban design that had previously received little attention were used more strongly. The position of the buildings in relation to cardinal directions is nearly perfect: the majority of living rooms will face southwest, while bedrooms, kitchens, and bathrooms are predominantly northeast facing," thereby maximizing access to sunlight at appropriate times of day. The view would also provide visual interest, as "the entire neighborhood opens up toward the most appealing parts of the Stalinstadt landscape, a backdrop formed by Diehlo Hill, with its lush vegetation, and the parks [on Leisure Time Island] behind the apartment building yards, which will convey, despite the relatively narrow space between buildings, the impression of living 'in the green'" (Härtel, n.d., 13). In 2020, Härtel reiterated this point when he told the local newspaper that because there was no existing street grid when he designed Housing Complex 5, he was able to freely choose the buildings' cardinal orientations. "It was because of this approach that Housing Complex 5 had the lowest turnover rate in the city," he said. "People stay in place when they're satisfied with their apartments" (Neiser 2020).

Similar environmental considerations were also essential to the relative locations of the city and its steelworks. As many informants told me, and as documents attest, the steelworks and city were arranged such that the factory's exhaust would be blown away from the city and into neighboring Poland. (While the border region is lightly populated, GDR planners did not take Polish welfare into account [Gansleweit 1986, 13].) But environmental considerations also took place on a smaller, more human scale. When plans were underway for Housing Complex 7 in 1982, the regional urban planning office in Frankfurt Oder issued a set of architectural revisions based on its assessment of the Housing Complex's sun exposure. The apartments on the second floors of Apartment Blocks (Wohnhäuser) 16, 20, and 25 had a twenty-minute "sunlight deficit" and would remain unchanged. But the apartments on the bottom three floors of Blockhouse 6, each with a thirty-five-minute sunlight deficit, would be redesigned "as community rooms for elderly residents or a similar purpose" (Büro für Städtebau Frankfurt Oder 1982).

The Group had met in the community room of one of the four remaining Blockhouses, though other Blockhouses have since been demolished (Lötsch 2020a). But the 1982 report stated that the Blockhouse apartments with thirty-five-minute deficits, as well as four apartments in other buildings with ninety-minute deficits and three that received no direct sunlight at all, would all become community spaces (Büro für Städtebau Frankfurt Oder 1982). The Group owed its existence, at least in part, to an architectural emic that was centered on a fully realized human being, one who needed access to sunlight—a resident who occupied space, rather than one who existed merely to transform space into an instrument of capitalist extraction.

The Subbotnik

Of course, the continued use of social infrastructures such as community rooms requires a populace willing to perceive them as such. Many of Eisenhüttenstadt's apartment buildings have communal spaces that are now informally used as storage for tenants, while others have been converted into penthouse apartments. When I visited Helga's building on Linden Avenue in 2015, the room where residents once prepared refreshments for parties was filled with patio furniture and other bulky, infrequently used items. Yet as the city center becomes repopulated and the city revitalized, the civic landscape has changed as well.

I first met Martin Maleschka in 2016, when our mutual friend Ben Kaden invited us to take photographs of the city's architecture. Martin is a photographer, architect, and Eisenhüttenstadt native, and his professional goal is to rehabilitate the public reputation of East German urban design. His architectural photography, which focuses on East German public art, has been widely exhibited at galleries across Germany, including at the Museum of Utopia and the Everyday. Both Ben and Martin, now in their early forties, have a deep respect for their city, and they would later display the photographs from our outing in a temporary exhibition, installed in an empty storefront as part of that year's City Festival. Both, however, lived elsewhere, Ben in Berlin and Martin in Cottbus, a nearby university town. And both recognized that their hometown, despite its positive attributes, was also facing its share of challenges—a widespread viewpoint at the time.

Youth Square had been the bustling center of Housing Complex 5, a large courtyard between the former grocery store and Juri Gagarin High School, which once served the neighborhood of close to six thousand residents. But the supermarket had not survived reunification, and the school shut down in 2009. At Youth Square, an elderly couple stopped us to engage in familiar griping. "What an eyesore," one of them said. Ben pointed out the landlord's West German area code, indicated by the phone number on a sign nailed to the plywood, which had narrowly escaped the abundant graffiti. The paving stones in the square were in haphazard disarray, and rust covered its sculptural metal dividing walls. In a colonnaded courtyard, wild saplings grew on the roof of a covered walkway, close to five feet high. Ben, Martin, and I walked around Housing Complex 5, where rows of *Plattenbauten* had been demolished over the previous decade. We found a front door ajar in one of the remaining high-rises and climbed the stairwell to get a better view of the empty space below. The resulting photographs had panoramic views of the surrounding area, but they also gawk at ruination, as the high-rise building towers incongruously over wide swaths of open space.

When I next saw Martin in 2023, he had moved to Eisenhüttenstadt, where he now lives on the top floor of the building we had explored years earlier. Although the building, one of the city's older and more vacant, had not been renovated, Martin arranged with the GeWi to have the apartment renovated before he moved in, and he loved the light and the expansive views—a testament to the success of Härtel's design choices. We discussed our shared excitement over the city's revitalization—the state of the renovated city center and the growing public interest in the city's utopian origins, as evidenced by the Museum of Utopia and the Everyday and the *Between Model and Museum* symposia. Hotel Lunik had recently been purchased by the city, and Martin was its unofficial ambassador, having worked with city leadership to conduct guided tours of the abandoned building.

Martin also told me about his *Subbotnik*, and as he did, he said he could feel goosebumps rising on his neck. *Subbotniks*, based on the Russian word for "Saturday," were an Eastern Bloc tradition where people gathered to perform volunteer labor in a collectively used space. In 2020, Youth Square was placed under historic preservation, and in 2023, Martin held his Subbotnik there on May 1, Labor Day. The project was a joint initiative between Martin, the Museum of Utopia and the Everyday, Oder-Spree County, and the Eisenhüttenstadt city government, and it was funded as part of a Brandenburg State arts initiative called "Living Building Culture" (Baukultur Leben) (Neiser 2023c). It was also organized in cooperation with the GeWi and EWG, and with young people via the city's high school (*Gesamtschule*), postsecondary school (*Fachschule*), and two youth clubs (Kulturland Brandenburg 2023, 12), many of whom showed up to participate. Shortly before the Subbotnik, stonemasons renovated Youth Square's paved surface (Neiser 2023d). On May 1, over two hundred Eisenhüttenstädters helped clean up the square, clearing away wheelbarrows full of weeds and rubble. Over the following months, the Museum of Utopia and the Everyday held a series of temporary outdoor exhibitions in the newly habitable space. The

FIGURE 57. Youth Square, 2015. Photograph by the author.

FIGURE 58. View from the high-rise in Housing Complex 5, 2015. Photograph by the author.

program started with a day of architectural tours and talks with artists, curators, and municipal leaders (Neiser 2023d). Then came a daylong series of dance performances—youth dance is a popular activity in Eisenhüttenstadt—followed by a participatory children's theater event. At ten o'clock at night, there was a drum and bass concert in the abandoned swimming pool of Juri Gagarin High School, followed by a series of sets by five DJs (Stadt Eisenhüttenstadt 2023).

The local newspaper reported that while a number of municipal leaders were in attendance for the Subbotnik's kickoff, Mayor Frank Balzer was over an hour late—he had been on Leisure Time Island for the beginning of the Metalworkers' Union Labor Day Festival (Neiser 2023e). The reporter, Janet Neiser, suggested that while some considered it inappropriate to hold an event that might compete with the union's annual festival, those in attendance believed that the volunteer labor suited the ethos of the holiday (Neiser 2023e). The two events underscored the complementary nature of the factory and the city, entities that operated somewhat autonomously but that were also inextricably intertwined. Yet while the fate of Eisenhüttenstadt's steelworks is tied primarily to ArcelorMittal, the fate of the city is in large part tied to its cultural leadership, and to the citizens who engage with local efforts. As residents collectively celebrate the city's utopian origins in places like Youth Square and the Museum of Utopia and the Everyday, they are also reenacting and perpetuating a culture of communitarianism whose origins are located in the construction of those same spaces.

An Invisible Border

East German urbanists perceived a binary distinction between housing as a social good and housing as a commodity. This distinction explains, in part, why private property continued to exist in East Germany, as elsewhere in the Eastern Bloc, and why collectively held state property conformed to a similar logic of ownership. Ownership in this context was synonymous with exclusive use, rather than the right to profit financially from one's holding (Strathern [2002] 2022; Humphrey 2002b; Cherkaev 2023). During the socialist era, East Germans mapped this division onto that of East Germany, where housing was intended to foster citizens' well-being, and West Germany, where human well-being was ancillary to the pursuit of capitalist value. But since reunification, this binary has been "fractally" reproduced (Gal 2002, 79; Gal and Irvine 2019, 19) in Eisenhüttenstadt, most visibly in the form of housing for asylum seekers. In 2015, as asylees from Syria and elsewhere began to enter Germany in record numbers,[4] the distinction between social and commodified housing became newly visible within the city.

In December 2015, a new playground went up nearly overnight on the grounds of what locals called the AWO dormitory. The charity Workers' Wellness (Arbeiterwohlfahrt, or AWO) had recently rented the unused dormitory as an overflow facility for the Central Foreigners' Reception Center (Zentrale Ausländerbehörde, or ZABH), in coordination with Oder-Spree County (Lötsch 2023b). When an asylum seeker enters Germany, they are assigned to temporary housing in one of the country's sixteen states. Brandenburg takes 3 percent of asylum seekers and has one facility—the ZABH in Eisenhüttenstadt—where people live short-term upon arrival (BAMF 2022). But in 2015, the ZABH had a capacity of around five hundred, and by July, around two thousand new residents were arriving each month (Lötsch 2015; Neiser 2015). The military set up tents, donated by the US Army, and built temporary barracks on Leisure Time Island. In the fall, state officials moved around three hundred people into the AWO dormitory, all families with children (Lötsch 2023b)—hence the playground.

During my fieldwork, I rented an apartment on Karl Marx Street, across the street from the AWO dormitory. From my window, I could see the swing set and monkey bars that had been erected next to the building's entrance. But from my front door, I could see another playground—a larger swing set and monkey bars, along with a seating area and concrete ping-pong table—in my apartment building's courtyard. Indeed, were it not for the presence of my building, which could be easily circumvented, the two playgrounds would have appeared directly across the street from one another; the distance between them could not have been more than fifty yards. But as the new playground went up, I was unsurprised by the redundancy. While the city's existing playgrounds had originally been built as "social condensers" (Murawksi and Rendell 2017),[5] it was already clear that asylum seekers were both spatially and socially marginalized—a position that, while imposed from without, was also reproduced by asylum seekers themselves. Despite the city's abundant public space, asylum seekers tended to gather in supermarket parking lots or in patches of uncultivated pine forest along the city's periphery. AWO dormitory residents made frequent use of their playground but seemed never to use the larger, more elaborate playground across the street.

Indeed, the edge of the historically protected zone acted as an invisible, informal boundary that dormitory residents did not cross. The apartment buildings along Karl Marx Street are positioned with their entryways facing the interior courtyard, while along the street is a strip of grass, more berm than lawn, between the building exteriors and the sidewalk. As the weather warmed in the spring of 2016, I frequently noticed residents of the dormitory eating meals or simply socializing on the berm next to the sidewalk, their backs to the buildings' exteriors. Karl Marx Street forms part of a B-grade highway, making its berm

FIGURE 59. The courtyard playground, 2016. Photograph by the author.

a particularly unpleasant place to spend one's time, especially given the unrestricted access to nearby courtyards.

The self-positioning of dormitory residents seemed to reflect a recursive identification with the "virtual" city (Langer 1957, 102; Douglas 1991, 292; Lynch 1964), an image of their place within the city made manifest in their spatial ordering. Anthropologists have long noted that spatial organization reflects elements of social organization (Bourdieu 1977; Keane 1995), and these interstitial, liminal spaces appeared available for use to people whose social position was also marginal. Sites such as the berm along Karl Marx Street were not simply peripheral; they were not even perceived as social spaces by the larger populace. But residents of the AWO dormitory stayed in Eisenhüttenstadt only temporarily—usually for around six weeks—and seemed not to access a sense of "rights to the city" (Lefebvre 1968; Harvey 2013), given the brevity and circumstances of their stay. Scholars note that housing for asylum seekers tends to exist in a state of permanent temporariness, which can disincentivize the development of a long-term future through investment in one's immediate surroundings (Ramsay 2020; Morris 2023).

Around the time that the playground was built, however, asylum seekers who were further along in their asylum process began to be housed in vacant apartments throughout the city. These apartments were rented by Oder-Spree County, which also paid the utility bills, and were administered by AWO.[6] Social workers furnished the apartments, mostly with secondhand items, and oversaw residents' housing assignments—often this involved moving pieces of paper around a whiteboard to make sure that roommates had compatible ages, language skills, and national backgrounds. Yet while some asylum seekers sought to fully express the rights entailed by apartment living,[7] others came up against the limits of rights that were merely illusory.

A City of Newcomers

I first met Basma in 2015, when she and her family were in temporary housing, sleeping on cots in the high school gym. Basma was an educated English speaker in her forties who had fled Syria around four years prior with her brother, husband, and three children. That October, her family was assigned an apartment in the building next door to my own, where they would stay until their asylum application was decided, likely another two or three months. Despite these limits, when I visited for the first time I found an apartment that seemed thoroughly lived in. The fourth-floor walk-up had two bedrooms, a kitchen, and a living room off a narrow hallway, with natural light coming in through casement windows, typical of apartments in the older parts of Complex 1. Basma told me how relieved she was to be settled after so many years in transit, and she led me from room to room showing me the things she had acquired in an effort to make the apartment feel like home: a box grater, a paper floor lamp, a pink tablecloth cinched with a rubber band, a clock on the living room bookshelf, beneath which was a stuffed bear wearing a T-shirt with the German flag. She served me tea and chocolates and told me that her brother was coming over later to repair the washing machine—the "continual vigilance" of making home (Douglas 1991, 305). As we chatted, she began to tell me about the beautiful waterfront views that were visible from her former home in Syria. Her family had lived there for only a year before escalating violence forced them to flee the country. "Now I try to think as if I never had that house. I don't ever think about that house," she said, implying that the memory would be too painful.

Yet here she was, not only thinking about that house but describing it to me as a key detail about her former life. While the development of home is not contingent on housing, housing can offer an essential anchor for the imagination of home, a process that begins, according to anthropologist Mary Douglas, by "bringing some space under control" (Douglas 1991, 289). But home is defined primarily by the social production of the household—a slice of urban space carved out through daily praxis in concert with the "virtual" (Langer 1957, 102), existing at the nexus between the material and the imagined. Douglas (1991,

FIGURE 60.   The mosaic *Our New Life*, by Walter Womacka (1958), located in the lobby of City Hall, 2016. Photograph by the author.

293–96) notes that the household produces its own temporality—not only its own daily rhythms but also a longer-term future evoked through its budgeting and storage, an incipient version of the commons. As such, home is also at the center of concentric circles of imagined belonging—household, neighborhood, nation—as well as nested scales of cyclical time. As Basma attended to her home with attention and care, she also constructed new circles of belonging and futurity that might come to coexist with the ones she left behind.

Moreover, Basma's acts of homemaking constituted an exercise of her right to fully inhabit the apartment on Karl Marx Street, to act on and in the city (Harvey 2013), starting with her home. The apartment offered her municipal recognition; even as an AWO subtenant, Basma could register her address, and, most importantly, her children could go to the local public school. But it also authorized her to take part in the everyday practices of habitation. I often ran into Basma outside the building, and her youngest son played on the courtyard playground. When he received a donated tricycle, his mother would let him ride it only in circles around the playground's perimeter—the boundary formed by Karl Marx Street also operated from within the courtyard. When the family's asylum application was approved, they made an arrangement through their social worker to take over the lease from the county, enabling them to stay long-term.

Basma's experience represented the fulfillment of an essential component of Eisenhüttenstadt's original vision: the full incorporation (McKowen and Borneman 2020) of migrants into the social body.[8] In 2014, the Documentation Center for Everyday Life in East Germany held an exhibition called *Arrival Eisenhüttenstadt: A City Founded by Immigrants*, which emphasized the city's role as a melting pot for people from various parts of Germany and Eastern Europe. When the city was founded in 1950, around 30 percent of the population were naturalized East German citizens, displaced from Eastern Europe by World War II. Yet the exhibition catalog emphasized the fact that, as Eisenhüttenstadt was a newly founded city, all of its early residents had necessarily relocated from elsewhere—even if some came only from nearby villages. As curator Axel Drieschner (2015, 6) wrote in the catalog, "Moving to a new city brings with it a complete reorientation to everyday life," no matter the distance from one's point of origin.

But during the socialist era, migrants occupied a starkly different set of social, political, and spatial positions than they do at present. Citizens who made reference to histories of displacement from Eastern Europe, such as those recounted in *Arrival Eisenhüttenstadt*, could be punished with up to eight years in prison; such references were perceived as a threat to East Germany's alliance with the Soviet Union (Schwartz 2008; Fox 2024). At the same time, immigrants from the Global South were publicly celebrated on postage stamps and in public art as icons of transnational socialist solidarity. A monumental mosaic in Eisenhüttenstadt's City Hall depicts Black and Asian socialists alongside their white comrades, as does stained glass in what is now the Museum of Utopia and the Everyday.

In reality, East Germany's immigration policy was decidedly less generous than its depictions of the "racial rainbow" would suggest (Slobodian 2015). In the 1960s, East Germany began offering three-to-five-year work visas to immigrants from Poland and Hungary, and in the 1970s it offered them to immigrants from Vietnam, Cuba, Angola, Algeria, and Mozambique, but migrants' social integration was tightly constrained (Poutrus 2005). Perhaps most notably, a 1987 treaty between East Germany and Vietnam stipulated that Vietnamese women who became pregnant while living in East Germany must either terminate their pregnancy or leave the country (Beyme 2020, 64). Nonetheless, some East Germans took transnational socialism seriously. At a town hall meeting in 2015, an elderly resident shouted that the city should support asylum seekers because "in Eisenhüttenstadt, we were once a city where solidarity was our highest priority." Other elderly attendees erupted in cheers.

During the socialist era, however, asylum rights originated not with the asylum applicant, as they do in Germany today, but rather with the state (Poutrus 2014). East Germany had a tightly controlled, militarized border, though its primary purpose was to prevent East Germans from leaving to seek asylum abroad. (This irony was not lost on Eisenhüttenstädters, who frequently joked that the efforts that migrants made to get into the country in 2015 mirrored the efforts that East Germans had once made to get out.) Asylum for foreigners in East Germany was overseen by the SED Politburo, which identified politically advantageous groups to whom asylum would be extended: in the 1950s, Greek and Spanish Communists, in the 1970s, Chileans who were expelled following Pinochet's coup. In Eisenhüttenstadt, Chilean asylees were housed in Hotel Lunik to indicate their elevated status within the body politic (Käthner 1980).

Housing for asylum seekers is now often defined by its difference from other forms of social housing, as migrants seeking asylum are often perceived as exceptional, set apart from other groups in need of shelter (Ramsay 2020). Their housing must be spare (people coming from elsewhere have not paid local taxes) but still humane, and most of all, it must be temporary, like the asylum process itself—or at least appear to offer temporary habitation in the form of dormitories, barracks, flat-pack and container houses (Morris 2023; Baumann 2020; Steigemann and Misselwitz 2020), or the tents that have traditionally populated refugee camps. It should appear as housing stripped down to its barest essential: shelter. As such, it offers its rotating sets of inhabitants the conditions of "bare life" (Agamben 1998) so often perceived as the foundation of "refugee-ness" (Malkki 1992, 35).

For residents of the AWO dormitory, the duplicated playground served as a reminder that their habitation operated in a register that was fundamentally distinct from that of their immediate neighbors. While many of my acquaintances saw the playground as a sign of AWO's sensitivity to asylum seekers' needs—and, indeed, the playground was well used and seemingly enjoyed—it also eliminated any ambiguity as to whether dormitory residents had a right to use the playground across the street. There was one set of rights for people who occupied the dormitory, and another for people who occupied the commodified real estate of the Housing Complex, whose habitation was a key priority for city leadership.

An Embryonic Community

As a volunteer with AWO, I occasionally helped social workers with tasks related to housing for asylum seekers. In February 2016, I was asked to help an Afghan family move out of one of the AWO apartments. The mother, father, and three school-age children had come up against a fractal reproduction (Gal 2002, 79; Gal and Irvine 2019, 19) of the binary between commodity and social good, as they inhabited their apartment not as customers but as wards of the state. The family seemed in good spirits as they loaded their suitcases into a van, but after they left, social workers explained that there had been trouble with the neighbors. It was not racially motivated, they insisted, but rather stemmed from the problem of night work.

Eisenhüttenstadt's steel plant runs continuously, and Eisenhüttenstädters who work the night shift can become irritable when woken up by neighbors not sensitive to their needs. I had recently borne the brunt of this anger myself when visiting a friend who, unbeknownst to me, shared a last name with a night-shift worker in his building. Not knowing that there were two doorbells with my friend's name, I repeatedly buzzed the doorbell for the night-shift worker, and when I arrived inside the building, I received an earful about my rude behavior— I should have known better than to ring a doorbell repeatedly, lest I disrupt a night-shift worker's sleep.

I gathered that something similar had happened to the Afghan family. A night-shift worker lived below them, and the children kept him awake as they played in the apartment during the day. It would be weeks before they could start school, and even then, they would be home by early afternoon. The neighbor complained to the GeWi, which relayed the complaints to AWO. Then a guest house on a rural property became available, and social workers agreed that it would be a more suitable home for the Afghan family—their children would have more room to play, and the move would resolve the ongoing strife with the neighbor. The AWO would make the apartment into a flat-share for four adult women, who were more likely to be compatible neighbors for the night-shift worker.

The social workers told me that people in Eisenhüttenstadt simply weren't used to living in apartment buildings with children—German children, too, would likely have garnered complaints from this neighbor. But it is difficult to imagine German children relocating in short order as a result of these complaints. German children's housing was not determined by social workers moving slips of paper around a whiteboard. The rights of their paying guardians might have come up against the rights of the night-shift worker to protected sleep, introducing friction to a conflict whose easy resolution, in the case of the Afghan family, was the result only of an imbalanced power dynamic.

Mary Douglas (1991, 288) examines the home in order to ask, "What makes solidarity possible?" She finds that the home is "an embryonic community," the site where nested, place-based notions of virtual belonging are first cultivated, and where the value of solidarity is first experienced in the collective management of household resources. As a household develops into a virtual community, its goal "is to achieve enough solidarity to protect the collective good" (Douglas 1991, 299). But what constitutes the collective good? And more importantly, who is included in the imagination of collective publics, which by their virtual nature exist for us as unarticulated affect (Fennell 2015, 7)? As of 2023, Eisenhüttenstadt had about 1,200 foreign-born residents, up from 760 in 2021 (Lötsch 2023b). At the same time, the strength of the far-right party Alternative for Germany (Alternativ fur Deutschland, or AfD) has risen sharply. In the 2013 parliamentary election, the AfD did not rank (Amt für Statistik Berlin-Brandenburg 2020, 50). In 2017 and 2021, it received nearly a quarter of Eisenhüttenstadt's votes (Landeswahlleiter Brandenburg 2021).[9]

In light of the local cultural engagement with mid-century utopianism, it is also essential that we examine the solidarity that can be cultivated in the nested collectives of the apartment building, the Housing Complex, and the city. While the Group was extremely welcoming to me, with members inviting me to their homes on numerous occasions, I was a PhD student, not an asylee, and I occupied a position of relative privilege. Basma hoped that her children would become integrated into the city's social networks when they started school, but when I visited in 2023, I found that another family had moved into their apartment. The Subbotnik in Youth Square sought to cultivate solidarity by enabling local youths to inhabit their city's socialist legacy, not only as they contributed to the cleanup but as they partied in an abandoned swimming pool while music played until early morning. By producing such social interactions, the Subbotnik also provided a set of concerns and a worldview that young people could appreciate as their cultural heritage—an alternative to right-wing culture. Eisenhüttenstadt's politics currently skew left, and since reunification the city government has been consistently traded among the mainstream liberal parties the Left (Die Linke), the Social Democrats (Sozialdemokratische Partei Deutschlands), and the Christian Democrats (Christlich Demokratische Union). But political fortunes can change quickly. And as the last century has shown, solidarity can be a fragile arrangement.

6

A MODEL OF TRANSFORMATION

Ecological economics suggests that climate change is in fact a cultural dilemma. As anthropologists assert, human beings have been living on this planet for hundreds of thousands of years, and most cultures prior to industrial modernity conceived of a way to do so that still allowed for the continued habitability of the environment. Economist Tim Jackson suggests that we might avert climate catastrophe by developing a new understanding of "prosperity" in the Global North. To achieve this, government and industry must sever the relationship between human flourishing and environmental degradation by decoupling economic growth from environmental harm (Jackson 2016, 158). As Amartya Sen's seminal work established, individuals cannot be relied on to solve the climate crisis through sheer willpower to consume less—"enough" is a baseline that shifts in different social contexts (Sen 1984). As the twentieth century has shown, a chicken for every pot soon becomes a laptop for every child, and even the chicken may not have been a sustainable goal.

Yet, says Jackson, if we are to believe that the limits to economic growth are only the limits of human ingenuity, let us imagine an economy in which human flourishing does not run counter to economic growth. Perhaps this is an economy in which care work is highly valued—perhaps at the behest of government—and thus the improvement of labor productivity among teachers, nurses, and social workers becomes reflected in calculations of economic output (Jackson 2016, 152). Perhaps this is an economy in which a decline in income inequality has led to increased leisure time, which in turn has reduced carbon emissions. (Jackson [2016, 193] notes that leisure activities tend to have a relatively low carbon

FIGURE 61. Steel prepared for shipment in the ArcelorMittal facility, 2015. Photograph by the author.

footprint.) This is not the economy that we currently live in. But we might take steps toward enacting it through policy decisions that decouple human flourishing from resource extraction. To return to ideas put forth in the introduction, this would mean paying attention to the relationship between ultimate ends and ultimate means in a world where most of the economy is focused on the intermediate (Daly [1973] 1980).

Eisenhüttenstadt's developments since the turn of the millennium provide one such model for improving human flourishing while diminishing resource extraction. This has not been done in the pursuit of ecologically responsible governance—or any other ideological motivator, city leaders have been quick to tell me. In 2023, shortly before her retirement, Verena Rühr-Bach called the city "small but great"—it rhymes in German, *klein aber fein*—though she insisted that city leadership had no aspiration to become so, as if I might mistake *klein aber fein* for the proud slogan of sustainable shrinkage. Rather, they had simply responded to a series of challenges—rising vacancy, an aging population, old debt—as best they could. Others in city leadership expressed a similar sentiment, noting that the city's socialist legacies, such as proprietary simplicity and the Housing Complex, have been retained in part due to historical contingencies that could well have turned out differently. Carbon-reduction efforts respond to national policy, as Germany aims to become "carbon-neutral" by 2045.[1] And yet, as they are, the developments of the 2010s represent a fundamental shift in the city's trajectory. Recall that socialist-era population projections estimated that Eisenhüttenstadt would have 110,000 inhabitants by the turn of the twenty-first century (Heilmeyer 2021, 19). Today's city of around 25,000 represents a fortuitous preservation of socialist urbanism's humane impulses without the growth mania that characterized the socialist era.

Here I consider urban developments in terms of ecological economics, examining how the consolidation of urban space minimizes the flow of throughput, a key instrument for severing the relationship between resource extraction and human flourishing. Such efforts are motivated by and contribute to long-standing cultural attention to throughput in the form of heat. As heating technologies have changed, citizens have become attuned to improving heat's durability through practices aimed at different stages of heat's journey as throughput: the human labor expended on coal stoves (*Ofenheizung*), the financial cost of natural gas, and the environmental toll of heat as the source of carbon emissions. I also examine ongoing efforts, in place since 2021, to transform Eisenhüttenstadt's steel facility into one of the world's first carbon-neutral steel manufacturing sites by 2050. These developments stand to have a significant impact not only on the city's imagined longevity but also on the emissions output of the German economy at large (Hirschl et al. 2023, 103).

Eisenhüttenstadt's plan for carbon-neutral heat by 2050, however, relies on the continued production of off-gas from the steelworks, which will cease to be produced as the blast furnace is converted to direct reduced iron (DRI). The dilemma speaks to the devil's bargains that must be made in the imposition of externalities, particularly as the stark reduction in carbon emissions across the German industrial sector masks the ongoing environmental harms of industrial resource extraction and the consumerism that it generates. In 2015, the city looked excitedly toward its soon-to-be-realized carbon neutrality, despite its planned expansion of heat sourced from blast-furnace outputs. "The goal of a CO_2-free district is, with our efforts, absolutely realizable by 2050," the Energy Renovation plan promised. "Eisenhüttenstadt, once the first New Town in the GDR, could today make a name for itself as a model city for urban structural transformation (based on the INSEK), and the Energy Transition" (Mann et al. 2015, xii).

Minimizing Throughput

As Urban Renewal projects were underway in the 2010s, so, too, were simultaneous efforts to reduce the city's carbon emissions. In 2015, in response to growing political pressure at the state, federal, and European Union levels,[2] the

FIGURES 62A, 62B, AND 62C. Residents respond to the consolidation of urban space. A 2004 postcard depicts Housing Complex 7 (*top*). Courtesy of Ben Kaden. Gudrun Hankowiak documents her courtyard in Housing Complex 7 shortly before its demolition (*middle*), early 2000s. Courtesy of Gudrun Hankowiak. A visitor to the former site of Housing Complex 7 (*bottom*), 2014. Photograph by the author.

city developed an Energy Renovation plan, with detailed instructions for how to lower the emissions associated with each one of the city's buildings. The plan was conceived as a complement to the 2014 comprehensive urban development plan (INSEK) and 2015 urban renewal plan (STUK), which outlined the city's large-scale demolitions and renovations. As Gabrielle Haubold, the former director of Urban Renewal, explained, by demolishing outlying areas and reconsolidating urban space around the central axis of Linden Avenue, the city could achieve multiple, interconnected goals that contributed to a reduction in environmental harm. The city would operate a smaller urban footprint, while its citizens would get around on foot or bicycle and expend less energy on heat. The Energy Renovation plan offered guidelines for how to maximize energy efficiency in renovated buildings and expand access to "*Hüttengas*," a term coined by the authors to describe off-gas from the steelworks, considered a carbon-neutral heating source. The plan highlighted these simultaneous efforts—the repopulation of the city center, the energy-efficient renovation of individual buildings, and the expansion of Hüttengas—as key to achieving carbon neutrality in the heating and electricity sectors by 2050.

Haubold was not the sole author of the Energy Renovation plan, but she was instrumental in its development, and it reflects her pride in the city's origins. Haubold's father, Herbert Härtel, served as the chief architect from 1958 to 1968, though in our many conversations she never revealed as much. Instead she focused on her decades of professional investment in the city, which spanned the eras of growth and shrinkage. Haubold worked as an architect on the team that designed Housing Complex 7 in the 1980s, and she oversaw its demolition when Urban Renewal East began in the early 2000s. Yet throughout, she also retained a reverence for the sense of collective possibility that she experienced in early childhood. In an essay about Housing Complex 6, Haubold writes from the perspective of an anonymous little girl who moves to Eisenhüttenstadt from a city where the houses are old and gray, and who is impressed by the "brightness" of the new Housing Complex. The girl's father leads her around an unfinished apartment building and points out the future sites of the library, post office, shops, and schools—"Totally modern," she thinks of the prefabricated concrete construction, parroting her father's language. Hüttengas would soon make hot water available around the clock and eliminate the daily hassles of coal heating (Haubold 1999, 188).

In the decades since Eisenhüttenstadt was founded, sensibilities about what constitutes a modern apartment have changed considerably. For instance, the Energy Renovation plan notes, during the GDR era, kitchens were small workspaces, whereas now they are central gathering places in the home; bathrooms were mere water closets, and guest bathrooms, once a rare luxury, are now

commonly sought after. As such, the plan stresses the importance of combining
the city center's small apartments into fewer, larger ones—this is why the renovations in Housing Complex 1, carried out in 2022, roughly doubled the size of
apartments from an average of 50 square meters (540 square feet) to 95 square
meters (1,022 square feet) (BBU 2021). But in 2015, such plans were only recently
underway. The Energy Renovation plan notes that "a highly insulated building
equipped with the latest technology is only energy efficient if efficient use is also
guaranteed." Despite a "compact spatial structure," Eisenhüttenstadt's residential
areas, particularly the city center, suffered from "unused and unheated apartments that worsen[ed] the buildings' energy balance" (Mann et al. 2015, 13).
A comprehensive analysis of heat-energy expenditures showed that buildings
with vacancy rates over 50 percent consumed around three times as much energy
per square meter as those with vacancy rates below 10 percent. In one particularly egregious example, an unrenovated building in Housing Complex 1, with
89 percent vacancy, consumed twenty times as much energy as nearby buildings with lower vacancy rates and basic insulation (4–7).[3] City officials would
have to increase the population density in order to minimize collective energy
expenditures.

In order to do so, the Energy Renovation plan turns to the Sixteen Principles
of Urban Planning, which are "made manifest in the city" (Mann et al. 2015, 16),
a recognition of latent possibility. Eisenhüttenstadt's role as "the first planned
city of the German Democratic Republic, under socialist auspices, is inextricably
tied to the goal of creating high-quality living spaces for workers" (16). Under
socialism, such spaces were compact, walkable, and intended to promote serendipitous interactions. Yet the quality of living space is defined by both social
and material concerns, and by the qualities of one's home as well as those of the
surrounding area. The Housing Complex's proportions are a unique asset, the
report explains. Ample green spaces and wide landscaped courtyards mitigate
summer heat, while the city's ratio of greenery to residents—eighty square meters
per resident, double the German national average of forty square meters (430
square feet)—has a positive effect on residents' physical and psychological well-
being. In a 2012 survey, close to 90 percent of residents said they felt comfortable
(*Wohlfühlen*) in their neighborhood. Only 65 percent, however, said they were
satisfied with the material condition of their apartment (Mann et al. 2015, 20). At
the time, 220 apartment buildings were slated for renovation in the coming years
(Stadt Eisenhüttenstadt and BBSM 2015, 62–63).[4] The Energy Renovation plan
stressed not only the importance of these renovations but also the need for them
to be undertaken in a way that maximized energy efficiency.

Thus, the GeWi, EWG, and city government worked together to analyze the
relative impacts of energy-efficiency efforts that had been implemented since

the 1990s. Their analysis showed the differential energy usage of buildings with various renovation measures (new doors and windows, facade insulation, different roof and cellar insulations, and combinations thereof) and informed efforts to improve energy efficiency as further renovations were carried out. The Energy Renovation plan noted that private landlords were excluded from the study, as they did not collect analogous data, highlighting the importance of cooperation between the three entities. It also noted the challenges posed by historic preservation, which limited the city's ability to install cost-effective insulation on buildings' exteriors (Mann et al. 2015, 53–55).

Indeed, insulation was seen as essential to the financial viability of the renovation projects. Some of the renovation costs would be reflected in tenants' rent, and city officials were keen to keep residents' utility bills down such that their overall monthly expenses remained within financial reach—particularly given the large proportion of elderly residents on meager incomes. Thus, the Energy Renovation plan described how city leadership would balance capital investments with projected monthly utility costs, noting that, for instance, the expansion of Hüttengas would help mitigate utility expenses for residents as buildings transitioned away from costly electric water-heating systems (Mann et al. 2015, 48–49). Since the plan's publication, both heat and electricity have become increasingly expensive in Germany, and the conservation of energy has only become a greater concern. The GeWi's winter 2023 newsletter highlights renovations in the city center aimed at improving heat efficiency. Descriptions of new windows, roof insulation, and cellar insulation are illustrated with side-by-side photos of an uninsulated exterior and a building swathed in construction tarps where exterior insulation was being installed—the historic preservation board having apparently conceded to the increasing cost of energy and the urgency of the climate crisis (GeWi 2023, 10).

Taken together, the demolition and renovation efforts speak to the work of sustainable shrinkage and right-sizing, minimizing what economists call "throughput": the transformation of natural resources into economic outputs and a natural correlate of urban sprawl. As noted above, individuals living in a sparsely populated apartment building expend more energy on heat without the added insulation of neighbors, and cities must still provide utilities and other municipal services to neighborhoods with high vacancy rates. The maintenance of such biopolitical infrastructures—the delivery of water, heat, electricity, and sanitation services—is often a key intermediary between resource extraction and human flourishing, and the efficient operation of such infrastructures is therefore key to achieving ecologically economic urban governance.

This attention to throughput attunes us to the relationship between ultimate ends and ultimate means. Rather than develop a political economy devoted to serving intermediate ends, Herman Daly ([1973] 1980, 11) suggests that we practice "ultimate political economy, or *stewardship*," in which we maintain awareness of how ultimate means (the environment) serve ultimate ends (human flourishing). Stewardship is based on John Stuart Mill's stationary state and resembles Jackson's redefined prosperity.[5] All three conceptions of urban thriving share a commitment to equitably distributing resources and curtailing heedless consumption. Resource depletion is understood as something that should serve humans rather than capital and that should be undertaken when its utility—its impact on human well-being—is highest (Jackson 2009; Daly [1973] 1980).

The image of a walkable, energy-efficient city center, where residents live in spacious apartments rather than energy-consuming single-family homes, speaks to a newfound awareness of ultimate means and ultimate ends connecting in the built environment—the material expression of a city built not to grow but to endure. Daly, drawing on Mill, places an emphasis on durability as one of the primary drivers of stewardship, as durability slows the rate of throughput, thereby minimizing its attendant environmental harms while maximizing its utility. Moreover, Daly notes, durability helps us live within the bounds of the laws of thermodynamics, a basic reality from which growth-oriented economists tend to hide. He points to the conservation of matter—the fact that the depletion of natural resources also leads to increased pollution—and the inevitability of entropy, which we experience in the form of energetic loss. The durability of material goods slows the extraction of natural resources and dampens the consumption of energy used to recycle materials (Daly [1973] 1980, 16–19). But when it comes to heat, energetic loss is experienced as a bodily condition in response to which a person is likely to turn up their thermostat.

Take It to Heart

Eisenhüttenstädters have long been attuned to throughput in the form of heat, particularly because of the human labor that heat indexes. As such, they are also attuned to the importance of conserving heat and improving its durability. During the GDR era, apartments in the city center were heated by coal stoves (*Ofenheizung*), as was common practice for buildings in Germany until the mid-twentieth century. I lived in such an apartment in Berlin in the late 2000s. Like the apartments in Eisenhüttenstadt, mine had what was essentially an internal chimney, a floor-to-ceiling stove about four feet square and covered in ceramic tiles, built into the corner of one room. The financial cost of the stove was negligible, but the labor it required was significant. My landlady, who lived above me, showed me how to use artificial kindling (*Feueranzunder*) to ignite a brick of coal; it was important to watch the brick and make sure it was lit properly, or else the fire might go out when the oven door closed. If successful, the brick would burn for a few hours. Eventually I would feel a growing chill and add a new brick. Every morning, I would sweep and dispose of the ashes, and every few days my landlady and I would haul bins of coal up from the cellar and stack the bricks next to the ovens in our respective apartments, our hands stained black.

When vacancy rates began to rise in Eisenhüttenstadt's city center in the 1980s, city officials pointed to coal stoves as a primary driver. Reports from the end of the socialist era express mounting concern as apartments in the city center stayed vacant for months on end (Rat der Stadt et al. 1990a, 1990b).[6] Eberhard Harz told me that the vast majority of these vacancies were on the fourth floor of four-story apartment buildings without elevators. Residents would rather not carry bins of coal up four flights of stairs only to lose most of their heat to a poorly insulated roof—not when there were modern high-rises in Housing Complexes 5, 6, and 7 with elevators and gas heating. Indeed, many informants told me that during the era of Ofenheizung, second- and third-story apartments were considered the most desirable. They had fewer stairs than the fourth floor and more sunlight than the first, but most importantly they had neighbors above and below to insulate the apartment and ease the burdens of maintaining a coal stove. Once, as we were walking beneath a columned entryway into the courtyard of Housing Complex 1, an acquaintance mentioned to me that she always felt bad for the people who lived above the entryways—despite being on the second story, she said, people in those apartments always suffered from cold feet.

During the GDR era, labor was not widely conceptualized as a commodity that people could sell. Rather, the state created jobs such that people could contribute to the socialist project—EKO was celebrated in part because of its ability to employ large numbers of people. But in July 1990, EKO's chairman, Karl Döring, gave a speech in which he braced his fellow citizens for a labor market that considered involuntary unemployment a matter of course. The primary challenge facing individuals and businesses, he explained, was that "people's labor would become a commodity" that not everyone could successfully sell—as evidenced by an unemployment rate of between 7.5 and 8 percent in the Federal Republic (quoted in Stiglich 2020, 186). Shortly thereafter came the transition to gas heating, installed as part of the city center renovations carried out in the 1990s.[7] Gas heating, like Ofenheizung, was mediated through labor. But unlike Ofenheizung, this labor did not directly contribute to the production of heat. Rather, it was sold, its proceeds used to pay the heating bill. And unlike Ofenheizung, gas heating could be financially burdensome.

Thus, Eisenhüttenstädters remained attuned to heat as the output of human labor—particularly as it began to take up an increasingly large proportion of the wages that residents earned. Over the course of the 2000s, average household heating costs in Germany nearly doubled, while consumer electricity prices rose by nearly 50 percent, introducing what the Berlin Renter's Association, in 2012, called "the new phenomenon of 'fuel poverty'" (Sethmann 2012; Der Bundes-regierung: Energie und Klimaschutz 2022).[8] In 2021, household heating costs doubled again. Germany's natural gas infrastructure relies on Russian-controlled pipelines, and following Russia's invasion of Ukraine, residential gas consum-ers saw costs increase from 7 cents per kilowatt-hour in 2020 to 16.25 cents per kilowatt-hour in 2023 (Bundesnetzagentur and Bundeskelleramt 2023).

Most of the comments about heat that I heard during my fieldwork came in the form of everyday complaints about its rising cost. But in 2015, as Syrian asylees began to be settled in Eisenhüttenstadt, I began to hear racist whisperings about their profligate heating habits: Syrians would try to recreate a Middle Eastern climate and mold would ensue, or else the cost would bankrupt social services. I occasionally volunteered as a translator for Syrian asylum seekers who spoke Eng-lish—there were few speakers of both Arabic and German in Eisenhüttenstadt—and helped people interface with municipal services. In 2016, I translated for a recent asylee, a man in his forties, as he signed the utility contracts for his apart-ment. The utility bills would be paid by the city's unemployment office, as was standard practice for unemployed residents, and would be calculated after usage. Thus, the unemployment office had an interest in the man's heating bills.

The unemployment officer, a woman in her fifties, was emphatic that I both convey the importance of conserving heat and also relay the complicated instruc-tions for maximizing the utility of its usage: The radiator must be turned off when leaving the house, it must never be turned above three even though the dial goes up to five, and one must never open the windows while the heat is on but also ventilate the kitchen and bathroom after use in order to prevent mold.[9] "Make sure he takes these instructions to heart," she told me. Turning to the man with earnest intensity, she lay her hand over her heart and repeated, "Take this to heart." Then she sheepishly ran through reasons why these practices may not have been obvious to the man, even though they would be obvious to most other Eisenhüttenstädters. After all, heat consumption had a significant impact on a household's finances. "We are GDR citizens, thrifty," she said, by way of explana-tion, evoking East German shortages and postreunification economic shocks in a curious use of the present tense.

As heat has become more expensive, residents also continue to rely on the insulating properties of neighbors. In winter 2022, the German federal govern-ment instituted price caps on natural gas, as access to heat was considered a matter of public safety (Neiser 2022c). In November 2023, I spoke with Annika, a curator at a local museum who was heading into her first winter in the city.

Annika had moved from Berlin, and as she adjusted to her new surroundings, she noticed an upside to living in the city center, with its large proportion of elderly residents: She barely had to heat her apartment. When she came home at the end of each workday, her retired neighbors had already settled in for the evening. Others were home during the day as well, and she suspected that many had poor circulation, given their degree of heat consumption. "I'm right in the middle of all this," she said, gesturing to the imaginary neighbors who insulated the space around her.

It was notable that Annika referred not to her reduced heating bills but to the pleasures of coming home to a warm apartment. She had certainly saved money, relative to the expense of heating a single-family home or an apartment in a highly vacant building. But the warmth that she experienced helped her recognize that her bodily well-being, too, was made better through her membership in the collective. The repopulation of the city center had created a mutually reinforcing cycle in which each resident's heat reduced the energy burdens of their neighbors—a process with financial, environmental, and affective consequences.

More broadly, city leadership has evinced a commitment to understanding energy as both an output and an analogue of human labor. Since 2003, the municipal utility provider (Stadtwerke Eisenhüttenstadt) has held the Grand Prix with Energy, a public festival organized around recreational athletics. On the last weekend before school holidays begin in early July, residents gather on Leisure Time Island for races catering to a wide range of ages, interests, and abilities: running, swimming, biking, walking, Nordic walking, wheelchair racing, and a "bambini run" for children under age six—the types of low-carbon activities that contribute to prosperity (Jackson 2009). The utility provider sets up a stage near the municipal swimming pool on Leisure Time Island, and food vendors serve bratwurst and beer. There are medal ceremonies for the various races, and entertainment throughout the weekend. Youth dance is a popular activity in Eisenhüttenstadt, and when I attended the Grand Prix in 2015, I watched a number of teenage troupes, including a group of unicyclists, in a well-attended, cheering crowd. Children played on the nearby playground as people in racing jerseys milled about among the food vendors. On the backdrop to the stage was a large image of a "Hüttecard," which all utility customers receive, a reminder of the multiple types of energy on which the event depended—the energy expended by medalists, dancers, and the utility's heat and electricity infrastructures.

The Grand Prix, in capitalizing on the ambiguous meaning of "energy," translates the dissipation of surplus into human experience, an act that reflects what theorist Georges Bataille calls the "law of general economy" (Bataille [1967] 1989, 27). According to Bataille, the dissipation of surplus is fundamental to life on earth but is often obscured by human culture, which views surplus—profit or

FIGURE 63. The Grand Prix with Energy, 2015. Photograph by the author.

waste—as the end result of economic activity, rather than as its progenitor. Yet all living things must either waste or expend their excess energy, Bataille asserts, and human cultures differ in how they choose to use this "accursed share": through war, human sacrifice, material destruction, or the excess energy's reinvestment in the social body. Bataille ([1967] 1989, 21) writes, "If the system can no longer grow, or if the excess cannot be completely absorbed in its growth, it must necessarily be lost without profit; it must be spent, willingly or not, gloriously or catastrophically." Throughput reflects how this excess is spent, to what extent it can be reinvested, and how quickly it exits the system as waste—a problem of both durability and culture.

Anthropologist Gretchen Bakke (2019), drawing on Bataille, suggests that fossil fuels have warped our perception of the energy contained in the "accursed share." The sun appears to provide limitless energy—it "gives without ever receiving" (Bataille [1967] 1989, 28)—and it furnishes human beings with the natural resources that sustain life and social reproduction. But fossil fuels also compress millennia of solar energy into materials that can be turned into waste almost instantly, and their energetic output dwarfs that of even the most robust mammals. While a preindustrial human would have operated on roughly two thousand calories per day, or 100 watts, a contemporary human is a "10,000-watt beast," consuming energy in the form of caloric intake but also heat, electricity, transportation, and manufacturing (Bakke 2019, 48). The thousandfold difference represents an extreme dissipation of excess to which we have become normalized.

The Grand Prix, in connecting the delivery of heat and electricity to the expenditure of athletic output, creates resonances between the energetic surpluses of infrastructural technologies and living organisms. The races and performances, funded by the proceeds of energy consumption, are also vehicles for the dissipation of the excessive energy enabled by that very consumption. At the same time, the burdens placed on human energy by those recreational activities make the finitude of natural resources apparent in human experience. Like the earth's energy reserves, human energy is experienced as both exhaustible and renewable, depending on circumstances. A runner can recover after a race through rest and caloric intake, but the Soviet soldiers buried nearby in Memorial Square were likely worked to death in Camp Stalag III B. Endurance is possible only when the collective surplus is reinvested in the system's well-being, rather than continually expended beyond what the system can support.

The Expansion of Hüttengas

Reinvestment and durability are also central to Hüttengas, a recycled industrial product that provides heat for much of the city. Hüttengas is off-gas from EKO's blast furnace, which is recaptured and burned in a power-heat coupling plant built in 1953 to serve the newly founded steelworks (VEO GmbH 2024). The burning Hüttengas (a mix of 45 to 60 percent N_2, 20 to 30 percent CO, 20 to 25 percent CO_2, and 2 to 4 percent H_2) powers a steam turbine that produces electricity, the majority of which is used to power the steelworks, though a smaller proportion is also purchased by Eisenhüttenstadt's utility provider. (The power-heat coupling plant produces about 750 gigawatt-hours; the city consumes roughly 81 gigawatt-hours, while EKO consumes around ten times as much, roughly 910 gigawatt-hours [Mann et al. 2015, 38–39].) In 1994, the power-heat coupling plant was spun off as an independent subsidiary of EKO as part of the privatization process; today 51 percent of the resulting company, Vulcan Energy Management, is owned by ArcelorMittal, and 49 percent is owned by Eisenhüttenstadt's municipal utility provider (VEO GmbH 2024). In 1997, Vulcan expanded its district heating (*Fernwärme*) system, developed in the 1960s: Hot water from the steam turbine is recaptured and used to heat both the city and the steelworks.

Vulcan has the capacity to heat the entire city (Mann et al. 2015, 40),[10] but its network is concentrated outside the city center. As of 2013, 99 percent of Housing Complex 6 was on district heating, as were 58 percent of Housing Complex 1, 16 percent of Complex 2, 32 percent of Complex 3, 61 percent of Complex 4, and

9 percent of Complex 5 (though having been substantially demolished, Housing Complex 5 consumed about half the overall energy of the other complexes) (50). The remaining areas are heated by natural gas. Thus, the Energy Renovation plan states that the expansion of district heating will be the most important contribution to the city's reduction of its carbon emissions. It even suggests rebranding Hüttengas as Hütte(N)Heat (*Hütte[N]Wärme*), with the N emphasized for sustainability, or *Nachhaltigkeit* (100–102).

But the fact that Hüttengas is considered carbon neutral is the result of a convenient imposition of externalities. The Energy Renovation plan includes a footnote: "Of course, considerable amounts of CO_2 are produced by the burning of blast-furnace and converter gas; however, they *belong to the carbon balance of the metallurgical process* and would be produced anyway, even if blast-furnace and converter gasses were flared off, as they must be, because they contain carbon monoxide" (Mann et al. 2015, 92; emphasis added). At present, the blast furnace is powered by coal; current investments are in the process of converting it to natural gas, which has lower emissions. It is projected to run on green hydrogen by 2050. At the same time, plans are currently underway to transform EKO's blast furnace into a direct reduced iron, electric arc furnace (DRI-EAF) process by 2050, which will eliminate the production of Hüttengas. In a DRI-EAF process, discussed in greater detail below, iron ore is reduced using hydrogen as a reactant and, as a result, the only byproduct produced is water—a zero-emissions iron refining process that threatens the future of the power-heat coupling plant, which is, in turn, key to Eisenhüttenstadt's promise of zero-emissions heat by 2050. City leadership is currently planning for this eventuality, still decades away (Lötsch 2023b). It remains possible that, decades from now, the steam-recapture process in the power-heat coupling plant may be converted to run on renewably sourced electricity, as the German federal government cites power-heat coupling plants as a key instrument in the energy transition (BMWK 2024).

At the same time, EKO's anointment as, potentially, the world's first carbon-neutral steel manufacturing plant has significantly changed the local outlook. As the city transformed over the 2000s, a sense of guarded optimism began to emerge. In 2015, a local news program asked notable Eisenhüttenstädters about the future of their hometown. Olympic shot-putter Udo Beyer reflected on the recent renovations, which brought an end to the chaotic period that had followed reunification, before announcing, approvingly, "I'll be glad if the city has one hundred years left in it" (Erler 2015). Today, such a prognosis no longer feels uncertain. The city's longevity has been reinvigorated by large-scale investments from government and corporations. Yet this longevity will also be enabled by the continued production of steel and thus the continued purchase of new automobiles and stainless-steel kitchen appliances, an externality apparently not considered in the press releases and news articles that promise carbon-neutrality (Lötsch 2023b; Neiser 2024; Evans et al. 2021; ArcelorMittal Eisenhüttenstadt 2021; Blaschek 2021).

The Promise of Green Steel

In March 2021, ArcelorMittal announced that it would transition its steel manufacturing facilities in Eisenhüttenstadt and Bremen into the world's first carbon-neutral steel manufacturing sites by 2050. The plan would also meet newly stringent European emissions standards—a reduction of 50 percent by 2030, relative to 2005 levels—as intermediate targets, such as the conversion of blast furnaces from coal to natural gas, were met. The announcement assuaged the fear, prevalent among Eisenhüttenstädters, that increasingly ambitious European emissions standards would lead ArcelorMittal to withdraw from the German market. By 2050, the plan announced, the two facilities would be processing one hundred thousand tons of carbon-neutral sponge iron into steel per year (Evans et al. 2021).

This industrial transformation hinges on the production of hydrogen, which has two primary applications in steel manufacturing: It can be used as an injection material in a traditional blast furnace, or it can be used as a reactant in a direct reduced iron (DRI) process. In order to produce steel, iron ore (Fe-O) must first be reduced into iron by separating its iron (Fe) and oxygen (O) molecules in a chemical reaction. In a traditional blast furnace, this is achieved by heating coking coal together with iron ore, which produces carbon dioxide as well as other off-gasses currently captured as Hüttengas (Mann et al. 2015, 38). But in a DRI process, iron ore is exposed to hydrogen (H_2), producing sponge iron with water (H_2O) and purified iron (Fe) as its chemical byproducts. In a DRI-EAF process, the sponge iron is then processed in an electric arc furnace, where it is heated via an electrical current and exposed to oxygen, creating a slag that can be removed, purifying iron into steel. If the hydrogen and electricity powering the DRI-EAF process are produced without carbon emissions, then the resulting steel is considered emissions-free. (DRI is sometimes used to process recycled materials, but mining, it seems, is another externality.)

Eisenhüttenstadt's blast furnace and, eventually, its DRI-EAF process will be powered by the East Brandenburg Hydrogen Cluster, a network of projects that include hydrogen electrolysis powered by renewable energy—hence its description as "green" hydrogen. In 2021, the State of Brandenburg issued a strategic plan for the development of its hydrogen economy and began broad efforts to fund hydrogen electrolysis facilities to supply the region's industrial sector. Projections for 2040 show an average industrial demand, across the state, of 9.9 terawatt-hours, of which ArcelorMittal's Eisenhüttenstadt facility would consume nearly half, at 4 terawatt-hours (MWAE 2022, 62).

In 2023, construction began on a project to build a hydrogen electrolysis plant that will serve only the ArcelorMittal facility, a €9.1 million project funded with €5.1 million from the Brandenburg State and the remainder from ArcelorMittal, Vulcan, and the energy provider McPhy Energy (Nüßlein 2023). As Germany transitions its electric grid to renewable sources, the hydrogen produced in Brandenburg's networks, at Bremen's facility, and at ArcelorMittal will be considered green hydrogen. In 2021, Germany's parliament pledged that 80 percent of its energy would be supplied by renewable sources by 2030, far above the 40 percent target issued by the European Parliament (MWAE 2022, 9). As of this writing, 52 percent of the country's energy is supplied by renewable sources, up from 31 percent in 2015 (Der Bundesregierung: Energie und Klimaschutz 2024). But the German federal government does not yet have a target date by which its grid will be completely renewable.

In 2021, Germany selected ArcelorMittal's plan as an Important Project of Common European Interest and submitted it to the European Parliament for funding. While the proposal was under review, the project's viability hung in the balance. When I visited Eisenhüttenstadt in 2023, the mood was unexpectedly grim. In 2022, energy prices in Germany had spiked, and as a result, Arcelor-Mittal had cut back work hours at its Eisenhüttenstadt facility, first in August and then again in October and December (Neiser 2022b). A headline in the local newspaper read, "More Pessimistic Than Ever: Mood in Industry in Steep Decline" (Matthes 2022). As always, many informants expressed skepticism that ArcelorMittal would stay in Germany, let alone move forward with its plan to make Eisenhüttenstadt's facility carbon neutral.

In early 2024, however, the plan's funding was approved. ArcelorMittal would transform its Bremen and Eisenhüttenstadt facilities at a total cost of €2.5 billion, €1.3 billion of which would be supplied by the European Parliament by way of the German Federal Ministry for Economic Affairs and Climate Action (Bundesministerium für Wirtschaft und Klimaschutz, or BMWK). The BMWK funding will go toward the DRI facility in Bremen and the construction of three EAFs, one in Bremen and two in Eisenhüttenstadt. The four facilities are scheduled to be operational by 2026 and will result in a 10 percent reduction in carbon emissions for the entire German steel sector (BMWK 2024).

These ongoing investments, supported at the highest levels of government, have made it unlikely that ArcelorMittal will pull out of its operations in Eisenhüttenstadt. The steel plant currently employs 2,700 people, about one-quarter of the total employment positions in the city (Stadt Eisenhüttenstadt and BBSM

2022, 18),[11] but it contributes significantly to the city's economy and is deeply entangled with its identity. Because of the high rates of steel employment during the GDR era, many people have memories of working in the steel plant or one of its subsidiaries, or they have friends or family members who share such memories with them. At the base of Linden Avenue is a slab of steel that reads, "This steel has been made here, and here will it stay!" The blast furnaces are the visual anchor for the city's central axis, visible on the horizon from Linden Avenue and from elevated viewpoints. Martin Maleschka, the architect and photographer, told me half-jokingly that from his high-rise apartment in Housing Complex 5, he looks out at the steel plant each morning "just to make sure it's still there."

In 2000, EKO held a millennium festival to thank the city's leadership for ushering the steelworks through the turbulent 1990s. The festival featured musical performances and an appearance by Chancellor Gerhard Schröder; around one hundred thousand people were in attendance (ArcelorMittal Eisenhüttenstadt 2024). Since then, EKO and the city government have jointly sponsored an annual City Festival (Stadtfest), an enormous undertaking that regularly sees around one hundred thousand attendees. Held over a weekend in August, the City Festival is a regional attraction and de facto reunion, as Eisenhüttenstädters who have moved away come back to visit friends and relatives and share in the festivities. The 2023 City Festival featured twelve amusement rides and close to eighty food and drink stands (Lötsch 2023c). Nearly a dozen outdoor stages feature a wide range of entertainment options, from rock bands to children's programming, and a large tent on Linden Avenue serves as the civic headquarters, where citizens gather to hear speeches from city leadership. While the City Festival is widely beloved, citizens have criticized its cost, which has ballooned to around €500,000. The majority is paid by ArcelorMittal, but in 2023, the city paid €145,000, just over double its allocated budget (Lötsch 2023c).

ArcelorMittal is featured prominently at the City Festival. When I attended in 2015, there were a number of booths where visitors could learn about EKO's history and the steel-making process, and the company's logo was visible on banners and tents throughout the festival grounds. The City Festival is also the only time of year when EKO offers tours of its facilities to the public—quite the draw, I found out, when I went to the sign-up booth and found that there was room only on the children's tour. I rode around EKO in a little green trolley, where grade-school children pushed their faces against the glass as we watched finely milled stainless steel get rolled and prepared for shipment. The adult tour had access to the hotter and more hazardous parts of the facility, while the children's tour included a visit to EKO's dedicated fire station.

During the socialist era, public festivals were an integral part of Eisenhüttenstadt's cultural landscape, and the City Festival seems to have recuperated that

FIGURES 64A AND 64B. Linden Avenue during the City Festival, 2015. Photographs by the author.

FIGURE 65. The civic tent on Linden Avenue, 2015. Photograph by the author.

FIGURE 66. The children's tour of EKO, 2015. Photograph by the author.

tradition. Herbert Härtel recalled that when he was designing Linden Avenue in the 1960s, his original plans called for the street to be only fifteen meters wide, under the logic that a narrow central street would maximize social interaction among residents. But East German officials forced him to widen the street to accommodate political demonstrations—there were obligatory public gatherings on Labor Day, Republic Day, and other occasions in which parades would flow down the city's main artery. Härtel says he now considers the change fortuitous, as the extra width allows Linden Avenue to host carnival rides, tents, and food stalls during the City Festival—an emblem of civic pride and a high point of the year.

More broadly, the turn toward green steel has allowed ArcelorMittal to step into the social role vacated by the socialist project. Its promises form the grounds on which urban longevity is imagined, while its economic force brings essential resources into the city. And as before, Eisenhüttenstadt's position as an exemplar has secured its near future, ensuring that despite the precarious position of the German industrial economy, resources will be directed toward the city's ongoing needs. This is perhaps a devil's bargain, given the leadership's goal of carbon neutrality and the environmental harms of steel manufacturing. But the city's overall well-being is dependent on that of the global conglomerate, which provides the scaffolding for this new iteration of exemplary urbanism.

CONCLUSION
A City of a New Kind

East German social life operated within a series of nested collectivities, each with its own set of concerns and domain of responsibility: the House Society within the Housing Complex, the work brigade within the factory within the nation. As scholars of the Soviet Union note, the fundamental logic of these nested collectivities rested on that of the household (*khoziaistvo*) and was distinct from Western economic logics in its reliance on top-down administration—the presence of a *khoziain*, or owner-manager, who, in theory, orchestrated activities in furtherance of the collective good (Collier 2011, 80–83; Cherkaev 2023, 75–78). In Eisenhüttenstadt, most of those nested collectives have disappeared from the social landscape. But the coordinated administration of real estate by the city government, the GeWi, and the EWG has kept the *khoziaistvo* of the city intact—enabled, fundamentally, by Urban Renewal East, in response to which the collaboration took form.

Socialist urban planners likely never foresaw that their nested social organization and modular imagination of urban growth would one day be instrumentalized in the model city's dismantling. Recall, however, that this was to be a city of a new kind—a "<u>city</u> in the fullest sense of the word" (Bauakademie der DDR 1951, 37). It would not require a minimum population before its citizens acquired the right to cosmopolitan amenities such as movies, theaters, dance halls, and hotels—the Friedrich Wolf Theater, built in 1953, was one of the city's first buildings, grounding social life in the larger collectives of the mass public, the nation, and the Eastern Bloc. Yet while the East German Building Academy claimed that its new type of city would defy the categorization of cities into sizes small,

FIGURE 67. Linden Avenue, then Lenin Avenue, 1961. The mural of the steelworker on the back of the Magnet Department Store would later be replaced by the Peace Dove mosaic. The text partially obscured by the linden trees reads, "Germany's First Socialist City" (Erste Sozialistische Stadt Deutschlands). Photograph by M. Fricke. Courtesy of Stadtarchiv Eisenhüttenstadt.

medium, and large, it nonetheless imagined that Eisenhüttenstadt would eventually become large (Bauakademie der DDR 1951, 37). The fact that city leadership has found a way for Eisenhüttenstadt to thrive as a small city speaks perhaps to the success of this original urban imagination. In place of the "socialist scaffold" (Zarecor 2018, 99) a well-populated, materially revitalized city center has been cultivated, which begets economic activity in a cycle of positive reinforcement.

Architects and urban planners are likely to credit the city's successful transformation to the built environment. As Herbert Härtel told me, "Architecture's impacts are in the well-being of residents." But Härtel also told me that when he began working as an architect in Eisenhüttenstadt in 1953, the mayor told him, "Remember that people do not enter their moving vans as members of the bourgeoisie and exit them as socialists." Residents' engagement in social infrastructures would be the most important factor in determining the success of architectural projects—without their eagerness to socialize with neighbors and their willingness to perform collective labor, an apartment building would be an anonymous collective, rather than the foundation for a House Society. Some of those residents, who grew up to become architects and urban planners, have reproduced the attention to collective good that once defined the city as a *kho-ziaistvo*, in which residents were attuned to the nested commons of the Housing Complex, House Society, and household. Still, it is important to remember that these concerns are being reproduced in a radically different social context. Angela, the former director of OFFIS, told me that her father had been a prominent dissident in the GDR. As a result, her educational prospects were nonexistent. When the Berlin Wall fell, she was a teenager looking toward a career as a barmaid. Instead she went to college, which in turn enabled her to pursue a career that has contributed enormously to the city's well-being.

Eisenhüttenstädters' attention to the socialist era's utopian origins is part of a larger cultural shift, motivated by widespread exhaustion with the unrelenting social and ecological damage wrought since the fall of the Eastern Bloc. This new iteration of *Ostalgie* questions the hasty process of reunification, which foreclosed the possibility of a reunified Germany that retained elements of both its component parts. I first noticed this narrative in *Bornholmer Street*, a 2014 film that aired on German television to celebrate the twenty-fifth anniversary of the fall of the Berlin Wall. The film tells the fictionalized story of Harald Jäger, the border guard who opened the Bornholmer Street crossing on November 9, 1989, amid mounting pressure from a crowd that had gathered under the state's promise of liberalized travel to the West. Toward the film's end, an East German couple, allowed into the West early in the night, are held by the border guards as they try to return home—reentry is prohibited. The border guards had assumed that anyone going West intended to emigrate. But the couple desperately explain that their children are in bed; they wanted to visit West Berlin only for a few hours, to see what all the fuss was about. They certainly didn't intend to leave East Germany forever.

In the intervening years, reconsiderations of the reunification period have regularly appeared in media and scholarship (Allen 2019; Lippmann et al. 2020; Mau 2021; Meakem 2024). In 2020, Netflix released *A Perfect Crime*, about the murder of Treuhand chair Detlev Karsten Rohwedder. Archival news footage from the 1990s shows East Germans openly weeping as they recount the trauma of mass unemployment, while former East German Finance Minister Christa Luft says that the East German economy "needed a shot of penicillin, not a lethal injection" (Schwochow 2014). In 2024, Jenny Erpenbeck's *Kairos*, set in the waning days of the East German state, became the first German winner of the International Booker Prize. The novel's protagonist, Katharina, is horrified by the homelessness she sees in the West and, later, by the bargain that East German leadership seems to have made, trading its demands for a new German constitution for "gummi bears, handbags, and scarves" (Erpenbeck 2023, 284). Katharina's mother insists that "in its quest for a durable form of social organization, humanity needs alternatives to Western consumer society" (265). Erpenbeck quotes the East German writer Christa Wolf, who in November 1989 wrote, "It's not too late for us to present a Socialist alternative to West Germany, in equal neighborliness with other European nations. We can still appeal to the anti-Fascist and humanitarian ideals that were our starting point" (quoted in Erpenbeck 2023, 271).

The artist Friedrich Liechtenstein, in a documentary podcast from the Museum of Utopia and the Everyday, says that the future promised by socialism was, from the start, unrealizable—but its realization was never the point. Cities like Eisenhüttenstadt should be read "not as models" for new modes of urban living, but "rather as critiques of the present." Indeed, he says, the goal of utopian projects is "to critique the future that seems most likely" at the moment in which utopian plans are conceived (RBB 2022). Eisenhüttenstadt's second iteration of utopian urbanism seems poised to critique a present that is heedlessly barreling toward catastrophe—though it does so with heavy internal contradictions. While the financialization of biopolitical resources such as housing and heat has forced residents and city leadership to be attuned to conservation, the city's economic well-being remains dependent on steel production. This entanglement contributes to a culture of limitless consumption in a dilemma common to post-cities. Susan Buck-Morss (2000, 115) writes that "by adopting the capitalist heavy-industry definition of economic modernization . . . Soviet socialism had no alternative but to try to produce a utopia out of the production process itself. In making this choice, the Soviets missed the opportunity to transform the very idea of economic 'development,' and of the ecological preconditions through which it might be realized."[1]

For decades following reunification, socialism pervaded Eisenhüttenstadt as a present absence. Residents lived with the remnants of socialist growth mania in the form of semi-empty tower blocks. In 1993, city leadership installed a one-to-one-thousand scale model of the city in the lobby of City Hall. In 2009, it updated the model to remove buildings that had been demolished, which were indicated in ghostly outlines. The model was kept under glass, recalling the derogatory remark that Eisenhüttenstadt was "under a cheese dome," preserved as an icon of obsolescence. But today the city seems defined not by the absence of socialism but by the presence of its legacy. In 2022, a new sculpture was installed on Linden Avenue: a one-to-one-thousand scale model of Housing Complexes 1 through 4, cast in bronze, including trees and architectural details. The project was funded by an initiative for the elderly and disabled and was intended as both a visual and tactile model (Peisker 2022). The sculpture sits on a pedestal in front of the Friedrich Wolf Theater, durable, available to a broadly imagined public, and meant to help residents familiarize themselves with the morphology of their city's original plan.

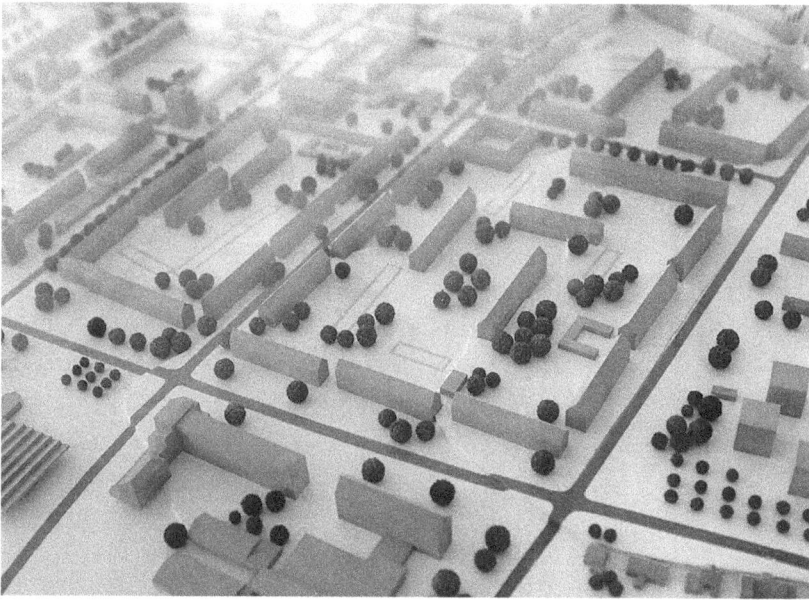

FIGURE 68. The model in City Hall, 2016. In the Peaceful Path Quarter in Housing Complex 4 (*center*), demolished buildings are marked by outlines. Photograph by the author.

FIGURE 69. The model on Linden Avenue, 2023. In the Peaceful Path Quarter in Housing Complex 4 (*bottom right*), this newer model shows only existing buildings. Photograph by the author.

In Liechtenstein's podcast, he recalls having been ashamed of his hometown until he visited an exhibition at the Getty Museum in Los Angeles that reminded him of the modernist utopian communitarianism that had defined his childhood. He then recites from the Ten Commandments of Socialist Morals and Ethics, which East German leadership issued in 1958. " 'You shall aid in eradicating the exploitation of man by man.' Sounds pretty good," he says, the ambient sounds of Linden Avenue in the background. " 'You shall protect and attend to people's property. You shall bring up your children in the spirit of peace and socialism'" (RBB 2022). The commandments are read piecemeal and out of order. But the past is made useful for the context at present.

Acknowledgments

This book has been over a decade in the making, and far too many people have helped me along the way than I can thank in these pages. First and foremost, I would like to thank the people in Eisenhüttenstadt who have inspired and supported my research over many years. Ben Kaden, Andreas Ludwig, and Gabriele Haubold first introduced me to the city's unique history early in my career. Archivist Gabriele Urban has been an invaluable resource throughout the research process. During my time in Eisenhüttenstadt, Helga Boehm, Manfred Dittman, Eberhard Harz, Wolf Krüger, Martin Maleschka, Angela Naundorf, Hartmut Preuß, Hendrick Pytel, Bettina Rettlich, Heike Steinhagen, Ina Trautmann, and most of all Gerlinde Gundlach showed me great kindness, friendship, and support for my research, as did members of the Group, particularly Detlef Juckel. I would also like to thank the curators at the Museum of Utopia and the Everyday; the staff at OFFIS; the people at AWO, particularly Mischa, Julia, Alwina, Susi, and Gazwa; the students and faculty at the Albert Schweizer Gymnasium; members of the city administration, notably Michael Reh; and others who contributed in a professional capacity, including Jens Beige, Oliver Funke, Herbert Härtel, and Verena Rühr-Bach. Finally, I am grateful to the many people who sat with me for interviews both personal and professional, without whom this book would not exist.

This book began in the Visual and Media Anthropology program at the Freie Universität Berlin, where I developed it under the mentorship of Undine Frömming and Kristian Petersen. At Columbia University, Brian Larkin and Catherine Fennell acted as unparalleled intellectual interlocutors. I am also grateful to the many others who taught me, worked with me, and learned alongside me, providing valuable feedback as I developed the ideas herein, including Monica Barra, Dominic Boyer, Alison Damick, Val Daniel, Deniz Duruiz, Julia Fierman, Severin Fowles, Molly Fox, Yulia Grinberg, Rebecca Journey, Peter Lagerqvist, Juan Carlos Mazariegos, Rosalind Morris, Katherine Rochester, and Emily Smith. While conducting research for this book, I was a scholar in residence in Visual and Media Anthropology at the Freie Universität Berlin and at the Center for Metropolitan Studies at the Technische Universität Berlin. An initial draft of chapter 3 was workshopped by the inaugural group of Heyman Center for Humanities fellows at Columbia University, where my peers provided valuable feedback.

While developing early drafts of this book at the New School for Social Research, I had the pleasure of working with wonderful colleagues and mentors, including Alex Aleinikoff, Jonathan Bach, Sarah Louise Earnshaw, Rachel Heiman, and Julia Morris. I am also grateful to my students at Lehigh University and my colleagues in the Department of Sociology and Anthropology.

The writing of this book was supported by a Hunt Fellowship from the Wenner-Gren Foundation. Research was funded by the Wenner-Gren Foundation, the Deutscher Akademischer Austauschdienst (DAAD), the Council for European Studies, and the National Science Foundation. Thanks also to the reviewers of the manuscript, and to the team at Cornell University Press, particularly Bethany Wasik and Jim Lance. Finally, this book is dedicated, with love and gratitude, to my family, who have supported me to the finish line, and who inspire me to imagine a better world.

Notes

INTRODUCTION

1. In December 2022, the Eisenhüttenstadt Real Estate Company (Eisenhütten-städter Gebaudewirtschaft, or GeWi) reported 1,100 vacancies among its total inventory of 6,849 apartments, for a vacancy rate of 16 percent. Of these vacancies, 420 were in buildings that had been purposely vacated prior to their planned demolition between 2023 and 2025. Excluding intended vacancies, the GeWi's rate was 7 percent. The Eisen-hüttenstadt Housing Cooperative (Eisenhüttenstädter Wohnungsbaugenossenschaft, or EWG), which holds around 5,000 apartments, similarly reported a vacancy rate of 12 per-cent, which would be 7.8 percent excluding purposely vacated buildings (Lötsch 2023b). Healthy vacancy is generally considered to be around 5 to 7 percent.

2. I use the term "post-cities" to refer to cities affected by twentieth-century legacies, commonly called postindustrial, postsocialist, postcolonialist, or combinations thereof. Cities with histories of heavy industry, from American Fordism to Eastern Bloc socialism, share common struggles with depopulation and sociocultural obsolescence. The term "post-cities" highlights these common struggles despite the cities' divergent histories.

3. The term "building generation" is sometimes used to describe the first generation of East Germans more broadly. In this context, the double entendre refers to the rebuilding of cities that were bombed by the Allies during World War II (Fulbrook 2014).

4. Many homes in Fürstenberg and Schönfließ, the medieval villages subsumed into the city in 1961, were privately owned throughout the socialist era and remain so.

5. "Informant" is the term that anthropologists use to describe their interlocu-tors. I use it here to refer to people I spoke with in Eisenhüttenstadt, often in a social context.

6. Since the turn of the twenty-first century, the question of whether we have entered an era of post-postsocialism has been raised and dismissed at regular intervals, with schol-ars generally agreeing that we cannot declare ourselves post-postsocialism, as the socialist era continues to affect the present (Hann et al. 2003; S. Phillips 2005; Chivens 2005).

7. Monday Demonstrations were peaceful protests against the East German state that contributed to German reunification.

8. While this event is often called the "European migrant crisis," scholars note the problematic nature of the term, which situates global migration as a European problem exacerbated by the presence of "undeserving" economic migrants (Fernando and Gior-dano 2016; Holmes and Castañeda 2016).

1. THE FIRST NEW TOWN

1. Unless otherwise specified, any references to Eisenhüttenstadt's local newspaper are to the *Märkische Oder Newspaper*, which covers the area between Märker Lake, east of Berlin, and the Oder River, which forms the border between Germany and Poland.

2. While the majority of homes in Fürstenberg are privately owned single-family residences, the EWG owns a number of apartment buildings in the area to which residents displaced by urban renewal have been relocated.

3. Kurt Leucht, who designed much of Eisenhüttenstadt, later said that Gropius and his cohort were "overrated" (*überschätzt*), having given themselves credit for ideas developed by an earlier generation of Scandinavian modernists (Leucht 1991).

4. Private car ownership became commonplace only in the later decades of the GDR. While Housing Complexes 6 and 7 had extensive parking lots, residents of Complexes 1 through 5 parked their cars in communal garages along the edge of the city center, an indication that cars were intended for use in the surrounding region but not within the city.

5. Red Flag (*Rote Fahne*) originated with the Spartacus League in the early twentieth century and was published by the German Communist Party, which was re-formed in the early 1990s.

6. This is in part due to the fact that Le Corbusier published the Athens Charter nearly a decade after the conference, and after he had put forth his plans for the Radiant City. This densely developed high-rise urban design would go on to influence urban development across the globe. Anthropologists, most notably Holston (1989) and Fennell (2015), as well as historian Lawrence Vale (2013, 2020), have noted that social factors complicate such techno-modernist utopian plans.

7. Other participants were Edmund Collein, Lothar Bolz, Waldemar Alder, Walter Piesternick, and Kurt Liebknecht (Durth et al. 1998).

8. Karl Döring, the former general director of Eisenhüttenstadt's steel plant, points out the hypocrisy of the embargo in his history of the EKO steel plant. East Germany was not officially recognized by the West until the 1970s, and a country that does not exist cannot be embargoed. Truman, Stalin, and Attlee signed a document at the Potsdam Conference on August 2, 1945, stating, "Despite the [Soviet] Zone of Occupation, Germany is to be considered as a unified economy" (Artikel III Teil B. Wirtschaftliche Grundsätze, Pkt. 14; quoted in Döring 2015, 123).

9. Canal systems connecting the Oder and the Spree, which runs through Berlin, were first built under the reign of Kaiser Karl IV (1316–78). These canals, however, required navigation over an enormous series of locks and could accommodate boats only up to .9 meters tall. A new canal, built between 1887 and 1891, continued to be used into the GDR era (Gansleweit 1986, 107).

10. In 1994, Werner Durth discovered a sketch for EKO Wohnstadt in which the city was to be located north of its current location, near Pohlizer Lake. Durth and historian Ruth May speculate that this may have been Ehrlich's original design (May 1999, 154–55).

11. Currency conversions have been conducted according to the methodology outlined in Marcuse 2018, using the resources at MeasuringWorth.com and accounting for inflation to 2022. I have chosen to convert Ostmarks to Deutschmarks at a rate of 5:1, the rate briefly available before Germany's monetary union and commonly used in informal markets.

12. 1953 also saw the development of a small area of single-family homes for elite EKO employees, which was heavily criticized (May 1999, 185).

13. The East German national newspaper *Neues Deutschland* boasted that Magnitogorsk's failure of technology and modernity was not to be repeated in Germany's Model Socialist City, which had the benefits of modern technology, not "primitive" Soviet tools, and the amenities of nearby Berlin, with "cafes, movie theaters, and civilization" (Pfannstiel 1977).

2. RETROFITTING THE HOUSING COMPLEX

1. In 1990, the name EKO was resignified from an abbreviation of Eisenhüttenkombinat Ost (Eastern Steelworks) to an acronym of E for *Eisen und Stahl* (iron and steel),

K for *Kaltgewaltzte Qualitätsbleche* (cold-rolled quality sheets), and *O* for *Oberflächen-veredelte Blecher, Bänder und Profile* (surface finished sheets, bands, and profiles) (Nicolaus 2020, 49).

2. In large East German cities, Housing Complexes were part of larger units called Housing Districts.

3. Those run by the Handelsorganization, the government agency for commerce.

4. Between 1971 and 1988, the proportion of East German men and women living to age seventy-five rose by 2 percent, and the proportion living to eighty-nine grew by 7 percent for women and 4 percent for men (Wiesner 2001, 27–29).

5. The term "New States" stands in contrast to the original states of the German Federal Republic, or West Germany, which absorbed East German states when Germany reunified. I use it here because it is used in the Urban Renewal East literature. My informants often referred to Urban Renewal East simply as Urban Renewal, and I will refer to it as Urban Renewal here, or as Urban Renewal East when disambiguation is necessary.

6. Fennell suggests that publics exist "sympathetically," that is, they are recognized through feeling (Fennell 2015, 7).

7. Heidi's attitude reflects McKowen and Borneman's (2020) notion that the "incorporation" of migrants into the social body is more important than their "integration," as incorporation entails change for both migrants and the existing social body.

8. The Left (Die Linke) is a far-left political party with an anticapitalist platform. It is considered the successor to the SED.

3. HISTORY IN THE URBAN LANDSCAPE

1. Anthropologist Alexei Yurchak ([2005] 2013, 36) recounts the plot of *Irony of Fate* as emblematic of the modularity of Soviet urban design. A drunk man from Moscow ends up in Leningrad, where he takes a taxi to his Moscow address, Second Street of Builders, which also exists in Leningrad. His key works in the equivalent apartment door, and he ends up falling in love with the inhabitant of the Leningrad apartment.

2. Wilhelm Pieck was the first president of the GDR. Klement Gottwald was the first leader of Communist Czechoslovakia. Georgi Dimitroff was the first leader of Communist Bulgaria. Walter Ulbricht was the first general secretary of the SED (effectively the leader of East Germany). Otto Grotewohl was the first prime minister of the GDR. Helmut Just was an East German border guard killed in the line of duty. Schehr, Thälmann, and Heckert were prominent members of the KPD who died before the founding of the East German state. Schehr and Thälmann were murdered in Nazi concentration camps, while Heckert died in exile in Moscow.

3. A further seventy-seven were only against renaming Thälmann Street, seventy-four were against renaming Helmut Just Street, and six were against renaming other streets (Boehme 1992).

4. As of 2020, fewer than half the 5.25 million eligible citizens have viewed their Stasi files, which Hertwig and Engel (2020, 3) point to as an example of "deliberate ignorance."

5. The KPD was the forerunner of the SED, or Socialist Unity Party, the official political party of East Germany. KPD members were persecuted by the Nazis. Participation in the KPD was outlawed in West Germany in 1956 (Major 1998).

6. The Konsomol was the Soviet youth organization.

7. As Eberhard Harz, the former chair of the GeWi, explained in an interview, and as the transcripts of city meetings attest (SVV 1990), the GeWi attempted to maintain a housing swap system to combat rising vacancy in the 1990s, but there was little uptake.

8. His letter ends: "The generation after us should not over and again—like us—have to needlessly pay for this [having streets named after politicians] . . . and also, because man

is by far not the most clever, highly developed, best life form in the world, we should not highlight the leaders of people; let us think only of the environmental and war-related damages wrought by the past and by our times."

9. *Acer saccharinum* (North America), *Acer negundo* (North America), *Acer ginnala* (East Asia), and *Acer capestre* (Western Asia and Central Europe) (Missouri Botanical Garden n.d.).

10. Between 1995 and 1996, 1,679 apartments were modernized at an average cost of 85,000 Deutschmarks per apartment (roughly $200,000) (Haubold 2000, 102).

4. HOUSING FOR THE SOCIAL REALM

1. Cockerill-Sambre became part of the Arcelor Group, a Luxembourg-based company, in 2001. In 2006, Arcelor merged with the Indian company Mittal Steel to become ArcelorMittal, as of 2020 the largest steel manufacturer in the world (Nicolaus 2020, 68).

2. EKO Stahl had a surplus of 389 million Ostmarks for Q1 1990, then projected a loss of 286 million Deutschmarks for Q2 (Stiglich 2020, 190).

3. Scholars have also interpreted city building as a social project that materialized the absence of private property. Zarecor (2011, 196) describes socialist cities as "a physical manifestation of the success of the socialist system." Anthropologist Michał Murawski (2018b, 920) suggests that socialist cities are best analyzed through the lens of "economic aesthetics," as their aesthetics were understood as the material manifestation of socialist socioeconomic relationships.

4. Scholars have similarly noted the incompleteness of Communist property relationships elsewhere in the Eastern Bloc (Murawski 2018a; Zarecor 2018; Verdery 2003).

5. Anthropologist Caroline Humphrey (2002b, 69) writes that "an idea of possessions as signifying human interdependence is dimly present everywhere, but [under capitalism] it is swamped by private property that is conceived competitively and exclusively."

6. Housing Complex 5 also has a number of civic buildings: sports facilities originally built for the Young Pioneers, an Evangelical church whose construction was approved by the GDR regime in 1976, and the Central Foreigners' Reception Center, which took over an unused police dormitory on the complex's periphery in 1991 (Keil et al. 1997e, 15).

7. In 1997 the facility would ultimately enable the construction of a hot rolling facility, the final stage in the production of highly refined steel (Nicolaus 2020, 48).

8. Of 180 apartments uninhabited due to minor disrepair, 134 belonged to the GeWi and 46 to the AWG. All of the 94 apartments uninhabited due to major disrepair belonged to the GeWi. The city government estimated that the necessary repairs would cost 18,000 Deutschmarks (roughly $3,000) (Rat der Stadt Eisenhüttenstadt et al. 1990b).

9. The renovation of buildings on Street of the Republic, in Housing Complex 3, would cost between €4 and €4.5 million (Lötsch 2020b).

10. Between 2002 and 2014, 6,089 apartments, the vast majority of which were owned by the EWG, were demolished, and 2,878 apartments, 1,438 of which were owned by the GeWi, were renovated (Stadt Eisenhüttenstadt and BBSM 2015, 7).

11. Specifically, these apartments are reserved for holders of *Wohnberechtigungsschein*, housing vouchers for low-income tenants.

12. Leucht's plans for Housing Complex 4, published in 1953, do not include the interior courtyard buildings. The buildings were added when Leucht's plans were revised by subsequent city architects during the complex's construction, which took place between 1957 and 1967 (Keil et al. 1997d).

13. A December 17, 1954, *Pravda* article was widely circulated in translation under the title "Billiger, Besser, Schneller Bauen!" (Build cheaper, better, faster!). It describes

the necessity of employing prefabricated concrete architecture to solve housing shortages across the Eastern Bloc (Berliner Wissenschafts-Verlag 1955, 186–88).

14. Marseille has been similarly derelict with the historically protected Wall Theater in Oldenburg, which he also owns (Zimmermann 2023).

15. DeSilvey and Edensor (2013) provide a comprehensive literature review of the anthropology of ruination as it developed over the previous decade.

16. Treuhand ceased operations in 1994, and its unsold real estate holdings were transferred to state-operated companies (Kellermann 2021). The Potsdam office of the Treuhand Property Company LLC (Liegenschaftsgesellschaft mbH) gained ownership of the Aktivist (Gericke 2004, 83).

5. INFRASTRUCTURES OF SOLIDARITY

1. This friend also told me that his father, a Polish immigrant who had been displaced after World War II, was deeply disapproving of the Pioneers, which he saw as an indoctrinating organization not dissimilar from the Hitler Youth. But he reluctantly allowed his son to participate, as the social cost of withholding participation would have been too high.

2. The *Hausgemeinschaft* has no relationship to the classic anthropological notion of the "house society" (Lévi-Strauss [1975] 1988) but instead refers to the social group contained within the apartment house.

3. Social cohesion was also diminished by a complex confluence of factors, including a rise in restrictions on cultural and economic exchange with the West, increasing state corruption, and the second generation's lack of attachment to the socialist project (Pfaff 2006; Fulbrook 2014).

4. In 2014, close to 239,000 people sought asylum in Germany. In 2015, close to 1,000,000 people sought asylum there (Statista 2024), primarily due to the escalation of the Syrian Civil War. While the number of asylum seekers afterward sank to around 300,000 annually, it rose again in 2022, with the Russian invasion of Ukraine. Between January and October 2022, slightly over 1.2 million people sought asylum in Germany, around 1,000,000 of whom were from Ukraine (Oliveira 2022).

5. The term "social condenser" was widely used in the early Soviet Union to describe architecture's ability to shape social life, bringing people into relation with each other through their shared use of space (Murawski and Rendell 2017).

6. Oder-Spree County official Rolf Lindemann, who oversaw housing for asylum seekers, explained that renting apartments in Eisenhüttenstadt was significantly more comfortable for residents and financially beneficial for the county. He estimated that for the same cost that it took to house one hundred people in the high school gymnasium, which required security guards and commercial laundry, cleaning, and catering services, the county could house around three hundred people in apartments, paying for their rent and utilities, as well as the one-time purchase of basic furniture. In both scenarios, AWO social workers assisted residents of county-administered housing. In 2023, Oder-Spree County rented 178 apartments for asylum seekers; 80 of these were in Eisenhüttenstadt, housing around five hundred asylum seekers from Ukraine (Lötsch 2023b).

7. Rights to the city, as conceived by scholars such as Lefebvre (1968) and Harvey (2013), are rooted in habitation—all inhabitants of a city have the right to both access its goods and shape its sociopolitical development—yet these rights are often limited by factors that place limits on habitation, such as cost, segregation, gentrification, and, particularly for asylum seekers, state oversight.

8. Anthropologists Kelly McKowen and John Borneman (2020) advocate for the use of the term "incorporation" to describe the successful integration of migrants into the

social body. Incorporation entails change for both migrants and nonmigrants, while the more commonly used "integration" entails change only for migrants.

9. In the 2017 parliamentary election, Eisenhüttenstadt's top parties were as follows: Christian Democrats (22.4 percent), AfD (23.8 percent), Social Democrats (26.8 percent), and the Left (18.9 percent). In 2021, the Christian Democrats had 12.2 percent of the vote, the AfD 23.4 percent, the Social Democrats 32.7 percent, and the Left 9.1 percent (Landeswahlleiter Brandenburg 2021). Economist Kim Kellermann (2021, 49) shows that communities that experienced higher rates of Treuhand-related job loss are more likely to support the AfD.

6. A MODEL OF TRANSFORMATION

1. In 2021, the German federal government set a target to reduce CO_2 emissions by 65 percent by 2030, relative to 1990. The country aims to have a zero CO_2 balance by 2045, meaning that it will release as much CO_2 as it sequesters on an annual basis (Der Bundesregierung: Energie und Klimaschutz 2021).

2. The 2015 Paris Climate Accords included a pledge for EU member states to collectively lower their carbon emissions by 40 percent by 2030; the market share of renewable energy would rise by 27 percent, and energy consumption would sink by 27 percent. At the time when the Energy Renovation was developed, German laws passed in 2007 and 2010 also included goals to lower greenhouse gas emissions by 80 percent by 2050, increase the market share of renewable energy to 60 percent by 2050, and reduce energy consumption by 50 percent relative to 2008 usage. In Brandenburg, a 2012 state law mandated that energy usage be reduced by 1.1 percent annually, resulting in a 23 percent reduction in energy usage by 2030; similar state targets were also in place to increase the market share of renewable energy sources to a minimum of 32 percent by 2030 (Mann et al. 2015, 5–7).

3. The study analyzed each building's square footage, heat source, degree of postreunification renovation, vacancy rate, and heat consumption in 2011, 2012, and 2013. Rosa Luxemburg Street 10–13, an unrenovated building in Housing Complex 1 that was 89 percent vacant, consumed 2,500 kilowatt-hours per square meter, nearly twenty times as much as the buildings in Housing Complex 1 that were renovated in the 1990s, which were around 8 to 12 percent vacant and used around 110–130 kilowatt-hours per square meter. Buildings in Complex 3 with vacancy rates above 50 percent consumed around 340 kilowatt-hours per square meter (Mann et al. 2015, 4–7).

4. While STUK lists each entryway as its own building (e.g., Rosa Luxemburg Street 10, 11, 12, 13), the Energy Renovation plan analyzes each apartment block (e.g., Rosa Luxemburg Street 10–13).

5. A true steady state would have limits set by the earth's carrying capacity, rather than by what seems achievable under current political and economic circumstances.

6. These reports were submitted in the context of the Housing Exchange. When residents wanted to move house, they would submit a request to the exchange, which would coordinate between the GeWi and EWG such that tenants could be swapped into suitable apartments. A resident might wait a few months for a suitable apartment to become available, and the reports note a growing shortage of apartments suitable for the elderly. The fourth-floor walk-up apartments that remained vacant were offered to residents on the exchange but were declined (Rat der Stadt et al. 1990a, 1990b).

7. In 1995 and 1996, the city installed new heating infrastructures in the city center as part of the broader renovation efforts discussed in chapter 3. Ofenheizung buildings in the city center were transitioned to natural gas heating (H. Haubold 2000, 90).

8. Annual household heating costs rose from an average of €684 in 2000 to €1,050 in 2012 and €1,122 in 2013 (BMWK 2022). The household electricity price index rose from 81 to 151 during that same period (BDEW 2023). Energy costs rose in part due to the surcharge (*Umlage*) that resulted from the federal Renewable Energy Law (Erneubare Energie Gestzt, or EEG), passed in 2000 and active until 2022, which promised renewable energy producers an above-market rate of return, distributed across their consumer base as the EEG surcharge. The surcharge grew slowly in the early 2000s, from around 0.4 cents per kilowatt-hour in 2003 to 1.3 cents per kilowatt-hour in 2009, and then spiked in the 2010s, reaching a high of 6.8 cents per kilowatt-hour in 2017 (Der Bundesregierung: Energie und Klimaschutz 2022; Netztransparenz.de 2022). While heat and electricity operate as separate infrastructures, their costs are both tied to the fluctuating price of natural gas; hence the blanket term "fuel poverty," sometimes translated as "energy poverty."

9. Eisenhüttenstädters, like most Germans, also tend to be preoccupied with ventilation as essential for mold prevention. In older buildings without modern HVAC systems, ventilation is achieved only by opening a window, which lets out valuable heat. Many of my informants struggled to find a balance between heating and ventilation. The Energy Renovation plan suggests improving ventilation systems such that residents do not have to open their windows in winter (Mann et al. 2015, 26).

10. The power-heat coupling plant can expend 170 megawatt-hours of heat, while the city tends to consume between 10 and 15 megawatt-hours. Even a record-cold day of minus fifteen degrees Celsius resulted in 30 megawatt-hours of heat consumption (Mann et al. 2015, 40).

11. The steel plant indirectly supports numerous other businesses that were once part of VEB EKO, such as Vulcan, the company that operates the power-heat coupling plant. In 2020, Eisenhüttenstadt had 12,133 employment positions, 6,110 of which were filled by nonresidents and 6,023 by residents, and 2,768 residents commuted outside the city for their work (Stadt Eisenhüttenstadt and BBSM 2022, 18).

CONCLUSION

1. In light of this missed opportunity, anthropologist Deana Jovanović (2018) describes how late-socialist, late-industrial cities must constantly negotiate between risk and hope—the risk is that the benefits of industrial production rarely outweigh its harms, yet residents hope for its continuation, as industry brings economic activity that contributes to human well-being.

Works Cited

Abram, Simone. 2014. "The Time It Takes: Temporalities of Planning." *Journal of the Royal Anthropological Institute* 20 (April). https://doi.org/10.1111/1467-9655.12097.

Abram, Simone, and Gisa Weszkalnys. 2013. *Elusive Promises: Planning in the Contemporary World.* Berghahn Books.

Adorno, Theodor W. 1959. "Was Bedeutet: Aufarbeitung Der Vergangenheit." *Gesammelte Schriften* 10 (2): 555–72.

Agamben, Giorgio. 1998. *Homo Sacer: Sovereign Power and Bare Life.* Translated by Daniel Heller-Roazen. Stanford University Press.

Ahmann, Chloe. 2018. " 'It's Exhausting to Create an Event Out of Nothing': Slow Violence and the Manipulation of Time." *Cultural Anthropology* 33 (1): 142–71. https://doi.org/10.14506/ca33.1.06.

———. 2022. "Vacancy: Introduction." *Anthropological Quarterly* 95 (2): 241–75. https://doi.org/10.1353/anq.2022.0015.

Alexander, Catherine, and Andrew Sanchez, eds. 2018. *Indeterminacy: Waste, Value, and the Imagination.* Berghahn Books.

Allen, Jennifer L. 2019. "Against the 1989–1990 Ending Myth." *Central European History* 52 (1): 125–47. https://doi.org/10.1017/S0008938919000062.

Allendorf, Leif. 1998. "»Altschulden« von Wohnungsgesellschaften zum Teil vom Tisch." Junge Welt, January 22. https://www.jungewelt.de/artikel/3204. altschulden-von-wohnungsgesellschaften-zum-teil-vom-tisch.html.

Amt für Statistik Berlin-Brandenburg. 2020. "Bundestagwahlen Im Land Brandenburg 2013." Last modified August 28. Statistischer Bericht BVII 1-4-4j/13. https://www.statistischebibliothek.de/mir/servlets/MCRFileNodeServlet/BBHeft_derivate_00022612/SB_B07-01-04_2013j04_BB.pdf.

Anand, Nikhil. 2017. *Hydraulic City: Water and the Infrastructures of Citizenship in Mumbai.* Duke University Press.

Anderson, Benedict. (1983) 2016. *Imagined Communities: Reflections on the Origin and Spread of Nationalism.* Verso Books.

Anton, Wolfgang. 1999. "Ein neuer, würdiger Name." In *Eisenhüttenstadt: "Erste sozialistische Stadt Deutschlands,"* edited by Arbeitsgruppe Stadtgeschichte Eisenhüttenstadt. Be.bra Verlag.

Appadurai, Arjun. 1990. "Disjuncture and Difference in the Global Cultural Economy." *Theory, Culture & Society* 7 (2–3): 295–310.

Appadurai, Arjun, and Neta Alexander. 2020. *Failure.* Polity.

Appel, Hannah, Nikhil Anand, and Akhil Gupta. 2018. "Temporality, Politics, and the Promise of Infrastructure." In *The Promise of Infrastructure,* edited by Hannah Appel. Duke University Press.

Arbeitsgruppe "Straßennamen." 1991. "Protokoll." May 23, 1991. Stadtverwaltung Eisenhüttenstadt. Stadtarchiv Eisenhüttenstadt.

ArcelorMittal Eisenhüttenstadt. 2021. "ArcelorMittal Eisenhüttenstadt— Klimaneutraler Stahl in Eisenhüttenstadt: Annalena Baerbock Besuchte

ArcelorMittal-Werk." June 28, 2021. https://eisenhuettenstadt.arcelormittal.
com.

———. 2024. "ArcelorMittal Eisenhüttenstadt—2000: EKO Stahl und Eisenhüttenstadt
Feiern Am 18. August Mit Einen Stadtfest Ihr 50-Jähriges Jubiläum." 2024.
https://eisenhuettenstadt.arcelormittal.com/.

Atkinson, Rick. 1993. "Treuhand: Eastern Germany's Bargain Basement."
Washington Post, September 25. https://www.washingtonpost.com/archive/
business/1993/09/26/treuhand-eastern-germanys-bargain-basement/48ae8e90-
287a-4e7e-83e0-a32ee64170bf/.

Augé, Marc. 2004. *Oblivion*. University of Minnesota Press.

"Ausbau erneuerbarer Energien beschleunigen." 2023. Die Bundesregierung
informiert, March 1, 2023. https://www.bundesregierung.de/breg-de/
schwerpunkte/klimaschutz/novelle-eeg-gesetz-2023-2023972.

"Ausgezeichnetes Wohnen in Eisenhüttenstadt—Quartier komplett saniert."
2022. *Märkische Oderzeitung*, May 19. https://www.moz.de/lokales/
eisenhuettenstadt/immobilien-in-oder-spree-ausgezeichnetes-wohnen-in-
eisenhuettenstadt-64506631.html.

Bach, Jonathan P. G. 2002. " 'The Taste Remains': Consumption, (N)ostalgia, and the
Production of East Germany." *Public Culture* 14 (3): 545–56.

———. 2017. *What Remains: Everyday Encounters with the Socialist Past in Germany*.
Columbia University Press.

Bakke, Gretchen. 2019. "Crude Thinking." In *The Rhetoric of Oil in the Twenty-First
Century*, edited by Heather Graves and David Beard. Routledge.

BAMF (Bundesamt für Migration und Flüchtlinge). 2022. "Erstverteilung der
Asylsuchenden (EASY)." February 2. https://www.BAMF.de/DE/Themen/
AsylFluechtlingsschutz/AblaufAsylverfahrens/Erstverteilung/erstverteilung-
node.html.

BASD (Bundesstiftung zur Aufarbeitung der SED-Diktatur). 2008. "Heckert, Fritz."
Accessed May 22, 2024. https://www.bundesstiftung-aufarbeitung.de/de/
recherche/kataloge-datenbanken/biographische-datenbanken/fritz-heckert.

Bataille, Georges. (1967) 1989. *The Accursed Share: Consumption*. Translated by
Robert Hurley. Zone Books.

Bateson, Gregory. (1936) 1958. *Naven: A Survey of the Problems Suggested by a
Composite Picture of the Culture of a New Guinea Tribe Drawn from Three Points
of View*. Stanford University Press.

Bauakademie der DDR. 1951. "Wohnstadt EKO: Ein Beispiel Fortschrittlichen
Städtebaus in Der DDR." Bauakademie der DDR. DH2/21423. Bundesarchiv
Deutschland.

———. 1956. "Entwurf Einer Beschlussvorlage Über Die Weitere Entwicklung von
Stalinstadt." Berlin. DH2/17312. Bundesarchiv Deutschland.

———. 1960. "Stalinstadt Bevolkerungsausberechnung 1960–1980." Bauakademie der
DDR. DH2/21427. Bundesarchiv Deutschland.

Baumann, Hanna. 2020. "Moving, Containing, Displacing: The Shipping
Container as Refugee Shelter." In *Rethinking Refugee Shelter*, edited by
Tom Scott-Smith and Mark E. Breeze. Berghahn Books. https://doi.org/
doi:10.1515/9781789207132-003.

Bauprogramm Wohnstadt. 1952. "Berechnung der Kapazität für Transportlagen und
Geräte für Baustoffumschlag." Brandenburg Landeshauptarchiv, Potsdam.

BBR (Bundesamt für Bauwesen und Raumordnung). 2008. *Stadtquartiere Im
Umbruch, Infrastruktur Im Stadtumbau—Chancen Für Neue Freiräume*. BBR.

BBU Verband (Berlin-Brandenburgischer Wohnungsunternehmen e.V.). 2009. "Gewohnt Gut 03/2009." March 13. https://bbu.de/themen/wettbewerbe/gewohnt-gut/38849.

———. 2011. "Eisenhüttenstädterwohnungsbaugenossenschaft Erhält Brandenburgischen BaukulturPreis 2011." October 24. https://bbu.de/beitraege/eisenhuettenstaedter-wohnungsbaugenossenschaft-erhaelt-brandenburgischen-baukulturpreis-2011.

———. 2013. "Gewohnt Gut 05/2013." August 5. https://bbu.de/themen/wettbewerbe/gewohnt-gut/267.

———. 2015. "Gewohnt Gut 09/2015 | BBU." September 14. https://bbu.de/themen/wettbewerbe/gewohnt-gut/39788.

———. 2021. "Gewohnt Gut 10/2021." October 21. https://bbu.de/themen/wettbewerbe/gewohnt-gut/48244.

———. 2022. "Gewohnt Gut 05/2022 | BBU." May 25. https://bbu.de/themen/wettbewerbe/gewohnt-gut/49131.

BDEW (Bundesverband der Energie- und Wasserwirtschaft). 2023. "Electricity Price Index for Households in Germany from 1998 to 2023." Statista. https://www-statista-com.ezproxy.lib.lehigh.edu/statistics/1346301/electricity-price-development-households-germany/.

Benjamin, Walter. (1933) 1999. "On the Mimetic Faculty." In *Walter Benjamin: Selected Writings; 1935–1938.* Harvard University Press.

———. 1968. "Theses on the Philosophy of History." In *Illuminations.*

———. 2002. *The Arcades Project.* Translated by Howard Eiland and Kevin McLaughlin. 3rd printing ed. Belknap Press of Harvard University Press.

Benveniste, Emile. (1958) 1971. "Subjectivity in Language." *Problems in General Linguistics* 1:223–30.

Berdahl, Daphne. 1999. *Where the World Ended: Re-Unification and Identity in the German Borderland.* University of California Press.

Berlant, Lauren. 2011. *Cruel Optimism.* Duke University Press.

Berliner Wissenschafts-Verlag. 1955. "Billiger, Besser, Schneller Bauen!" *Ost-Probleme* 7 (5): 186–201.

Bernhardt, Christoph. 2005. "Planning Urbanization and Urban Growth in the Socialist Period: The Case of East German New Towns, 1945–1989." *Journal of Urban History* 32 (1): 104–19. https://doi.org/10.1177/0096144205279201.

Beyme, Klaus von. 2020. "DDR-Migrationspolitik." In *Migrationspolitik: Über Erfolge und Misserfolge.* Springer Fachmedien Wiesbaden. https://doi.org/10.1007/978-3-658-28662-0_5.

Blaschek, Rainer. 2021. "ArcelorMittal Eisenhüttenstadt—Auf Dem Weg Zu Klimaneutralem Stahl." April 15. https://eisenhuettenstadt.arcelormittal.com/Nachhaltigkeit/Auf-dem-Weg-zu-klimaneutralem-Stahl/.

BMWK (Bundesministerium für Wirtschaft und Klimaschutz). 2022. "Heating Expenditure per Private Household in Germany from 2000 to 2020 (in Euros per Year)." Statista. https://www-statista-com.ezproxy.lib.lehigh.edu/statistics/1323561/heat-costs-private-household-germany/.

———. 2024. "Press Release: Go-Ahead for Green Steel Production." February 23, 2024. https://www.bmwk.de/Redaktion/EN/Pressemitteilungen/2024/02/20240223-go-ahead-for-green-steel-production.html.

Boehme, Helga. 1992. "Antrag Auf Bürgerentscheid." Stadtarchiv Eisenhüttenstadt.

Borneman, John. 1991. *After the Wall: East Meets West in the New Berlin.* Basic Books.

———. 1992. *Belonging in the Two Berlins: Kin, State, Nation*. Cambridge Studies in Social and Cultural Anthropology. Cambridge University Press. https://doi.org/10.1017/CBO9780511607714.

Bourdieu, Pierre. 1977. *Outline of a Theory of Practice*. Translated by Richard Nice. Cambridge University Press.

Boyer, Dominic. 2006. "Ostalgie and the Politics of the Future in Eastern Germany." *Public Culture* 18 (2): 361–81. https://doi.org/10.1215/08992363-2006-008.

Boym, Svetlana. 2007. "Tatlin, or, Ruinophilia." *Cabinet*, Winter 2007–2008. https://cabinetmagazine.org/issues/28/boym2.php.

———. 2008. *The Future of Nostalgia*. Basic Books.

BpB (Bundeszentrale für politische Bildung). 2005. "Die 16 Grundsätze des Städtebaus." April 3. https://www.bpb.de/themen/nachkriegszeit/wiederaufbau-der-staedte/64346/die-16-grundsaetze-des-staedtebaus/.

Braun, Kerstin. 2011. "EWG Eisenhüttenstadt Erhält den Deutschen Preis für Denkmalschutz." 2011. https://bbu.de/nachricht/37342.

Brückweh, Kerstin. 2019. "Haus ohne Grund. Wo 'der Westen' und 'der Osten' sich treffen." *Zeitgeschichte Online*, March 18. https://doi.org/10.14765/zzf.dok-2551.

Buchli, Victor. 1999. *An Archaeology of Socialism*. London: Routledge. https://doi.org/10.4324/9781003084525.

Buchli, Victor, and Gavin Lucas. 2001. *Archaeologies of the Contemporary Past*. Routledge. https://doi.org/10.4324/9780203185100.

Buck-Morss, Susan. 1991. *The Dialectics of Seeing: Walter Benjamin and the Arcades Project*. MIT Press.

———. 2000. *Dreamworld and Catastrophe: The Passing of Mass Utopia in East and West*. MIT Press.

BUNBR (Bundesministerium für Umwelt, Naturschutz, Bau und Reaktorsicherheit). 2016a. "Bundesprogramm Zur Förderung Des Stadtumbau Ost." http://www.staedtebaufoerderung.info/StBauF/DE/Programm/Stadtumbau/StadtumbauOst/Foerderung/Foerderung2016.pdf?__blob=publicationFile&v=3.

———. 2016b. "Eisenhüttenstadt." http://www.staedtebaufoerderung.info/StBauF/DE/Programm/Stadtumbau/Praxis/Kommunale_Praxisbeispiele/Massnahmen/Eisenhuettenstadt/Eisenhuettenstadt_node.html.

———. 2016c. "Stadtumbau Ost Grundlagen." http://www.staedtebaufoerderung.info/StBauF/DE/Programm/Stadtumbau/StadtumbauOst/Programm/Grundlagen/grundlagen_node.html.

Bundach, Heinz. 1991. "Brief an Bürgermeister Werner." May 14. Stadtarchiv Eisenhüttenstadt.

Bundesnetzagentur and Bundeskelleramt. 2023. "Gas Prices in Germany from 2011 to 2023 by Consumer Group (in Euro Cents per Kilowatt Hour)." Statista. https://www-statista-com.ezproxy.lib.lehigh.edu/statistics/1319491/gas-prices-consumer-groups-germany/.

Büro für Städtebau Frankfurt Oder. 1982. "Komplexer Wohnungsbau Eisenhüttenstadt, Büro für Städtebau Frankfurt(O)." September 1. Brandenburg Landeshauptarchiv, Potsdam.

Butler, Judith. 1997. *Excitable Speech: A Politics of the Performative*. Psychology Press.

BVBS (Bundesministerium für Verkehr, Bau, und Stadtentwicklung). 2009. "Städtebauliche Sanierungs- Und Entwicklungsmaßnahmen 2009 Neue Länder." https://www.staedtebaufoerderung.info/SharedDocs/downloads/DE/WeitereProgramme/SanierungUndEntwicklung/Foerderung2009_neueBL.pdf?__blob=publicationFile&v=2.

BWSB (Bundesministerium für Wohnen, Stadtentwicklung und Bauwesen). 2018. "Eisenhüttenstadt: Räumlicher Schwerpunkt: Innenstadt—Wohnkomplexe (WK) I-IV." June. https://www.staedtebaufoerderung.info/DE/ WeitereProgramme/Stadtumbau/Praxis/Praxisbeispiele/Eisenhuettenstadt/ Eisenhuettenstadt.html.

———. 2021. "Stadtumbau Ost." Bundesinstitut für Bau-, Stadt- und Raumforschung. http://www.staedtebaufoerderung.info/DE/ProgrammeVor2020/Stadtumbau/ StadtumbauOst/stadtumbauOst.html;jsessionid=713892CB3CEFF3DA1ECBEC 64F01F3AF4.live11292?nn=3626310.

———. 2022. "Der Deutschlandatlas - Wie Wir Wohnen - Baulandpreise." https://www. deutschlandatlas.bund.de/DE/Karten/Wie-wir-wohnen/043-Baulandpreise. html.

———. 2024. "Stadtumbau Ost." Bundesinstitut für Bau-, Stadt- und Raumforschung. http://www.staedtebaufoerderung.info/DE/WeitereProgramme/Stadtumbau/ StadtumbauOst/stadtumbauOst.html;jsessionid=7441FC24579F446867CF6378 168B81E3.live11292?nn=3626310.

CEUDA (Centre for Excellence in Universal Design). 2020. "What Is Universal Design, Irish National Disability Authority." https://universaldesign.ie/ what-is-universal-design/.

Chari, Sharad, and Katherine Verdery. 2009. "Thinking Between the Posts: Postcolonialism, Postsocialism, and Ethnography After the Cold War." *Comparative Studies in Society and History* 51 (1): 6–34.

Chatterjee, Partha. 2006. *The Politics of the Governed: Reflections on Popular Politics in Most of the World.* Columbia University Press.

Cherkaev, Xenia A. 2023. *Gleaning for Communism: The Soviet Socialist Household in Theory and Practice.* Cornell University Press.

Chivens, Thomas. 2005. "After Post-Socialism? Transition's Obscured Inevitability." *Anthropology of East Europe Review* 23 (2): 26–29.

CIAM (Congress Internationaux d'Architecture Moderne). 1946. *Charter of Athens (1933).* Translated by J. Tyrwhitt. Library of the Graduate School of Design, Harvard University. https://www.getty.edu/conservation/publications_ resources/research_resources/charters/charter04.html.

Colditz, Heinz, and Martin Lücke. 1958. *Stalinstadt: Neues Leben, neue Menschen.* Kongress-Verlag.

Collier, Stephen J. 2011. *Post-Soviet Social: Neoliberalism, Social Modernity, Biopolitics.* Princeton University Press.

Cuevas-Wolf, Cristina. 2017. "John Heartfield's Thälmann Montages: The Politics Behind Images of International Antifascism." *New German Critique* 44 (2 [131]): 1–24.

Daly, Herman E. (1973) 1980. *Economics, Ecology, Ethics: Essays Toward a Steady-State Economy.* W. H. Freeman.

———. (1977) 1991. *Steady-State Economics: Second Edition with New Essays.* Island.

———. 1993. "Steady-State Economics: A New Paradigm." *New Literary History* 24 (4): 811–16. https://doi.org/10.2307/469394.

———. 2014. *Beyond Growth: The Economics of Sustainable Development.* Beacon.

Daniel, E. Valentine. 2013. "The Coolie: An Unfinished Epic." In *Imperial Debris,* edited by Ann Laura Stoler. On Ruins and Ruination. Duke University Press.

"Das Deutsche Volk Formt Selbst Sein Schicksal." 1949. *Tägliche Rundschau,* October 7. http://germanhistorydocs.ghi-dc.org/docpage.cfm?docpage_id=3208& language=german.

Dawdy, Shannon Lee. 2010. "Clockpunk Anthropology and the Ruins of Modernity." *Current Anthropology* 51 (6): 761–93. https://doi.org/10.1086/657626.

———. 2016. *Patina: A Profane Archaeology*. University of Chicago Press.

DBP (Deutscher Bauherrenpreis). 2015. "Deutscher Bauherrenpreis Hohe Qualität— Tragbare Kosten Im Wohnungsbau Eisenhüttenstadt, Alte Ladenstraße." http:// www.deutscherbauherrenpreis.de/projekt/eisenhuttenstadt-alte-ladenstrase/.

DEAL (Doughnut Economics Action Lab). 2022. "Cities & Regions." https:// doughnuteconomics.org/themes/1.

Der Bundesregierung: Energie und Klimaschutz. 2021. "Climate Change Act: Climate Neutrality by 2045." Die Bundesregierung informiert. June 25. https://www.bundesregierung.de/breg-de/schwerpunkte/klimaschutz/ climate-change-act-2021-1936846.

———. 2022. "Wegfall der EEG-Umlage entlastet Stromkunden." Die Bundesregierung informiert. May 28. https://www.bundesregierung.de/breg-de/themen/ tipps-fuer-verbraucher/eeg-umlage-faellt-weg-2011728.

———. 2024. "Wo steht Deutschland bei der Energiewende." Die Bundesregierung informiert. March 27. https://www.bundesregierung.de/breg-de/schwerpunkte/ klimaschutz/faq-energiewende-2067498.

Der Oberbürgermeister. 1992. "Amtliche Mitteilung." Stadtverwaltung Eisenhüttenstadt.

DeSilvey, Caitlin, and Tim Edensor. 2013. "Reckoning with Ruins." *Progress in Human Geography* 37 (4): 465–85. https://doi.org/10.1177/0309132512462271.

Destatis. 2022a. "Arbeitslosenquote Neue Länder und Berlin." Statistisches Bundesamt. https://www.destatis.de/DE/Themen/Wirtschaft/Konjunkturindikatoren/ Arbeitsmarkt/arb230a.html.

———. 2022b. "Life Expectancy in Germany Has Decreased Since the Beginning of the Pandemic." Federal Statistical Office. https://www.destatis.de/EN/ Press/2022/07/PE22_313_12621.html.

Döring, Karl. 2015. *EKO: Stahl Für Die DDR, Stahl Für Die Welt*. Edition Berolina.

Douglas, Mary. 1991. "The Idea of a Home: A Kind of Space." *Social Research* 58 (1): 287–307.

Drieschner, Axel. 2015. *Ankunft Eisenhüttenstadt: Eine Stadt gegründet von Zuzüglern; Zeitgeschichte in Lebensbildern*. Städtisches Museum Eisenhüttenstadt.

Drieschner, Axel, and Barbara Schulz. 2002. "Denkmal oder Altlast? Eine Kraftwerksruine in Eisenhüttenstadt erzählt von Rüstungswirtschaft, Zwangsarbeit und Krieg." *Kunsttexte.de - Journal für Kunst- und Bildgeschichte*, no. 1: 1–11. https://doi.org/10.48633/ksttx.2002.1.85495.

———. 2004. "Granit Für 'Germania.'" *Markisches Oder Zeitung*, February 13. Stadtarchiv Eisenhüttenstadt.

———. 2008. "Rüstungswirtschaft Und Zwangsarbeit in Fürstenberg (Oder) 1940–45." Mittelpunkt Kriegswichtiger Industrien. Städtisches Museum Eisenhüttenstadt. http://www.gedenkstaettenforum.de/nc/gedenkstaetten-rundbrief/rundbrief/ news/ruestungswirtschaft_und_zwangsarbeit_in_fuerstenberg_oder/.

DSP (Deutscher Städtebaupreis). 2018. *Deutscher Städtebaupreis 2018: Sonderpreis/ Belobigung, Eisenhüttenstadt/Stärkung Der Innenstadt-Wohngebiete Im Wandel*. https://staedtebaupreis.de/wp-content/uploads/2018/09/14-B-SP-Eisenh%C3%BCttenstadt.pdf.

Durkheim, Emile. (1895) 1982. *The Rules of Sociological Method*. Translated by W. D. Halls. Free Press.

Durth, W., J. Düwel, N. Gutschow, and S. Klimek. 1998. *Architektur Und Städtebau Der DDR*. Architektur Und Städtebau Der DDR, Vol. 1. Campus Verlag.

Dzenovska, Dace. 2020. "Emptiness: Capitalism Without People in the Latvian Countryside." *American Ethnologist* 47 (1): 10–26. https://doi.org/10.1111/amet.12867.

Eddy, Melissa. 2013. "East German Model City Rusts, Quarter-Century After Berlin Wall's Fall." *New York Times*, November 3. https://www.nytimes.com/2013/11/04/world/europe/east-german-model-city-rusts-quarter-century-after-berlin-walls-fall.html.

Edensor, Tim. 2005. "The Ghosts of Industrial Ruins: Ordering and Disordering Memory in Excessive Space." *Environment and Planning D: Society and Space* 23 (6): 829–49.

"Eisenhüttenstädter Wohnungsbaugenossenschaft Erhält Brandenburgischen Baukulturpreis 2011 | Fachinformation." 2011. BBU.de. 2011. https://bbu.de/beitraege/eisenhuettenstaedter-wohnungsbaugenossenschaft-erhaelt-brandenburgischen-baukulturpreis-2011.

Erler, Michael, dir. 2015. "Eisenhüttenstadt—Stahl, Brot Und Frieden." *Der Osten—Entdecke Wo Du Lebst*. MDR.

Erpenbeck, Jenny. 2023. *Kairos*. Translated by Michael Hofmann. New Directions.

Evans, Sophie, Arne Langer, and ArcelorMittal Corporate. 2021. "ArcelorMittal Plans Major Investment in German Sites, to Accelerate CO2 Emissions Reduction Strategy and Leverage the Hydrogen Grid." March 29. https://corporate.arcelormittal.com/media/.

EWG (Eisenhüttenstädter Wohnungsbaugenossenschaft e.G.). 2022a. "Die Geschichte Hinter Dem Aktivisten—EWG Besser Wohnen." https://www.ewg-besser-wohnen.de/2022/06/22/die-geschichte-hinter-dem-aktivist/.

———. 2022b. "5 Mal Ausgezeichnet—Einfach Besser—EWG Besser Wohnen." https://www.ewg-besser-wohnen.de/2022/06/07/5-mal-ausgezeichnet-einfach-besser/.

EWG eG. 2019. "Besser Wohnen I Sanierung »Quartier Friedensweg« in Eisenhüttenstadt." YouTube video, 6:04, January 18. https://www.youtube.com/watch?v=EB2FPMeCTaQ.

———. 2021. "Herzlich Willkommen Daheim - Gelb und Blau." YouTube video, 3:45, June 24. https://www.youtube.com/watch?v=sJpknCYIvGY.

Fehérváry, Krisztina. 2009. "Goods and States: The Political Logic of State-Socialist Material Culture." *Comparative Studies in Society and History* 51 (2): 426–59. https://doi.org/10.1017/S0010417509000188.

Fennell, Catherine. 2015. *Last Project Standing: Civics and Sympathy in Post-Welfare Chicago*. University of Minnesota Press.

Fernando, Mayanthi, and Cristiana Giordano. 2016. "Refugees and the Crisis of Europe." Society for Cultural Anthropology. June 28. https://culanth.org/fieldsights/series/refugees-and-the-crisis-of-europe.

Fortun, Kim. 2012. "Ethnography in Late Industrialism." *Cultural Anthropology* 27 (3): 446–64. https://doi.org/10.1111/j.1548-1360.2012.01153.x.

Foucault, Michel. 2009. *Security, Territory, Population: Lectures at the Collège de France 1977—1978*. Translated by Graham Burchell. Edited by Michel Senellart. Picador.

Fox, Samantha M. 2020. "Street Lighting and the Uneasy Coexistence of Socialist and Capitalist Urban Imaginaries." *Environment and Planning D: Society and Space* 38 (4): 646–63. https://doi.org/10.1177/0263775820909140.

———. 2024. "A City of Newcomers: Migration and Solidarity in the Former East Germany." *City & Society* 36 (2): 67–77. https://doi.org/10.1111/ciso.12484.

Friedman, Thomas L. 2005. *The World Is Flat: A Brief History of the Twenty-First Century*. Farrar, Straus and Giroux.

Fromm, Günter. n.d. [late 1980s]. "Denkmale Und Denkmalpflege in Eisenhüttenstadt Stadtteil Fürstenberg Oder." *Eisenhüttenstadt Stadtspiegel*. Stadtarchiv Eisenhüttenstadt.

———. 1999. "Nieder mit der Regierung! Der 17. Juni in Stalinstadt und Fürstenberg/ Oder." In *Eisenhüttenstadt: "Erste sozialistische Stadt Deutschlands,"* edited by Arbeitsgruppe Stadtgeschichte Eisenhüttenstadt. Be.bra Verlag.

———. 2002a. "Abschied von Den Genossen." *Märkische Oderzeitung*, September 9.

———. 2002b. "Diskussion Um Links-Opfer." *Märkische Oderzeitung*, September 5.

Fukuyama, Francis. (1992) 2006. *The End of History and the Last Man*. Simon and Schuster.

Fulbrook, Mary. 2005. *The People's State: East German Society from Hitler to Honecker*. Yale University Press.

———. 2014. *A History of Germany, 1918–2014: The Divided Nation*. John Wiley & Sons.

Gal, Susan. 2002. "A Semiotics of the Public/Private Distinction." *Differences* 13 (1): 77–95. https://doi.org/10.1215/10407391-13-1-77.

Gal, Susan, and Judith T. Irvine. 2019. *Signs of Difference: Language and Ideology in Social Life*. Cambridge University Press. https://doi.org/10.1017/97811086 49209.

Ganschow, Jörg. 1990. "Antrag Zur Stadtverordnetenversammlung Am 14. November." Stadtarchiv Eisenhüttenstadt.

Gansleweit, Klaus-Dieter. 1986. *Eisenhüttenstadt und Seine Umgebung*. Akademie der Wissenschaften der DDR, Institut für Geographie und Geoökologie, Arbeitsgruppe Heimatforschung, Akademie-Verlag GmbH.

Gericke, Frank. 1998. *Eisenhüttenstadt Architektur-Skulptur*. Stadtverwaltung Eisenhüttenstadt.

———. 2004. *50 Jahre Eisenhüttenstädter Wohnungsbaugenossenschaft e.G.* Eisenhüttenstädter Wohnungsbaugenossenschaft.

"Gesetzblatt der DDR NR.: 129/1953." 1953. In *50 Jahre Eisenhüttenstädter Wohnungsbaugenossenschaft e.G.*, 7. EWG e.G.

GeWi (Gebäudewirtschaft Eisenhüttenstadt). 2023. "GeWi-Info: Mieterzeitung Der Eisenhüttenstädter Gebäudewirtschaft GmbH." Winter. Gebäudewirtschaft Eisenhüttenstadt GmbH.

Giedion, Sigfried. 1995. *Building in France, Building in Iron, Building in Ferroconcrete*. Getty Publications.

Goffman, Erving. 1974. *Frame Analysis: An Essay on the Organization of Experience*. Harvard University Press.

Gook, Ben. 2015. *Divided Subjects, Invisible Borders: Re-Unified Germany After 1989*. Rowman & Littlefield.

Graeber, David, and David Wengrow. 2021. *The Dawn of Everything: A New History of Humanity*. Farrar, Straus and Giroux.

Gropius, Walter. (1919) 2019. "Programm Des Staatlichen Bauhauses in Weimar." Translated by Katherine Rochester. In *Bauhaus: Building the New Artist*. The Getty Research Institute. https://www.getty.edu/research/exhibitions_events/ exhibitions/bauhaus/new_artist/history/.

Günel, Gökçe. 2019. *Spaceship in the Desert: Energy, Climate Change, and Urban Design in Abu Dhabi*. Experimental Futures: Technological Lives, Scientific Arts, Anthropological Voices. Duke University Press.

Günther, Julia, and Frank Nestmann. 2000. "Quo vadis, Hausgemeinschaft? Zum Wandel nachbarschaftlicher Beziehungen in den östlichen Bundesländern." *Gruppe. Interaktion. Organisation. Zeitschrift für*

Angewandte Organisationspsychologie 31 (3): 321–37. https://doi.org/10.1007/s11612-000-0028-x.

Halbwachs, Maurice. (1925) 1992. *On Collective Memory*. University of Chicago Press.

Hann, Chris, Caroline Humphrey, and Katherine Verdery. 2003. "Introduction: Postsocialism as a Topic of Anthropological Investigation." In *Postsocialism as a Topic of Anthropological Investigation*. Routledge.

Härtel, Herbert. n.d. "Der Sozialistische Wohnungsbau: Chefarchitekt Härtel, Stalinstadt, Erläutert Am Wohnkomplex V Die Perspektive Des Wohnungsbaues in Unserer Stadt." *Stadtspiegel Eisenhüttenstadt*. Keil et Al Wohnkomplex V. Stadtarchiv Eisenhüttenstadt.

Harvey, David. 2006. "Neo-liberalism as Creative Destruction." *Geografiska Annaler: Series B, Human Geography* 88 (2): 145–58. https://doi.org/10.1111/j.0435-3684.2006.00211.x.

———. 2013. *Rebel Cities: From the Right to the City to the Urban Revolution*. Verso.

Haubold, Gabriele. 1999. "Moderne Zeiten oder Das Ende der Gemütlichkei." In *Eisenhüttenstadt: "Erste sozialistische Stadt Deutschlands,"* edited by Arbeitsgruppe Stadtgeschichte Eisenhüttenstadt. Be.bra Verlag.

———. 2014. "Straßen Und Ihre Menschen." *Bunt & Komplex*, December, 2014/4 edition.

Haubold, Hans-Wolfgang. 2000. *Die Planstadt: Eisenhüttenstadt Die Wohnkomplexe I-IV*. Gebaudewirtschaft Eisenhüttenstadt.

Haupt- und Finanzausschuß. 1991. "Umbenennung von Straßen Und Plätzen in Eisenhüttenstadt." Stadtarchiv Eisenhüttenstadt.

Heilmeyer, Florian. 2021. "Zukunft Gesucht: 70 Jahre Eisenhüttenstadt." *BaunetzWoche*, April 22.

Hensel, Jana. 2002. *Zonenkinder*. Rowohlt Taschenbuch Verlag.

Hermann, Tobias. 2021. "Bundesarchiv Internet—Übernahme Der Verantwortung Für Die Stasi-Unterlagen Durch Das Bundesarchiv." https://www.bundesarchiv.de/DE/Content/Meldungen/2021-06-16_integration-stua.html.

Hertwig, Ralph, and Christoph Engel. 2020. "Homo Ignorans: Deliberately Choosing Not to Know." In *Deliberate Ignorance: Choosing Not to Know*, edited by Ralph Hertwig and Christoph Engel. Massachusetts Institute of Technology and the Franklin Institute for Advanced Study.

Hirschl, Bernd, Christoph Lang, Gregor Weyer, Raoul Hirschberg, and Martina Richwien. 2023. "Gutachten Zum Klimaplan Brandenburg Erarbeitung Einer Klimaschutzstrategie Für Das Land Brandenburg Endbericht." Institut für ökologische Wirtschaftsforschung, Berlin.

Hirt, Sonia. 2013. "Whatever Happened to the (Post)Socialist City?" *Cities: Current Research on Cities*, no. 32 (July): 29–38. https://doi.org/10.1016/j.cities.2013.04.010.

Holmes, Seth M., and Heide Castañeda. 2016. "Representing the 'European Refugee Crisis' in Germany and Beyond: Deservingness and Difference, Life and Death." *American Ethnologist* 43 (1): 12–24. https://doi.org/10.1111/amet.12259.

Holston, James. 1989. *The Modernist City: An Anthropological Critique of Brasilia*. University of Chicago Press.

Howest, Frank. 2006. "Eisenhüttenstadt: Auf Und Umbau Einer Geplanten Stadt." PhD diss., Ruhr-Universität Bochum. http://www-brs.ub.ruhr-uni-bochum.de/netahtml/HSS/Diss/HowestFrank/diss.pdf.

Humphrey, Caroline. 2002a. "Rituals of Death as a Context for Understanding Personal Property in Socialist Mongolia." *Journal of the Royal Anthropological Institute* 8 (1): 65–87. https://doi.org/10.1111/1467-9655.00099.

——. 2002b. *The Unmaking of Soviet Life: Everyday Economies After Socialism.* Cornell University Press.

——. 2004. "Cosmopolitanism and Kosmopolitizm in the Political Life of Soviet Citizens." *Focaal* 2004 (44): 138–52. https://doi.org/10.3167/092012904782311245.

——. 2006. "On Being Named and Not Named: Authority, Persons, and Their Names in Mongolia." In *An Anthropology of Names and Naming,* edited by Barbara Bodenhorn and Gabriele vom Bruck. Cambridge University Press.

Huyssen, Andreas. 2003. *Present Pasts: Urban Palimpsests and the Politics of Memory.* Stanford University Press.

——. 2006. "Nostalgia for Ruins." *Grey Room,* no. 23 (April): 6–21. https://doi.org/10.1162/grey.2006.1.23.6.

Jackson, Tim. 2016. *Prosperity Without Growth: Foundations for the Economy of Tomorrow.* Routledge.

——. 2021. *Post Growth: Life After Capitalism.* Polity.

James, William. (1890) 1983. "The Hidden Self." In *Essays in Psychology,* edited by Frederick Burkhardt. Harvard University Press.

Jarausch, Konrad H. 1999. "Care and Coercion: The GDR as Welfare Dictatorship." In *Towards a Socio-Cultural History of the GDR,* edited by Konrad H. Jarausch. Berghahn Books. https://doi.org/doi:10.1515/9781782384793-006.

Jencks, Charles. 1977. *The Language of Post-Modern Architecture.* Academy Editions.

Joyce, Patrick. 2003. *The Rule of Freedom: Liberalism and the Modern City.* Verso.

Kaden, Ben. 2017. "Die Roten Fahnen von Stalinstadt. Eine Ansichtskarte." *Retrace Blog.* June 19. https://retraceblog.wordpress.com/2017/06/19/stalinstadt-1960/.

——. 2020a. *Karten zur Ostmoderne / DDR-Philokartie 1.* Sphere Publishers.

——. 2020b. "Die Stadt Im Spiegel Ihrer Ansichtskarten." August 21–22. Zwischen Modell Und Museum, Friedrich Wolf Theater, Eisenhüttenstadt: Kunstverein Neuzelle.

Käthner, Klaus. 1980. *30 Jahre Eisenhüttenstadt.* Rat der Stadt Eisenhüttenstadt.

——. 1991. "Warum Solch Ein Streit Um Einen Straßennamen?" *Märkische Oderzeitung,* July 9.

Kauschke, Marion. 1991. "Brief an Bürgermeister Werner." May 21. Stadtarchiv Eisenhüttenstadt.

Keane, Webb. 1995. "The Spoken House: Text, Act, and Object in Eastern Indonesia." *American Ethnologist* 22 (1): 102–24.

——. 2003. "Semiotics and the Social Analysis of Material Things." "Words and Beyond: Linguistic and Semiotic Studies of Sociocultural Order," edited by Paul Manning, special issue, *Language & Communication* 23 (3–4): 409–25. https://doi.org/10.1016/S0271-5309(03)00010-7.

Keil, Bärbel, Marita Beschoner, Karin Fischer, Lotti Herde, and Gudrun Noack. 1997a. "Entwicklung Der Wohnkomplexe I Bis VIII." Stadtarchiv Eisenhüttenstadt.

——. 1997b. "Entwicklung Der Wohnkomplexe I Bis VIII: WK I." Stadtarchiv Eisenhüttenstadt.

——. 1997c. "Entwicklung Der Wohnkomplexe I Bis VIII: WK II." Stadtarchiv Eisenhüttenstadt.

——. 1997d. "Entwicklung Der Wohnkomplexe I Bis VIII: WK III." Stadtarchiv Eisenhüttenstadt.

——. 1997e. "Entwicklung Der Wohnkomplexe I Bis VIII: WK IV." Stadtarchiv Eisenhüttenstadt.

——. 1997f. "Entwicklung Der Wohnkomplexe I Bis VIII: WK V." Stadtarchiv Eisenhüttenstadt.

———. 1997g. "Entwicklung Der Wohnkomplexe I Bis VIII: WK VI." Stadtarchiv Eisenhüttenstadt.

———. 1997h. "Entwicklung Der Wohnkomplexe I Bis VIII: WK VII." Stadtarchiv Eisenhüttenstadt.

Kellermann, Kim Leonie. 2021. "Trust We Lost: The Treuhand Experience and Political Behavior in the Former German Democratic Republic." Working Paper 3/2021. WUU Munster: CIW Discussion Paper. https://www.econstor.eu/handle/10419/231373.

Khatchadourian, Lori. 2022. "Life Extempore: Trials of Ruination in the Twilight Zone of Soviet Industry." *Cultural Anthropology* 37 (2): 317–48. https://doi.org/10.14506/ca37.2.10.

Klement, Franz. 1993. "Städtebaulicher Ideenwettbewerb: Stadtzentrum Eisenhüttenstadt." Stadt Eisenhüttenstadt, Der Oberbürgermeister und Amt für Stadtplanung und Stadtentwicklung. Stadtarchiv Eisenhüttenstadt.

Klimaschutz, BMWK-Bundesministerium für Wirtschaft und. 2024. "Kraft-Wärme-Kopplung." https://www.bmwk.de/Redaktion/DE/Artikel/Energie/moderne-kraftwerkstechnologien.html.

Klinenberg, Eric. 2018. *Palaces for the People: How Social Infrastructure Can Help Fight Inequality, Polarization, and the Decline of Civic Life.* Crown.

Knox, Hannah. 2020. *Thinking Like a Climate: Governing a City in Times of Environmental Change.* Duke University Press.

Köhlner, H. 1991. "Brief an Redakteur Der *Märkische Oderzeitung.*" April 28. Stadtarchiv Eisenhüttenstadt.

Koselleck, Reinhart. 2004. *Futures Past: On the Semantics of Historical Time.* Translated and with an introduction by Keith Tribe. Columbia University Press.

Kotkin, Stephen. 1997. *Magnetic Mountain: Stalinism as a Civilization.* Revised ed. University of California Press.

Krüger, H. 1991. "Brief an Bürgermeister Werner." May 14. Stadtarchiv Eisenhüttenstadt.

Kulturland Brandenburg. 2023. "Eisenhüttenstadt: Bühne Der Baukultur." *Kulturland Brandenburg Magazine, Baukultur Leben Themenjahr 2023.*

Ladd, Brian. 1990. *Urban Planning and Civic Order in Germany, 1860–1914.* Harvard University Press.

Land Brandenburg. 2004. *Gesetz Über Den Schutz Und Die Pflege Der Denkmale Im Land Brandenburg (Brandenburgisches Denkmalschutzgesetz - BbgDSchG).* GVBl.I. Vol. 4. https://bravors.brandenburg.de/gesetze/bbgdschg.

Landeswahlleiter Brandenburg. 2021. "Ergebnisse Bundestagswahlergebnisse Nach Landkreisen Und Kreisfreien Städten in 67 0 120 120—Eisenhüttenstadt, Stadt." September 26. https://www.wahlergebnisse.brandenburg.de/wahlen/BU2021/afspraes2/ergebnisse_gemeinde_120670120120.html.

Langer, Suzanne. 1957. *Philosophy in a New Key.* Harvard University Press.

Larkin, Brian. 2013. "The Politics and Poetics of Infrastructure." *Annual Review of Anthropology* 42 (1): 327–43. https://doi.org/10.1146/annurev-anthro-092412-155522.

LBV (Landesamt für Bauen und Verkehr). 2011. "Infopool Stadtentwicklung: 'Junges Wohnen' in Eisenhüttenstadt." https://lbv.brandenburg.de/1161_3192.htm.

———. 2016. "Infopool Stadtentwicklung: Generationen-Wohnen Im Zentrum." http://www.lbv.brandenburg.de/1161_4493.htm.

———. 2018. "Infopool Stadtentwicklung: Flächenhafter Rückbau." https://lbv.brandenburg.de/1161_1210.htm.

Le Corbusier. (1931) 1986. *Towards a New Architecture.* Dover.

Lefebvre, Henri. (1968) 1996. "The Right to the City." In *Writings on Cities*. Translated and edited by Eleonore Kofman and Elizabeth Lebas. Blackwell Publishers.

——. (1974) 1992. *The Production of Space*. Translated by Donald Nicholson-Smith. Wiley.

Leitz, Michael, dir. 2022. *70 Jahre Eisenhüttenstadt*. Alpha-Doku. ARD 1.

Leucht, Kurt W. 1956. "Anlagen." Forschungsinstitut für Städtebau und Siedlungswesen. DH2/21424. Bundesarchiv Deutschland.

——. 1957. *Die erste neue Stadt in der Deutschen Demokratischen Republik: Planungsgrundlagen und -ergebnisse von Stalinstadt*. Verlag Technik.

——. 1990. Personal correspondence with Gabriele Haubold. December 8.

——. 1991. "Interview with Kurt Leucht, Unpublished." Dresden. Personal correspondence of Gabriele Haubold.

Lévi-Strauss, Claude. (1975) 1988. *The Way of the Masks*. Translated by Sylvia Modelski. University of Washington Press.

Liebmann, Heike, Anja Nelle, Christoph Haller, Christopher Knappe, and Ulrike Hagemeister. 2012. "10 Jahre Stadtumbau Ost—Berichte aus der Praxis." Bundesinstitut für Bau-, Stadt- und Raumforschung. https://www.bbsr.bund.de.

Lippitz, Ulf. 2021. "Flächendenkmal Eisenhüttenstadt: Ganz schön verplant." *Der Tagesspiegel*, March 23. https://www.tagesspiegel.de/gesellschaft/ganz-schon-verplant-4239166.html.

Lippmann, Quentin, Alexandre Georgieff, and Claudia Senik. 2020. "Undoing Gender with Institutions: Lessons from the German Division and Reunification." *Economic Journal* 130 (629): 1445–70. https://doi.org/10.1093/ej/uez057.

Livingston, Julie. 2019. *Self-Devouring Growth: A Planetary Parable as Told from Southern Africa*. Critical Global Health: Evidence, Efficacy, Ethnography. Duke University Press.

Lonzek, K. 1991. "Brief an Bürgermeister Werner." April 24. Stadtarchiv Eisenhüttenstadt.

LOS (Landkreis Oder-Spree). 2021. "Neue Dachmarke: Museum Utopie und Alltag." Landkreis Oder-Spree. May 19. https://www.landkreis-oder-spree.de/Service-Aktuelles/Aktuelles/Mitteilungen/.

Lötsch, Stefan. 2015. "System kommt an seine Grenzen." *Märkische Oderzeitung*, January 23. https://www.moz.de/lokales/eisenhuettenstadt/_system-kommt-an-seine-grenzen_-49846456.html.

——. 2019. "Kaffeeklatsch mit Nachbarn." *Märkische Oderzeitung*, May 25. https://www.moz.de/lokales/eisenhuettenstadt/begegnung-kaffeeklatsch-mit-nachbarn-48984858.html.

——. 2020a. "Die Stahlstadt Schrumpft Weiter." *Märkische Oderzeitung*, January 5. https://www.moz.de/artikel-ansicht/dg/0/1/1776166/.

——. 2020b. "Immobilienmarkt: Gebäudewirtschaft in Eisenhüttenstadt Saniert Auf Sicht | MMH." *Märkische Oderzeitung*, February 9. https://www.moz.de/lokales/eisenhuettenstadt/immobilienmarkt-gebaeudewirtschaft-in-eisenhuettenstadt-saniert-auf-sicht-51019032.html.

——. 2021. "Gefahr für prägenden Baum in Einkaufsstraße von Eisenhüttenstadt." *Märkische Oderzeitung*, April 7. https://www.moz.de/lokales/eisenhuettenstadt/naturschutz-gefahr-fuer-praegenden-baum-in-einkaufsstrasse-von-eisenhuettenstadt-56096820.html.

——. 2022a. "Ausgezeichnetes Wohnen in Eisenhüttenstadt—Quartier komplett saniert." *Märkische Oderzeitung*, May 19. https://www.moz.de/lokales/eisenhuettenstadt/immobilien-in-oder-spree-ausgezeichnetes-wohnen-in-eisenhuettenstadt-64506631.html.

———. 2022b. "Gibt es Hoffnung für das ehemalige Hotel Lunik?" *Märkische Oderzeitung*, February 10. https://www.moz.de/lokales/eisenhuettenstadt/immobilie-in-oder-spree-gibt-es-hoffnung-fuer-das-ehemalige-hotel-lunik-in-eisenhuettenstadt_-62570437.html.

———. 2022c. "Statt Abriss—Warteliste für bezahlbare, sanierte Wohnungen in Eisenhüttenstadt." *Märkische Oderzeitung*, May 25. https://www.moz.de/lokales/eisenhuettenstadt/wohnen-miete-eisenhuettenstadt-statt-abriss-_-warteliste-fuer-bezahlbare_-sanierte-wohnungen-in-eisenhuettenstadt-64629011.html.

———. 2023a. "Bevölkerung in Eisenhüttenstadt: Attraktive Stadt? Zahl der Einwohner wächst 2022 deutlich." *Märkische Oderzeitung*, February 11. https://www.moz.de/lokales/eisenhuettenstadt/bevoelkerung-in-eisenhuettenstadt-attraktive-stadt_-zahl-der-einwohner-waechst-2022-deutlich-69145741.html.

———. 2023b. "Mehr als 1700 neue Einwohner—Ausländeranteil nimmt deutlich zu." *Märkische Oderzeitung*, May 2. https://www.moz.de/lokales/eisenhuettenstadt/bevoelkerung-in-eisenhuettenstadt-mehr-als-1700-neue-einwohner-_-auslaenderanteil-nimmt-deutlich-zu-70504333.html.

———. 2023c. "Wohnen in Eisenhüttenstadt: Zu viel oder zu wenige Wohnungen—ist Gebäude-Abriss bald überflüssig?" *Märkische Oderzeitung*, February 16. https://www.moz.de/lokales/eisenhuettenstadt/wohnen-in-eisenhuettenstadt-zu-viel-oder-zu-wenige-wohnungen-_-ist-gebaeude-abriss-bald-ueberfluessig_-69204599.html.

Lowenthal, Lotte. 1957. "East Germany." *The American Jewish Year Book* 58:296–99.

Ludwig, Andreas. 1999a. "Eisenhüttenstadt: Industrieller Kern und neue Stadt." In *Eisenhüttenstadt: "Erste sozialistische Stadt Deutschlands,"* edited by Arbeitsgruppe Stadtgeschichte Eisenhüttenstadt. Be.bra Verlag.

———. 1999b. "Genossenschaften in der DDR." In *Eisenhüttenstadt: "Erste sozialistische Stadt Deutschlands,"* edited by Arbeitsgruppe Stadtgeschichte Eisenhüttenstadt. Be.bra Verlag.

———. 2000. *Eisenhüttenstadt: Wandel einer industriellen Gründungsstadt in fünfzig Jahren*. Brandenburgische Landeszentrale für Politische Bildung.

———. 2004. "Genossenschaften in Der DDR." In *50 Jahre Eisenhüttenstädter Wohnungsbaugenossenschaft e.G.*, edited by Frank Gericke. EWG e.G.

Lynch, Kevin. 1964. *The Image of the City*. MIT Press.

Major, Patrick. 1998. *The Death of the KPD: Communism and Anti-Communism in West Germany, 1945–1956*. Clarendon.

Malkki, Liisa. 1992. "National Geographic: The Rooting of Peoples and the Territorialization of National Identity Among Scholars and Refugees." *Cultural Anthropology* 7 (1): 24–44.

———. 1995. "Refugees and Exile: From 'Refugee Studies' to the National Order of Things." *Annual Review of Anthropology* 24 (1): 495–523. https://doi.org/10.1146/annurev.an.24.100195.002431.

Mann, Matthias, Daniel Knopf, and Thüringer Institut für Nachhaltigkeit und Klimaschutz GmbH. 2015. *Integrierten Quartierskonzept Zur Energetischen Stadtsanierung Der Wohnkomplexe 1 Bis VI in Eisenhüttenstadt*. Stadtverwaltung Eisenhüttenstadt.

Manz, Karl Heinz. 1991. "Brief an Bürgermeister Werner." September 11. Stadtarchiv Eisenhüttenstadt.

Marcuse, Harold. "Historical US Dollars to German Marks Currency Conversion." 2018. University of California, Santa Barbara. https://marcuse.faculty.history.ucsb.edu/projects/currency.htm#infcalc.

Märkischer Sonntag. 2015. "Jetz Kann Die Stadt Attraktiver Werden: Kooperationsvertrag Sichert Stadtumbau," February 7.

Marx, Karl, and Friedrich Engels. (1848) 1978. "Manifesto of the Communist Party." In *The Marx-Engels Reader,* edited by Robert C. Tucker. Norton.

Mathews, Andrew S. 2018. "Landscapes and Throughscapes in Italian Forest Worlds: Thinking Dramatically About the Anthropocene." *Cultural Anthropology* 33 (3): 386–414. https://doi.org/10.14506/ca33.3.05.

Matthes, Ina. 2022. "Krise in Brandenburg: So Pessimistisch Wie Nie – Stimmung in Der Wirtschaft Rutscht Ins Tief | Moz.De." *Märkische Oderzeitung,* October 22. https://www.moz.de/nachrichten/brandenburg/krise-in-brandenburg-so-pessimistisch-wie-nie-_-stimmung-in-der-wirtschaft-rutscht-ins-tief-67260669.html.

Mau, Steffen. 2021. "Over Three Decades Since Reunification, Germany Is Still Fractured: An Interview with Steffen Mau." *Jacobin,* March 10. https://jacobin.com/2021/10/german-reunification-east-west-berlin-wall-anniversary.

Mauss, Marcel. (1925) 2002. *The Gift: The Form and Reason for Exchange in Archaic Societies.* Translated by W. D. Hall. Routledge Classics.

May, Ruth. 1999. *Planstadt Stalinstadt: Ein Grundriss der frühen DDR, aufgesucht in Eisenhüttenstadt.* IRPUD.

McConica, James. 2011. "Thomas More as Humanist." In *The Cambridge Companion to Thomas More,* edited by George M. Logan. Cambridge University Press.

McKowen, Kelly, and John Borneman, eds. 2020. *Digesting Difference: Migrant Incorporation and Mutual Belonging in Europe.* Global Diversities. Springer International. https://doi.org/10.1007/978-3-030-49598-5.

McLellan, Josie. 2006. Review of "The People's State. East German Society from Hitler to Honecker." *History in Focus,* no. 10 (February). https://archives.history.ac.uk/history-in-focus/cold/reviews/mclellan.html#1.

MDFE (Land Brandenburg Ministerium der Finanzen und für Europa). 2019. "Görke: Hilfe zum Abbau der Altschulden ostdeutscher Wohnungsunternehmen fortsetzen." August 24. https://mdfe.brandenburg.de/mdfe/de/ministerium/presse/pressemitteilungen/pressemitteilung/~24-08-2019-goerke-hilfe-zum-abbau-der-altschulden-ostdeutscher-wohnungsunternehmen-fortsetzen.

Meakem, Allison. 2024. "A Tale of Two Germanies." *Foreign Policy* (blog), June 5. https://foreignpolicy.com/2023/10/01/germany-east-west-reunification-book-review-katja-hoyer-michael-kater/.

Mill, John Stuart. (1848) 1986. "John Stuart Mill on the Stationary State." *Population and Development Review* 12 (2): 317–22. https://doi.org/10.2307/1973114.

Ministerium für Aufbau. 1950. "Festlegung des Standortes Für Das Hüttenkombinat Ost (Fürstenberg/Oder)." Ministerium für Aufbau, Berlin. Rep 601/6065. Brandenburg Landeshauptarchiv, Potsdam.

Ministerium für Bauwesen. 1958. "Grünplanung: Bautechnischer Erläuterungsbericht Und Erläuterung Zum Kostenplan." Zentrales Entwurfsbüro Für Hochbau. Berlin. Stadtarchiv Eisenhüttenstadt.

Missouri Botanical Garden. n.d. "Plant Finder." Accessed May 23, 2024. https://www.missouribotanicalgarden.org/plantfinder/plantfindersearch.aspx.

More, Thomas. (1516) 1965. *Utopia.* Translated by Paul Turner. Reprint, Penguin Classics.

Morris, Julia Caroline. 2023. *Asylum and Extraction in the Republic of Nauru.* Cornell University Press.

MOZ Redakteure. 1991. "Straßen-Umbenennung: 'Was Kann Denn Der Lenin Dafür?'" *Märkische Oderzeitung,* May 25.

Mrázek, Rudolf. 2018. *Engineers of Happy Land: Technology and Nationalism in a Colony.* Princeton University Press.

Muehlebach, Andrea. 2012. *The Moral Neoliberal: Welfare and Citizenship in Italy.* Chicago Studies in Practices of Meaning. University of Chicago Press.

Müller-Enbergs, Helmut. 2008. *Inoffizielle Mitarbeiter Des Ministeriums Für Staatssicherheit.* BSTU. http://www.nbn-resolving.org/urn:nbn :de:0292-97839421302647.

Mumford, Lewis. 1922. *The Story of Utopias.* Boni and Liveright. http://archive.org/ details/storyutopias00mumfgoog.

———. 1961. *The City in History: Its Origins, Its Transformations, and Its Prospects.* Houghton Mifflin Harcourt.

Munn, Nancy D. 2013. "The 'Becoming-Past' of Places: Spacetime and Memory in Nineteenth-Century, Pre-Civil War New York." *HAU: Journal of Ethnographic Theory* 3 (2): 359–80. https://doi.org/10.14318/hau3.2.025.

Murawski, Michał. 2018. "Marxist Morphologies: A Materialist Critique of Brute Materialities, Flat Infrastructures, Fuzzy Property, and Complexified Cities." *Focaal* 2018 (82): 16–34. https://doi.org/10.3167/fcl.2018.820102.

Murawski, Michał, and Jane Rendell. 2017. "The Social Condenser: A Century of Revolution Through Architecture, 1917–2017." *Journal of Architecture* 22 (3): 369–71. https://doi.org/10.1080/13602365.2017.1326680.

Muth, Prof. Dr. 1991. "Änderungen von Straßennamen." Ministerium des Innern, Land Brandenburg. Stadtarchiv Eisenhüttenstadt.

MWAE (Ministerium für Wirtschaft, Arbeit und Energie des Landes Brandenburg). 2022. *Maßnahmenkonkrete Strategie Für Den Aufbau Einer Wasserstoff Wirtschaft Im Land Brandenburg.* Potsdam.

Nadolni, Florence. 2021. "Museum Utopie Und Alltag: Kulturgemeinschaften in Brandenburg." June 7. *Kulturstiftung Der Länder Podcast.* Kulturstiftung der Länder—Stiftung des bürgerlichen Rechts.

Navaro-Yashin, Yael. 2009. "Affective Spaces, Melancholic Objects: Ruination and the Production of Anthropological Knowledge." *Journal of the Royal Anthropological Institute* 15 (1): 1–18. https://doi.org/10.1111/j.1467-9655.2008.01527.x.

———. 2012. *The Make-Believe Space: Affective Geography in a Postwar Polity.* Duke University Press.

Neiser, Janet. 2015. "Es Ist Katastrophal." *Märkische Oderzeitung,* July 20. https://www. moz.de/artikel-ansicht/dg/0/1/1407439/.

———. 2019. "Bauen: Lunik führt Bürgermeister nach Hamburg," January 10. https:// www.moz.de/lokales/eisenhuettenstadt/bauen-lunik-fuehrt-buergermeister- nach-hamburg-49171966.html.

———. 2020. "Interview Zur DDR–Geschichte: Einstiger DDR–Chefarchitekt Sorgt Sich Schlaflos Um Sein Eisenhüttenstadt." *Märkische Oderzeitung,* August 9. https://www.moz.de/lokales/eisenhuettenstadt/ddr-geschichte-schlaflos-in-der- planstadt-eisenhuettenstadt-51181862.html.

———. 2022a. "Ein Viertel bei Mietern besonders beliebt—Warteliste für Interessenten." *Märkische Oderzeitung,* March 28. https://www.moz.de/lokales/ eisenhuettenstadt/wohnen-in-eisenhuettenstadt-ein-viertel-bei-mietern- besonders-beliebt-_-warteliste-fuer-interessenten-63536575.html.

———. 2022b. "Kurzarbeit in Eisenhüttenstadt zurück—neue Entwicklungen am Stahl–Standort Bremen." *Märkische Oderzeitung,* September 29. https://www. moz.de/lokales/eisenhuettenstadt/arcelormittal-eisenhuettenstadt-kurzarbeit- zurueck-_-sorgen-beim-betriebsrat-und-forderung-nach-preisdeckel-fuer- strom-und-gas-66808985.html.

———. 2022c. "ArcelorMittal Germany: Kurzarbeit in Eisenhüttenstadt zurück –
neue Entwicklungen am Stahl-Standort Bremen." *Märkische Oderzeitung*,
September 29. https://www.moz.de/lokales/eisenhuettenstadt/arcelormittal-
eisenhuettenstadt-kurzarbeit-zurueck-_-sorgen-beim-betriebsrat-und-
forderung-nach-preisdeckel-fuer-strom-und-gas-66808985.html.

———. 2023a. "Ehemaliges Hotel Lunik in Gefahr—Landkreis erhöht Druck."
Märkische Oderzeitung, March 31. https://www.moz.de/lokales/
eisenhuettenstadt/immobilien-in-eisenhuettenstadt-ehemaliges-hotel-lunik-in-
gefahr-_-landkreis-erhoeht-druck-69982879.html.

———. 2023b. "Ein Stückchen DDR wird freigelegt—das passiert am 1. Mai."
Märkische Oderzeitung, April 26. https://www.moz.de/lokales/eisenhuettenstadt/
lost-place-in-eisenhuettenstadt-ein-stueckchen-ddr-wird-freigelegt-_-das-
passiert-am-1.-mai-70407705.html.

———. 2023c. "Eisenhüttenstadt räumt auf, Jugend begeistert—Lost Place lebt."
Märkische Oderzeitung, May 1. https://www.moz.de/lokales/eisenhuettenstadt/
tag-der-arbeit-eisenhuettenstadt-raeumt-auf_-jugend-begeistert-_-lost-place-
lebt-70494519.html.

———. 2023d. "Neue Initiative zum ehemaligen Hotel Lunik—offener Brief an Ulrich
Marseille." *Märkische Oderzeitung*, February 17. https://www.moz.de/lokales/
eisenhuettenstadt/immobilie-in-eisenhuettenstadt-neue-initiative-zum-
ehemaligen-hotel-lunik-_-offener-brief-an-ulrich-marseille-69227861.html.

———. 2023e. "Was der Architekt Martin Maleschka für den Platz der Jugend
geplant hat." *Märkische Oderzeitung*, March 3. https://www.moz.de/lokales/
eisenhuettenstadt/lost-places-in-eisenhuettenstadt-was-der-architekt-martin-
maleschka-fuer-den-platz-der-jugend-geplant-hat-69479969.html.

———. 2024. "Habeck in Bremen—Zusage für grünen Stahl, auch für
Eisenhüttenstadt." *Märkische Oderzeitung*, February 5. https://www.moz.de/
lokales/eisenhuettenstadt/arcelormittal-habeck-im-stahlwerk-bremen-_-
hoffnung-auf-foerderzusage-in-eisenhuettenstadt-72968947.html.

Netztransparenz.de. 2022. "Surcharge Under the Renewable Energy Sources Act for
Household Electricity Customers in Germany from 2003 to 2022 (in Euro Cents
per Kilowatt Hour)." Statista.

Nicolaus, Herbert. 2020. "Stahl-Zeiten: 70 Geschichten aus 70 Jahren
Unternehmensgeschichte ArcelorMittal Eisenhüttenstadt." ArcelorMittal
Eisenhüttenstadt GmbH.

Nitschke, Niklas. 2021. "'Eisenhüttenstadt—Between Model and Museum.' The
Ideal City as Site for Artistic Research and Intervention: On Two Exhibitions
and Symposia." *Journal for Artistic Research* (December 30). https://doi.
org/10.22501/jarnet.0052.

Nüßlein, Christopher. 2023. "ArcelorMittal, Veo and McPhy Set Up Pilot Electrolysis
Plant in Eisenhüttenstadt—ICOB: Investor Center Ostbrandenburg GmbH"
ICOB: Investor Center Ostbrandenburg GmbH (blog), April 5. https://www.
icob.de/arcelormittal-veo-und-mcphy-errichten-pilot-elektrolyseanlage-in-
eisenhuettenstadt/.

Ojani, Chakad. 2023. "The Promise of Fog Capture: Ground-Touching Clouds
as a Material (Im)possibility in Peru." *Cultural Anthropology* 38 (2):
225–50.

Oliveira, Astrid Prange de. 2022. "Faktencheck: Kommen 2022 mehr Flüchtlinge als
2015/2016?" DW.com. November 16. https://www.dw.com/de/faktencheck-
kommen-2022-mehr-fl%C3%BCchtlinge-als-2015-2016/a-63747379.

Oliver-Smith, Anthony. 1996. "Anthropological Research on Hazards and Disasters." *Annual Review of Anthropology* 25 (1): 303–28. https://doi.org/10.1146/annurev. anthro.25.1.303.

Ophir, Adi. 2005. *The Order of Evils: Toward an Ontology of Morals.* Zone Books.

Oushakine, Serguei Alex. 2014. "'Against the Cult of Things': On Soviet Productivism, Storage Economy, and Commodities with No Destination." *Russian Review* 73 (2): 198–236. https://doi.org/10.1111/russ.10727.

Pehnert, Lutz, dir. 2016. "Geheimnisvolle Orte: Eisenhüttenstadt." Rundfunk Berlin-Brandenburg (RBB). https://www.rbb-online.de/geheimnisvolle_orte/archiv/ eisenhuettenstadt.html.

Peirce, Charles Sanders. 1931. *Principles of Philosophy and Elements of Logic.* Edited by Charles Hartshorne and Paul Weiss. Vol. 1 of *Collected Papers of Charles Sanders Peirce.* Belknap Press of Harvard University Press.

Peisker, Andrea. 2022. "Ein Tastmodell Für Eisenhüttenstadt." *Bunt & Komplex,* March, 2/22 edition.

Pence, Katherine, and Paul Betts. 2008. *Socialist Modern: East German Everyday Culture and Politics.* University of Michigan Press.

Pérez Fernández, Federico. 2023. "The Archaeology of Decay: Ruinous Knowledge and the Violence of Urban Planning." *American Anthropologist* 125 (3): 505–18.

Pfaff, Steven. 2006. *Exit-Voice Dynamics and the Collapse of East Germany: The Crisis of Leninism and the Revolution of 1989.* Duke University Press.

Pfannstiel, Margot. 1951. "Wohnstadt Für 25 000 Einwohner." *Neues Deutschland,* October 7.

———. 1977. "Ein Besuch Mit Vielen Folgen." *Neues Deutschland.*

Phillips, Kristin D. 2023. "Southern Politics, Southern Power Prices: Race, Utility Regulation, and the Value of Energy." *Economic Anthropology* 10 (2): 197–212. https://doi.org/10.1002/sea2.12279.

Phillips, Sarah D. 2005. "Postsocialism, Governmentality, and Subjectivity: An Introduction." *Ethnos* 70 (4): 437–42. https://doi.org/10.1080/ 0014184050041 9725.

Poutrus, Patrice G. 2005. "Die DDR, Ein Anderer Deutscher Weg? Zum Umgang Mit Ausländern Im SED-Staat." In *Zuwanderungsland Deutschland, Migrationen 1500–2005,* edited by Rosmarie Beier. Deutsches Historisches Museum.

———. 2014. "Asylum in Postwar Germany: Refugee Admission Policies and Their Practical Implementation in the Federal Republic and the GDR Between the Late 1940s and the Mid-1970s." *Journal of Contemporary History* 49 (1): 115–33.

Protokoll des III. Parteitages der SED. 1950. "Der Fünfjahrplan 1951–1955." Berlin (Ost). http://germanhistorydocs.ghi-dc.org/docpage.cfm?docpage_id=3274& language=german.

Pudack, M. 1992. "Brief an Bürgermeister Werner." January 25. Stadtarchiv Eisenhüttenstadt.

Quinn, Leon Roman. 2002. "The Politics of Pollution? Government, Environmentalism and Mass Opinion in East Germany, 1972–1990." PhD diss., University of Bristol.

Raatz, Christine. 2011. "DDR Lebt in Straßennamen Weiter." *Sächsische Zeitung,* December 11. http://www.sz-online.de/sachsen/ddr-lebt-in-strassennamen-weiter-904710.html.

Rabinow, Paul. (1989) 1995. *French Modern: Norms and Forms of the Social Environment.* University of Chicago Press.

Rada, Uwe. 2023. "Hotel Lunik in Eisenhüttenstadt: Wie der Palast der Republik." *Die Tageszeitung,* May 14. https://taz.de/!5931537/.

Ramsay, Georgina. 2020. "Time and the Other in Crisis: How Anthropology Makes Its Displaced Object." *Anthropological Theory* 20 (4): 385–413. https://doi.org/10.1177/1463499619840464.

Rat der Stadt Eisenhüttenstadt. 1977. "Der Rat Beschließt Die Kreisdenkmalliste." Stadtarchiv Eisenhüttenstadt.

——. 1984. "Denkmalschutzgebieteserklärung Der Wohnkomplexe I, II, und III, Eisenhüttenstadt." Stadtarchiv Eisenhüttenstadt.

Rat der Stadt Eisenhüttenstadt, Abteilung Wohungspolitik und Wohnungsgewirtschaft. 1990a. "Analyse Der Wechselwohnungen." Stadtarchiv Eisenhüttenstadt.

——. 1990b. "Analyse Der Wechselwohnungen Der 31.3.1990." Stadtarchiv Eisenhüttenstadt.

Rat der Stadt Stalinstadt. 1955. "Entwurfsbüro Für Hochbau Stalinstadt Des Rates Des Bezirkes Frankfurt/Oder: Planzenliste." Stadtarchiv Eisenhüttenstadt.

Raworth, Kate. 2017. "A Doughnut for the Anthropocene: Humanity's Compass in the 21st Century." *Lancet Planetary Health* 1 (2): e48–49. https://doi.org/10.1016/S2542-5196(17)30028-1.

RBB (Rundfunk Berlin-Brandenburg). 2022. "Sprudelnde Fontänen." February 27. *Liechtenstein in Stalinstadt.* ARD Audiothek. https://www.ardaudiothek.de/sendung/liechtenstein-in-stalinstadt/10306275.

Remenz, Johannes. n.d. [late 1980s]. "Denmale in Sozialistischen Städtebau." *Eisenhüttenstadt Stadtspiegel.* Stadtarchiv Eisenhüttenstadt.

Richter, Jenny, Heike Förster, and Ulrich Lakemann. 1997. *Stalinstadt-Eisenhüttenstadt: Von der Utopie zur Gegenwart; Wandel industrieller, regionaler und sozialer Strukturen in Eisenhüttenstadt.* Schüren.

Richter, Jörn, and Norbert Engst. 2024. "Fritz–50." May 23. https://www.fritz-50.de/.

Ricoeur, Paul. 2009. *Memory, History, Forgetting.* University of Chicago Press.

Ringel, Felix. 2018. *Back to the Postindustrial Future: An Ethnography of Germany's Fastest-Shrinking City.* Berghahn Books.

——. 2022. "The Time of Post-Socialism: On the Future of an Anthropological Concept." *Critique of Anthropology* 42 (2): 191–208. https://doi.org/10.1177/0308275X221095930.

Robbins, Joel. 2013. "Beyond the Suffering Subject: Toward an Anthropology of the Good." *Journal of the Royal Anthropological Institute* 19 (3): 447–62. https://doi.org/10.1111/1467-9655.12044.

Rockstroh, R. 1991. "Brief an Bürgermeister Werner." June 26. Stadtarchiv Eisenhüttenstadt.

Roesler, Jörg. 1994. "Privatisation in Eastern Germany—Experience with the Treuhand." *Europe-Asia Studies* 46 (3): 505–17.

Roesler, Jörn. 1997. " 'Eisen Für Den Frieden.' Das Eisenhüttenkombinat Ost in Der Wirtschaft Der DDR." In *Aufbau West—Aufbau Ost: Die Planstädte Wolfsburg Und Eisenhüttenstadt in Der Nachkriegszeit.* Deutsches Historisches Museum. http://www.dhm.de/archiv/ausstellungen/aufbau_west_ost/katlg16.htm.

Sammartino, Annemarie. 2018. "The New Socialist Man in the Plattenbau: The East German Housing Program and the Development of the Socialist Way of Life." *Journal of Urban History* 44 (1): 78–94. https://doi.org/10.1177/0096144217710231.

Saussure, Ferdinand de. 1959. *Course in General Linguistics.* Translated by Wade Baskin. Philosophical Library.

Schaefer, Thomas. 1993. "Mieten in Ostdeutschland: Zwischen Instandsetzungsstau und Mieterinteressen; eine Tagung der Friedrich-Ebert-Stiftung,"

Wirtschaftspolitische Diskurse, no. 59 (April 14). https://library.fes.de/fulltext/fo-wirtschaft/00343toc.htm.

Schlaubejournal. 1991. "Können Wir Uns Denn Änderungen Leisten?" April 23. Stadtarchiv Eisenhüttenstadt.

Schretzenmayr, Martina. 1998. "Wohnungsbau in Der Ehemaligen DDR." *disP—The Planning Review* 34 (133): 40–48. https://doi.org/10.1080/02513625.1998.10556676.

Schulz, Johannes. 2022. "'Vergangenheitsbewältigung' Revisited: Distinguishing Two Paradigms of Working Through the Past." *Philosophy & Social Criticism* 50 (2). https://doi.org/10.1177/01914537221117562.

Schütrumpf, Jörn. 1997a. "Kurt W. Leucht, Planer von Stalinstadt, Der 'Ersten Sozialistischen Stadt Deutschlands.'" In *Aufbau West—Aufbau Ost: Die Planstädte Wolfsburg und Eisenhüttenstadt in Der Nachkriegszeit*, edited by Rosmarie Beier. Deutsches Historisches Museum. http://www.dhm.de/archiv/ausstellungen/aufbau_west_ost/katlg09.htm.

———. 1997b. "'Wo einst nur Sand und Kiefern Waren . . .' >Vergangenheitsbewältigung< im Eisenhüttenkombinat Ost." In *Aufbau West—Aufbau Ost: Die Planstädte Wolfsburg und Eisenhüttenstadt in Der Nachkriegszeit*, edited by Rosmarie Beier. Deutsches Historisches Museum. http://www.dhm.de/archiv/ausstellungen/aufbau_west_ost/katlginh.htm.

Schwartz, Michael. 2008. "Vertriebene im doppelten Deutschland. Integrations- und Erinnerungspolitik in der DDR und in der Bundesrepublik." *Vierteljahrshefte für Zeitgeschichte* 56 (1): 101–51. https://doi.org/10.1524/vfzg.2008.0004.

Schwarz, Frank. 2004. "Ein Ort ohne Eigenschaften: Gutachter stellten Imagestudie vor/Neuer Name für die Stadt empfohlen." *Märkische Oderzeitung*, March 31.

Schwenkel, Christina. 2018. "The Current Never Stops: Intimacies of Energy Infrastructure in Vietnam." In *The Promise of Infrastructure*, edited by Hannah Appel. Duke University Press.

———. 2020. *Building Socialism: The Afterlife of East German Architecture in Urban Vietnam*. Duke University Press.

Schwochow, Christian, dir. 2014. *Bornholmer Straße*. ARD Degeto Film, Mitteldeutscher Rundfunk (MDR), Rundfunk Berlin-Brandenburg (RBB).

Scott, David. 2014. *Omens of Adversity: Tragedy, Time, Memory, Justice*. Duke University Press.

Scott, James C. 1999. *Seeing Like a State: How Certain Schemes to Improve the Human Condition Have Failed*. Yale University Press.

Sen, Amartya. 1984. "The Living Standard." *Oxford Economic Papers* 36:74–90.

———. 2001. *Development as Freedom*. Oxford University Press.

Sethmann, Jens. 2012. "Das Neue Phänomen Der Energiearmut." *MieterMagazin*, November. https://www.berliner-mieterverein.de/magazin/online/mm1112/111212.htm.

Shapiro, Nicholas, and Eben Kirksey. 2017. "Chemo-Ethnography: An Introduction." *Cultural Anthropology* 32 (4): 481–93. https://doi.org/10.14506/ca32.4.01.

Simmel, Georg. 1972. *Georg Simmel on Individuality and Social Forms*. Edited by Donald N. Levine. University of Chicago Press.

Sloane, Paul, Penny Roberts, and William Recktenwald. 1994. "Gary Takes Over as Murder Capital of U.S." *Chicago Tribune*, January 3.

Slobodian, Quinn. 2015. *Comrades of Color: East Germany in the Cold War World*. Berghahn Books.

Smith, Monica L. 2020. *Cities: The First 6,000 Years*. Penguin.

Smith, Neil. 1996. *The New Urban Frontier: Gentrification and the Revanchist City*. Psychology Press.

Stadt Eisenhüttenstadt. 2010. "Statistischer Jahresbericht."
———. 2013. "Bebauungsplan Der Innentwicklung 'Wohngebeit Fuerstenberger
    Strasse.'" 33, 5/10. Bereich Stadtentwicklung/Stadtumbau.
———. 2018. "Stadtumbau." https://www.eisenhuettenstadt.de/Leben-Wohnen/
    Wohnen-und-Bauen/Stadtentwicklung/Stadtumbau/.
———. 2021. "Kultur." https://www.eisenhuettenstadt.de/Freizeit-Tourismus/Kultur/.
———. 2023. "Pressemitteilung: Festakt Und Festival Zum Themenjahr 'Baukultur
    Leben' in Eisenhüttenstadt." May 27. https://www.eisenhuettenstadt.de/index.
    php?object=tx,2852.5&ModID=7&FID=2852.19561.1.
Stadt Eisenhüttenstadt and BBSM (Brandenburgische Beratungsgesellschaft
    für Stadterneuerung und Modernisierung). 2015. *Stadtumbaustrategie
    Eisenhüttenstadt 2015–2025 Mit Ausblick Auf 2030 (Stadtumbaukonzept—4.
    Fortschreibung 2014).* http://www.eisenhuettenstadt.de/images/4/neu%20
    Bearbeitung/3_Stadtumbau/Stadtumbaustrategie.pdf.
———. 2022. *Integriertes Stadtentwicklungskonzept (2. Fortschreibung).*
    Eisenhüttenstadt. https://www.eisenhuettenstadt.de/media/custom/2852_
    4301_1.PDF?1653908367.
Stadt Eisenhüttenstadt, Der Stadtverordnetenvorsteher. 1992. "Umbennenung von
    Straßen in Eisenhüttenstadt." Stadtarchiv Eisenhüttenstadt.
Stadtverwaltung Eisenhüttenstadt. 2023. "Pressemitteilung: Hotel Lunik und
    Bettenhäuser Gehören Nun Zur Stadt." June 22.
Stadtverwaltung Eisenhüttenstadt, Abteilung Stadtentwicklung/Stadtumbau. 2024.
    "Sanierung Overview, Leerstand Nach WK." Csv.
Star, Susan Leigh. 1999. "The Ethnography of Infrastructure." *American Behavioral
    Scientist* 43 (3): 377–91.
Statista. 2024. "Jährlich neu registrierte Flüchtlinge in Deutschland bis 2018."
    March 26. https://de.statista.com/statistik/daten/studie/663735/umfrage/
    jaehrlich-neu-registrierte-fluechtlinge-in-deutschland/.
Statistisches Amt der DDR. 1990. "Lebenserwartung in Der Deutschen
    Demokratischen Republik (DDR) Bei Der Geburt Nach Geschlecht von 1952
    Bis 1989." https://de.statista.com/statistik/daten/studie/249309/umfrage/
    lebenserwartung-in-der-ddr/.
Steigemann, Anna Marie, and Philipp Misselwitz. 2020. "Architectures of Asylum:
    Making Home in a State of Permanent Temporariness." *Current Sociology* 68 (5):
    628–50. https://doi.org/10.1177/0011392120927755.
Stiglich, Larissa. 2020. "After Socialism: The Transformation of Everyday Life in
    Eisenhüttenstadt, 1975–2015." PhD diss., University of North Carolina at
    Chapel Hill.
Stoler, Ann Laura. 2009. *Along the Archival Grain: Epistemic Anxieties and Colonial
    Common Sense.* Princeton University Press. https://www.jstor.org/stable/j.
    ctt7rtrg.
———. 2013. *Imperial Debris: On Ruins and Ruination.* Duke University Press.
———. 2016. *Duress: Imperial Durabilities in Our Times.* Duke University Press.
Strathern, Marilyn. (2002) 2022. *Property, Substance, and Effect: Anthropological Essays
    on Persons and Things.* Edited by Eric Hirsch. Classics in Ethnographic Theory.
    HAU.
SVV (Stadtverordnetenversammlung Eisenhüttenstadt). 1990. "Beschlussvorlage."
    Stadtverwaltung Eisenhüttenstadt. Stadtarchiv Eisenhüttenstadt.
SVV Stalinstadt. 1961. "Beschluß." Stadtarchiv Eisenhüttenstadt.
Taussig, Michael T. 1993. *Mimesis and Alterity: A Particular History of the Senses.*
    Psychology Press.

TEDx Talks. 2014. "The Economics of Enough: Dan O'Neill at TEDxOxbridge." YouTube video, 12:51, June 13. https://www.youtube.com/watch?v=WIG33QtLRyA.

Till, Karen E. 2005. *The New Berlin: Memory, Politics, Place.* University of Minnesota Press.

Trouillot, Michel-Rolph. 1997. *Silencing the Past: Power and the Production of History.* Beacon.

———. (2003) 2016. *Global Transformations: Anthropology and the Modern World.* Springer.

Tsing, Anna Lowenhaupt. 2015. *The Mushroom at the End of the World: On the Possibility of Life in Capitalist Ruins.* Princeton University Press.

———. 2017. "The Buck, the Bull, and the Dream of the Stag: Some Unexpected Weeds of the Anthropocene." *Suomen Antropologi: Journal of the Finnish Anthropological Society* 42 (1): 3–21.

TV:Schwerin. 2019. "'Fritz Heckert'—Eine Legende." YouTube video, 6:11, November 29. https://www.youtube.com/watch?v=p07y5v7taew.

Urbistat. 2022. "Altersklassen Nach Geschlecht Gemeinde von Eisenhüttenstadt, Alterungsindex Und Durchschnittsalter Der Ansässigen." https://ugeo.urbistat.com/AdminStat/de/de/demografia/eta/eisenhuttenstadt/20188535/4.

US Census Bureau. 2020. "QuickFacts: The Villages CDP, Florida." Accessed October 24, 2022. https://www.census.gov/quickfacts/fact/table/thevillagescdpflorida/POP010220#POP010220.

US Department of State. 1949. "Foreign Relations of the United States, 1949, Council of Foreign Ministers; Germany and Austria, Volume III 740.00119 Control (Germany)/4–649." Office of the Historian. Accessed May 9, 2025. https://history.state.gov/historicaldocuments/frus1949v03/d60.

Vale, Lawrence J. 2013. *Purging the Poorest: Public Housing and the Design Politics of Twice-Cleared Communities.* Historical Studies of Urban America. University of Chicago Press.

———. 2020. *After the Projects: Public Housing Redevelopment and the Governance of the Poorest Americans.* Oxford University Press.

VEO GmbH. 2024. "Über uns – VEO GmbH." https://www.veo-eh.de/ueber-uns/.

Verdery, Katherine. 1996. *What Was Socialism, and What Comes Next?* Princeton University Press.

———. 2003. *The Vanishing Hectare: Property and Value in Postsocialist Transylvania.* Cornell University Press.

Volksstimme. 2011. "Woher kommen die Altschulden aus DDR-Zeiten?" November 18. https://www.volksstimme.de/sachsen-anhalt/woher-kommen-die-altschulden-aus-ddr-zeiten-448860.

Von Schnitzler, Antina. 2016. *Democracy's Infrastructure: Techno-Politics and Protest After Apartheid.* Princeton University Press.

Wakeman, Rosemary. 2016. *Practicing Utopia: An Intellectual History of the New Town Movement.* University of Chicago Press.

Wiedemer, Rochus. 2004. *Warum Stadtumbau Ost?* KW Institute for Contemporary Art Berlin. Accessed June 14, 2024. https://www.schader-stiftung.de/themen/stadtentwicklung-und-wohnen/fokus/konversion/artikel/warum-stadtumbau-ost.

Wierling, Dorothee. 2008. "Age as the Eternal Enemy: Conflicts in the Education Dictatorship of the 1960s." In *Socialist Modern: East German Everyday Culture and Politics*, edited by Katherine Pence and Paul Betts. University of Michigan Press.

———. 2009. "How Do the 1929ers and the 1949ers Differ?" In *Power and Society in the GDR, 1961–1979*, edited by Mary Fulbrook. Berghahn Books.

Wiesner, Gerd. 2001. *Der Lebensverlängerungsprozess in Deutschland: Stand - Entwicklung - Folgen*. Beiträge zur Gesundheitsberichterstattung des Bundes. Robert Koch Institut.

Wood, Ellen Meiksins. 2002. *The Origin of Capitalism: A Longer View*. Verso.

Wortprotokoll Der Sondersitzung Der SVV Am 14.04. 1990. Stadtverwaltung Eisenhüttenstadt. Stadtarchiv Eisenhüttenstadt.

Young, James E. 2000. *At Memory's Edge: After-Images of the Holocaust in Contemporary Art and Architecture*. Yale University Press.

Yurchak, Alexei. (2005) 2013. *Everything Was Forever, Until It Was No More: The Last Soviet Generation*. Princeton University Press.

Zarecor, Kimberly Elman. 2011. *Manufacturing a Socialist Modernity: Housing in Czechoslovakia, 1945–1960*. University of Pittsburgh Press.

———. 2018. "What Was So Socialist About the Socialist City? Second World Urbanity in Europe." *Journal of Urban History* 44 (1): 95–117. https://doi.org/10.1177/0096144217710229.

Zeiderman, Austin, and Katherine Dawson. 2022. "Urban Futures." *City* 26 (2–3): 261–80. https://doi.org/10.1080/13604813.2022.2035964.

Zimmermann, Felix. 2023. "Leerstehendes Traditionskino: Verfallende Pracht." *TAZ (Die Tageszeitung)*, May 14, 2023. https://taz.de/!5933804/.

Zitelmann, Rainer. 2021. "Enteignung Und Mietenstopp: Grün Und Links Glorifizieren Größte Fehler Der DDR." *Focus*, July 11. https://www.focus.de/politik/historischer-vergleich-enteignung-und-mietenstopp-gruen-und-links-glorifizieren-groesste-fehler-der-ddr_id_24399204.html.

Index

Note: Page numbers in *italics* refer to figures and tables.

www.ingramcontent.com/pod-product-compliance
Lightning Source LLC
Chambersburg PA
CBHW030404270326
41926CB00009B/1266